The Shape of
German Romanticism

The Shape of
German Romanticism

Marshall Brown

Cornell University Press
Ithaca and London

Cornell University Press gratefully acknowledges a grant from the Andrew W. Mellon Foundation that aided in bringing this book to publication.

First published 1979 by Cornell University Press.
Published in the United Kingdom by Cornell University Press Ltd., 2-4 Brook Street, London W1Y 1AA.

International Standard Book Number 0-8014-1228-5
Library of Congress Catalog Card Number 79-14313

Printed in the United States of America

Librarians: Library of Congress cataloging information appears on the last page of the book.

To Jane

Contents

Acknowledgments

Copies of a number of the works cited in this study are relatively scarce. I have used most extensively the Yale and Harvard university libraries; for certain texts I have drawn on the libraries of the universities of California at Los Angeles, North Carolina, and Virginia and the Boston Public Library. To the staffs of these libraries as well as to those of Boston University and Mount Holyoke and Smith colleges I owe many thanks for their generous assistance. I also want to thank *JEGP* for permission to reprint, with slight revisions, my essay "The Eccentric Path."

Stuart Atkins introduced me to the German romantics in a class he taught with rare commitment and intensity. Geoffrey Hartman's inspirational teaching provided my initiation into American and European critical theory, and his influence has sustained, though I hope not overwhelmed, all of my writing. Cyrus Hamlin was a "doctor-father" in the best sense of the phrase and has remained my most alert and critical friend. Other friends and acquaintances have read part or all of the manuscript, and each has contributed a measure, often a large measure, of encouragement and welcome advice: Dagmar and Jeffrey Barnouw, Dorrit Cohn, Neil Flax, Marjorie Grene, Dieter Henrich, Gertrude Kurshan, Maynard Mack, Jr., Paul de Man, Donald Marshall, Charles Rosen, Maria Tatar, Christie and Eugene Vance, René Wellek. Theodore Ziolkowski and an anonymous reader furnished detailed and persuasive critiques that prompted two extensive and entirely beneficial reworkings of the text. My parents, true students of Thoreau in this, have ceaselessly exhorted me to simplify, simplify. I have done what I could to satisfy them, and Jeanne Duell and the staff of Cornell University Press have furthered my efforts with exceptional patience and thoroughness. Those who know my wife know that few paragraphs have been unimproved by her loving watchfulness.

MARSHALL BROWN

Charlottesville, Virginia

9

Abbreviations

Ath. Fr.	Friedrich Schlegel, *Athenäums-Fragmente*, in *KA*, vol. 2
HKA	Joseph Freiherr von Eichendorff, *Historisch-kritische Ausgabe*
KA	Friedrich Schlegel, *Kritische Ausgabe*
LN	Friedrich Schlegel, *Literary Notebooks*
MuR	Johann Wolfgang von Goethe, *Maximen und Reflexionen*, in *Werke*, vols. 18–19
PhL	Friedrich Schlegel, *Philosophische Lehrjahre*, in *KA*, vols. 18–19
VB	Novalis, *Vermischte Bemerkungen*, in *Schriften*, vol. 2

Note on Citations and Translations

Quotations are identified by page, paragraph, or line numbers, except that quotations from the following collections are cited by fragment number: *Ath. Fr.*, *Blütenstaub* (in Novalis, *Schriften*, vol. 2), *Glauben und Liebe* (in Novalis, *Schriften*, vol. 2), *Ideen* (in *KA*, vol. 2), *LN*, *MuR* (cited according to Max Hecker's enumeration), *PhL*, and *VB*.

All translations are my own. So far as English idiom permits, I have tried to render as literally as possible the idiosyncrasies and, on many occasions, the infelicities of the original texts.

The Shape of
German Romanticism

Introduction

Yes—the theory of the center—the romantic theory of
the center. . . .

—Georg Lukács, *Die Seele und
die Formen*

The brilliance of the romantic age in Germany is at once the despair
and the joy of its historians. Few periods parallel it in either greatness or range of writings. Hand in hand with philosophical treatises
of notorious difficulty and profundity go long and short poems in
numerous genres, seminal works in numerous types of prose fiction
and imaginative nonfiction, comedies and tragedies in prose and
verse—some innovative in form, others based on Greek, English,
French, and Spanish models. Most of the major authors were serious students of the philosophical systems of the age, and of much
else as well: of the sciences, history, linguistics, art and art history,
politics, the nascent discipline of abnormal psychology. At times,
particularly in the last five years of the eighteenth century, the ferment was so intense that a chronology must be calibrated not in
years but in days; claims of priority and demonstrations of influence would have to stand or fall on the speed of the mails. Where
even a chronicle is difficult to conceive, for events at once so complex and so disparate, how can we arrive at a historical synthesis?
What is the focus, if any, of the romantic enterprise? Where is the
center of its manifold activities? How can it be understood as a
coherent movement?

Since the time of Mme de Staël and Heine, romanticism has generally been described in terms of systems of belief and content-
oriented categories like the infinite, nature, music, medievalism.
Such categories are reductive; they emphasize isolated motifs and
often neglect the integrity of literary works. Nor do they achieve
their usual goal, the definition of a common romantic system of
belief. For each category evokes its opposite. Next to the poetry of

13

nature was a poetry of the city.[1] Alongside the ideal of the infinite and formless was an ideal of form. Beside authors who took music as a model lived others who looked to painting. Even the same authors fit into different categories at different times. It once was routine (and still is regrettably common) for historians confronting these contradictions to reify them historically, pitting a "classical school" centered on Goethe and Schiller in Weimar against one or more "romantic schools" located in Jena and elsewhere. Yet Weimar and Jena, only a few dozen kilometers apart, were also close intellectually; and the constellations of allied figures and sub-movements shifted constantly. Rarely did a romantic author see himself as part of a consolidated bloc opposing a second bloc; more typical of the romantic flux—and of the historian's quandary—is the series of toasts in the introduction to Tieck's arch-romantic collection *Phantasus* (*Schriften* IV, 87–89), offered to authors of both "camps" and to those of the uncertain middle: Goethe and Schiller, Jacobi and Jean Paul, both Schlegels, Shakespeare, and Novalis. Ultimately, the very excitement of the period frustrates any attempt to precipitate a "romantic school" out from the romantic movement. It is unhelpful to look for fixed groupings where individual authors are ceaselessly experimenting and where no single author can be held to a fixed position. Romanticism must be seen as a whole, including Weimar authors (not only Goethe and Schiller, but also Herder and Moritz, Jean Paul and Humboldt) together with their occasional antagonists in Jena. The richness of the period is irreducible.

Faced with the proliferation of competing interests and personalities, the romantics themselves raised the question of a focus. "The phenomenon of all phenomena," says Ludoviko in Friedrich Schlegel's *Gespräch über die Poesie*, is "that humanity struggles with all its force to find its center" (*KA* II, 314); and Schlegel's notebooks, in particular, abound in contributions to the struggle, finding the center variously in religion, poetry, nature, and so

---

1. Urban romanticism is the subject of numerous books by Marianne Thalmann, including *The Literary Sign Language of German Romanticism*, trans. Harold A. Basilius (Detroit, 1972), one of the best books available in English on the period.

forth.[2] The list of these centers—possible, probable, and definite—seems nearly endless and maddeningly contradictory. Indeed, from very early on, hostile historians have held against the romantics their urgent search for a center, as if to be aware of a danger were necessarily to fall victim to it and intellectual virtuosity were inevitably accompanied by dilettantish dissipation of genius. A history of the romantic movement written by one of the angry young men of 1848, for instance, contains a long polemical examination of "this call for a midpoint, a center of literature, which fills this whole age of the romantics."[3] If the romantics were constantly looking for a center in medievalism and nationalism, in Catholicism, or in self-conscious form, Prutz argues, then this shows that they were frivolous and elitist, out of touch both with their own talent and with their contemporaries. The "loss of center," upon which Prutz dwells, has remained a commonplace of criticism that underlies, among many others, well-known treatments of the romantic influence on modern art by Hans Sedlmayr (who coined the phrase in his book *Der Verlust der Mitte*), Ernst Gombrich, and Robert Rosenblum.

If "center" represents a governing principle or idea, then both those who defend the coherence of a restricted "romantic school" and those who attack romanticism for its lack of focus can be seen to be writing ideological criticism. What is sought by the one and felt to be lacking by the other is a unified body of doctrine. I have already suggested that to hope to delineate a unified doctrine runs counter to the romantic spirit of intellectual experimentation. Rather than seeking common belief systems in such widely differing authors, we need to look for a common repertoire of accessible ideas and a common organization of the mental universe, a shared "archive," as Michel Foucault has called it; rather than a common

2. "Poetry is thoroughly central in every respect" (*LN* 1827); "religion is the central center, that is clear" (*PhL* IV, 1435); "only nature is central" (*PhL* III, 439), mythology or love is the center of poetry (*KA* II, 312; *PhL* IV, 725); reason is in the center (*PhL* IV, 1397); the golden age or the encyclopedia is the central center (*LN* 1382; *PhL* IV, 706); music is center and periphery (*LN* 1416); "yoni is the present, center, fullness" (*PhL* Beilage VII, 15).

3. Robert Prutz, *Vorlesungen über die deutsche Literatur der Gegenwart* (Leipzig, 1847), lecture 2, p. 101.

ideology, a common approach to ideology. Criticism that starts
from doctrines is beginning with the results, not the sources, of reflection. We need to investigate how the doctrines are generated,
what practices underlie romantic preachings, into what forms romantic thought may be cast. These are the questions through which
I wish to approach the synergy of speculation and poetic achievement that characterizes the romantic period in Germany.

I wish to show that the notion of an organizing center served the
romantics as a dynamic impulse governing their processes of
thought and composition. They were united in a common formal
postulate or what might be termed, in quasi-Kantian parlance, a
schematism of the imagination. Regardless of differences of temper-
ament and ideology—differences that were as great in the romantic
generation as in any other—the authors strove to cast their beliefs
and perceptions into particular centrally organized patterns. Indeed, the restless experimentation of early romanticism can be
viewed as part of the effort to adapt all aspects of experience to the
given form. A number of German romantic authors yield nothing
to Emerson, Dickinson, or Yeats in their explicit and abiding fascination with centers and with the curves that can be generated
from them.

To a certain extent the importance of centrality for romanticism
has long been recognized. Alongside the hostile critics of the "lost
center" persuasion are a number of critics who have used the notion
of the center constructively to illuminate various aspects of romanticism. Among their works are the brief chapter on the romantic
ellipse, "Die romantische Zahl," in Ricarda Huch's *Blütezeit der
Romantik* (1899); comments and discussions scattered throughout
the works of Oskar Walzel, which were pursued in greater detail,
for the Jena romantics, by his pupil Marie Joachimi-Dege in the first
chapter of *Die Weltanschauung der deutschen Romantik* (1905);
Dietrich Mahnke's learned reverse history of the idea of the divine
center beginning with Novalis and ending with the pre-Socratics,
Unendliche Sphäre und Allmittelpunkt (1937); and a seminal chapter in Georges Poulet's *Metamorphoses of the Circle* (originally
published in French in 1961). These—as well as many detailed
accounts in specialized studies of individual authors—reveal the

pervasiveness of the notion of centrality in the romantic period.[4] But no full-scale analysis has been attempted of this category as it appears in both early and late romanticism. The need is not so much to document the extent of concern with central forms (with some difficulty such documentation can be culled from the specialized studies) as to scrutinize thoroughly the implications of centrality. Generally, too much is taken for granted about the significance of the center and the relations between central point and surrounding world, and as a result much of the specificity of romantic formalism is overlooked. Received notions of organic form, of arabesque, and of circuitous journey can be considerably refined by minute sifting of the evidence; while formal analysis of completed works can be advantageously complemented by philological examination of the innumerable programmatic utterances of both poets and philosophers.

The center is not an isolated notion. It brings with it, for the romantics, a flotilla of associated notions and images that must simultaneously be objects of study. Not just one single formal postulate is involved, but a whole network of spatial and temporal relations that structure romantic writing and that, in addition, shift with time. The romantic center is the node of an intricate and highly specific experiential pattern.

It was Friedrich Schlegel, not by nature the most systematic of thinkers, who termed the center a "systematic category," that is, part of the basic armature to which his thought was, or should be, subjected: "Beginning, ending, centering figures belong to the systematic style, likewise cycling" (*LN* 910).[5] "Systematic categories are the concepts—method, center, beginning, end.—Center, outlines, cycles, lines.— Foundation and result are systematic *facta*" (*LN* 925). "In every systematic work there must be a prologue, an

4. For comparable treatments of English-language texts see Meyer H. Abrams's account of circular narrative structures in *Natural Supernaturalism* (New York, 1971), which discusses German parallels in chap. 4, and R. A. Yoder's brilliant analysis of the much-studied circles of American romanticism in "The Equilibrist Perspective: Toward a Theory of American Romanticism," *Studies in Romanticism* 12 (1973), 705–40.
5. *Centrirende* ("centering") is my conjectural emendation; the edition reads *contrirende*.

epilogue and a centrologue (or a parekbasis.–)" (*LN* 933). As may be seen, these categories cover a wide variety of phenomena. They are both concepts and facts and pertain to both rhetoric and literary form. They are the common currency of romanticism, the medium of exchange between different areas of concern. Furthermore, although centrality is related to temporal categories (beginning, ending, foundation, and result), it is even more closely associated with spatial notions (outlines and geometrical shapes, and also the parekbasis, or movement outward in a play). The study of centrality leads to an understanding of what, to borrow a term, might be called the spatial forms of German romanticism. Indeed, the incessant making and unmaking of patterns in Schlegel's voluminous notebooks give the impression of a man who was concerned with form before content or who was even totally unconcerned with content. That this is the case—and that form is to be understood primarily as spatial form—is confirmed by the following entry, which I "quote" in full. "A philosophical work," writes Schlegel, "must have a definite geometrical form." And he goes on to construct the figure reproduced below (*PhL* VI, 142).

```
        +           ∓              −
                    ○
        +           ∓              −
                    ○
                    I
        +                          −
                    2
        +                          −
                    3
                    ∓
        +           =              −
                    ×
              ×              ≦
            + +            + + ?
        ×           ×              ×
```

Schlegel's lucubrations, the fascination with astronomy examined in the section "The Eccentric Path," and the abstract spatial configurations of romantic painters all attest to the capital importance of geometry to the romantic imagination.[6] Throughout the period recourse to Euclid was a ready means of clarifying the underlying structure of any difficult or problematic idea. Euclid could help, for instance, to explain the origin of life. The relation of prototype to developed species, as we are told in a late work by one of the last romantic scientists, is like that of egg to adult, of soul to body, or of center to circumference:

For indeed every point is only an ideal determination of space, but in and of itself, as Euclid already said, never spatially representable, since understandably everything in a drawing that we are accustomed to name a "point" represents . . . a spatial mass that in turn must still always have *its* ideal center *in it*. . . . The sphere is unthinkable without a center and the center (which in and of itself is never in any way spatially representable) is inconceivable without a sphere.[7]

Even more to the point—and here Hegel can be cited—geometrical shapes provide the analogy that shows how formalization is possible outside the natural sciences:

That a definite particularity indeed constitutes the peculiar principle of a people, this is the side which must be empirically received and demonstrated in a historical manner. To accomplish this presupposes not merely a practiced abstraction, but even before that an intimate acquaintance with the idea; one must be, so to speak, a priori conversant with the sphere wherein the principles fall, just as (to name the greatest man in this kind of discovery) Kepler already had to have a previous a priori familiarity with ellipses, with cubes and quadratics and with the notions of the relationships among them before he could discover in the empirical data his immortal laws, which consist in modifications of those spheres of conception.[8]

It is, however, in some of the muddiest waters of romanticism—the writings of Schelling and his followers the *Naturphilosophen*—that we can learn most directly what is meant by a systematic category. Lorenz Oken, the leading force in German science in the

6. Wieland Schmied has recently documented one leading painter's "love for geometry," in *Caspar David Friedrich* (Cologne, 1975), pp. 27–29.
7. Carl Gustav Carus, *Physis: Zur Geschichte des leiblichen Lebens* (Stuttgart, 1851), pp. 11–12.
8. G. W. F. Hegel, *Vorlesungen über die Philosophie der Geschichte*, ed. Eva Moldenhauer and Karl Markus Michel (Frankfurt, 1970), p. 87.

first half of the nineteenth century, began his career with an ambi-
tious program for the study of all fields of science predicated on the
"categorical" assumption that the line is identity, the circle antithesis, and the ellipse totality. Joseph Görres, eventually a distinguished nineteenth-century publicist and Catholic philosopher, admired Oken's ambition but corrected the categories: the ellipse, he
claims, is the true antithesis, and the circle is totality. In the light
of history, their disagreement seems insignificant; what concerns us
is the belief (as stated by Oken) that in isolation empiricism and
speculation are both useless, that natural philosophy is the conjunction of empiricism and speculation, and that "if any knowledge is
allotted to us, then we can only obtain it through mathematics."[9]
Later, in presenting a new method for geological classifications,
Oken argued against Linnaeus's analytical classifications based on
selected traits. In their stead he favored a system based on the
Gesamtcharakter or what we might call the "gestalt" of minerals;
we must perceive the principle of organization (of a rock!) before
we can understand its function. Most of Oken's writings start with
a brief account of the mathematical or pseudomathematical foundations of their organization, and his first full-length work includes
a blanket claim that all the more substantive branches of knowledge
and of speculation depend upon mathematical forms. Although the
claim becomes characteristically vague toward the end, the geometrical underpinning is evident: "Mathematics is far removed from
acknowledging itself to be dependent upon philosophy, or even a
branch thereof, since it is its intellectual counterpart [*geistiges
Gleichbild*]. Each of its theorems is without any modification a the-
orem in science, in art, and in ethics, which as the unity of virtue
and justice stands above both, not as their equilibrium, but as their
highest power, as the focus of a (stereotic) ellipse."[10]
The thesis of the present work, then, is that a series of related
formalizations underlies all the German writings that we recognize
as romantic and that these formalizations can be described and

9. Laurentius Oken, *Übersicht des Grundrisses des Systems der Naturphilosophie
und der damit entstehenden Theorie der Sinne*, in *Gesammelte Schriften*, ed.
W. Keiper, (Berlin, 1939), I, 4–23; the portions summarized are pp. 5–7, the
quotation is on p. 6. Görres's review is found in his *Schriften* II², 167–69.
10. Oken, *Die Zeugung* (Bamberg, 1805), p. 26.

studied on the basis of explicit programmatic utterances of the romantics themselves.

These fundamental "shapes" have both a systematic and a historical dimension. That is, their inner logic first generates a network
of structural configurations representing different aspects of early
romanticism, and these configurations then also change with time.
The first part of my analysis elaborates the logical and psychological implications of centrality, and the second traces the substitution,
after 1800, of the ellipse with two centers for the circle as the basic
romantic curve. It is not always easy, however, to distinguish between elaborations of a basic structure and changes in the structure;
indeed, part of my argument is that certain unstable patterns were
elaborated in the final years of the eighteenth century and that the
instability of these patterns led to the shift in the basic structure. As
will be seen, the later romantics were well aware of this fundamental change—that "the circle had become an ellipse." Nevertheless,
the historical picture is far less clear-cut than might be desired, for
in fact circular structures continued to be elaborated after they had
been, in some sense, superseded by elliptical structures. Without
being forced, the evidence will not conform to any simpler scheme.
And that is, after all, only common sense: generations overlap, influences cross, individual thinkers entertain and explore more than
one notion at once, sometimes forging ahead, sometimes falling
back on more familiar developed patterns. It seems inevitable that
historical development will never be perfectly synchronized and
that ideas will always coexist at different stages of maturity. Indeed, it is more remarkable that the shift to the ellipse took place
on a broad front and can be dated with considerable precision to
about the year 1800 than that older patterns continued to exist
after the watershed year.

In view of the large number of quotations it did not seem profit-
able to date each in the text. Apart from the earliest pioneering
novels mentioned in the final chapter, passages concerning elliptical
and bicentral structures all postdate the rediscovery about 1800 of
the seventeenth-century theosophist Jakob Böhme. Those passages
given in the first part of this work however, derive indiscriminately
from early and later romanticism; whatever helped to lay bare the
implications of romantic centrality I assigned to its place in the sys-

tem of ideas. The section called "The Open Circle" deals with some of the more problematic variants of the romantic circle. These are the inherently unstable formal models that led to the emergence of the ellipse. They were explored in theory and practice primarily in the years immediately preceding the rediscovery of Böhme, and most of the material discussed here dates from this brief period. But again, I have drawn on both earlier and later writings illustrating these problematic variants of the romantic circle in order to clarify their nature. (In "The Eccentric Path" the evidence ranges rather more widely; here a philological argument is made to determine the fixed meaning of a phrase that surfaced as a popular slogan in the closing years of the century.)

At the center of this history of romanticism lies a study of influence. It too needs to be properly understood. The story of the rediscovery of Böhme has often been told, but rarely with the proper emphases. There was, to be sure, a general surge of interest in Böhme's work after 1800. But the texts show unmistakably that the sudden feverish excitement was associated with one particular idea, which I have called the doctrine of two centers, and which appears only in a few scattered passages in Böhme's writings and hardly at all in his most famous work, *Aurora*. In Böhme the romantics found not so much a major thinker, a system, or even (as is sometimes said) a writing style as a single image. The latter fired their imagination because it was precisely what was needed to resolve the formal problems with which they were then struggling. One is tempted to say that if the romantics had not found the doctrine of two centers, they would have had to invent it. Superficially, Böhme's influence seems to be an outside contingency that intervened to change the course of romanticism; in fact, it finds its place as part of the immanent, logical unfolding of a formal structure, beginning well before 1800 and continuing well after the (generally quite rapid) subsiding of enthusiasm for Böhme's own writings. Our most influential theoretician of influence has recently written that "an 'influence' across languages is, in our time, almost invariably a cunning mask for an influence-relation within a language"; [11] in the case of

11. Harold Bloom, "Poetic Crossings, II: American Stances," *Georgia Review* 30 (1976), 790.

Böhme it may be urged that an influence across time masks a development inherent in the romantic system.

I should like to use Hegelian terms to summarize the nature of the historical process through which centrality is traced. It must be stressed that the process is not single but double. The circular patterns of early romanticism continue to develop even while they seem to be yielding to elliptical ones. And this double logic of history, partially continuing and partially reversing itself, is reflected at every level. The same words may be used (tolerance, for example) or the same forms exploited (folk song is a case in point), but the values become entirely different.[12] In its formal sense, as in its religion, its politics, and indeed its prevailing mood, the later romantic generation seems now to perpetuate, now to betray, the concerns of the earlier. This is the paradox—repeated, surely, in every historical juncture—that needs to be accounted for.

Hegel's name for the forward movement is the familiar punning word *Aufhebung*: a resolution of contradictions that preserves identities and suspends differences. Dialectical *Aufhebung* is dynamic, even propulsive, and in what I have called the dialectic of objectivity will be seen a series of such sublations, hyperbolic movements in which the romantic position redefines itself in ever more extreme forms. But *Aufhebung* is by nature an assertive process, a series of affirmations of successive stances, and cannot adequately explain the negativity often attributed to writers after 1800. The world-weariness of later romanticism has often been noted for its decadence, *Spätzeitlichkeit*, or belatedness.[13] Its betrayals of early romanticism—the Oedipal revenge of children against their poetic fathers in the flamboyant metaphor of Harold Bloom's antithetical criticism—have also been examined. Neither world-weariness nor betrayals, though, are part of the dialectical process itself. They belong to a second logic that unfolds, as I have suggested, simultaneously with dialectical *Aufhebung* and in recognizable counterpoint to it. This second logic is regressive. It is a reflective movement of

12. On tolerance, see "The Dialectic of Objectivity" below. An excellent account of the shifting ideology of the folk song is in Alexander von Bormann, *Natura Loquitur* (Tübingen, 1968), pp. 48–74.
13. See, for instance, Emil Staiger, "Schellings Schwermut," in *Die Kunst der Interpretation* (Zurich, 1971), pp. 154–75.

consciousness, or something akin to consciousness, searching for the stable ground of the dialectic, for the root of its propulsiveness. A French phrase, *mise en abyme*, has recently come into critical fashion to describe this reflective grounding, but the Hegelian name is perhaps even more subtly expressive. It is another pun, *Zugrundegehen*, which means grounding and also destruction. For in being grounded the dialectic is also being undermined; what it gains in stability it loses in dynamism. The two kinds of historical logic are perpetually at odds: the Prolific (the soaring exuberance of dialectical sublation) is constantly being dragged to earth (but also given shape and form) by the Devourer, which is the ground. Hence from the Hegelian perspective the generational conflict is but one representation of the dual logic of historical process. The younger romantics were simply completing the mission of their predecessors, for instance, by writing the kinds of books that the latter had demanded. But the mission of the early romantics lived through the energy of incompleteness, and therefore the later romantic fulfillment can easily be seen as a *Zugrunderichten*, or a retaliatory destruction.

History is always chasing its own tail, moving forward and backward at once. The materials I have collected and the constraints of a linear exposition combined to impose on me the effort of sorting out these two aspects of the historical process. In trying to untangle the skein of events I am sensible of having had to select arbitrarily and to simplify greatly. But I hope at least to have brought some order and sense to our understanding of romanticism and to have done so in a way that remains faithful to the texts and close to the spirit of the writers' own analyses of their aims and accomplishments.

I. The Romantic Circle

I sought above all, in accord with my innate tendency, for a thread or, as it might also be called, for a point from which to proceed, a maxim to hold onto, a circle from which there could be no erring.

—Goethe, review of Geoffroy de Saint-Hilaire, *Principes de Philosophie Zoologique*

Circle and Line

Our earth is one of the middle planets.
—Herder, *Ideen zur Philosophie
der Geschichte der Menschheit*

The romantic center always belongs to a circle or a sphere, not to a line. Franz von Baader, as usual citing Jakob Böhme as the spokesman for his own views, says explicitly, "Center in J. Böhme is always circle, frame, ground."[1] From this, its simplest but also most significant property, derive many of the characteristic attributes of the romantic center. In a circle the center is a unique point with special properties unlike those of the infinitely many points on the periphery or in the body of the circle. When a wheel rotates, for example, only the center is immobile: "Movement of the periphery is one with repose of the center, blockage of movement in the periphery is one with unrest in the center."[2] In a line the end points are unique, and the midpoint tends to resemble the other points along the line. A plucked string is immobile at the two ends; although the center does vibrate more vigorously than the other points on the string, this difference is one of degree, not one of kind. The center of a circle is primary; the center must be fixed before the circle can be drawn. The center of a line is secondary and is determined with respect to the two endpoints.

The contrast between these two versions of centrality was already decisive in the works of St. Augustine.[3] Man's position, according to the theologians, is in the middle of the universe, halfway up the

1. Franz von Baader, *Fermenta Cognitionis* I, 10, in *Werke* II, 164.
2. Baader, "Beiträge zur Elementarphysiologie," *Werke* III, 210. See also Eichendorff's quatrain "Weltgeschichte" from the group entitled "Andeutungen": "Inmitten steht die Sonn und wandelt nicht, / Ringsum sehnsüchtig kreisen die Planeten" ("Amidst them stands the sun and does not move, / Round about with yearning circle the planets").
3. See the related discussion of Augustine by Walther Rehm in *Experimentum Medietatis* (Munich, 1947), p. 7. Meyer Abrams's *Natural Supernaturalism* (New York, 1971), pp. 83–94, illuminates the Augustinian affinities of the English romantics.

great chain of being, between the animals and the divine realm: "For I was superior to these, but inferior to you—you my true delight whenever I submit to you—and you made me ruler of the things which you created beneath me. And this was the proper mean and middle region of my health, that I remain in your image and that in serving you I command my body" (*Confessions*, bk. VII, chap. vii). Man violates his middle status when he commits the sin of pride and, in punishment for wishing to exceed his allotted position, he is cast down to the very bottom of creation. This was Job's sin, and Augustine's words as he describes it echo the book of Job (15:26–27): "But when I proudly rose against you and ran upon the Lord with the fat neck of my shield, even these lowest things were placed above me and they were heavy and nowhere was there loosening or breathing" (*Confessions* VII, vii).

Now, the first act of pride was eating from the tree of knowledge, which was in the middle of Paradise. Its location is the symbol of man's subjection to the mediation of God. "For should the soul," says Augustine in reference to the original sin in his first commentary on Genesis, "leave God and turn toward itself and wish to enjoy its power as though without God, then it would swell with pride, which is the beginning of all sin" (*De Genesi contra Manichaeos* II, ix). According to his later commentary on the same passage, man learns of good and evil "through experiencing the punishment" that results ("per experimentum poenae") (*De Genesi ad Litteram* VIII, vi). Augustine uses the *double entendre* suggested by this in a notable chapter of the *De Trinitate*: "Per illud suae medietatis experimentum," he says, "the soul learns from its punishment the difference between the good which has been deserted and the evil which has been committed" (XII, xi). Fallen man experiments with his middle status, trying to trade in his natural mediocrity for the central position, the "mediation" of Christ and of the tree that is the type of Christ.

Mediocrity, mediation; despite the similar etymology, the two concepts differ enormously. For the orthodox Christian, man belongs in the middle, not in the center. For the romantics, on the other hand, the true center and end of man were never the human center in the middle of a line, but always the divine center, the privileged point in the circle, the point of mediation.

In the works of Johann Gottfried Herder the tension between the traditional orthodox conception and the incipient romantic conception is especially clear.[4] "Virtue" for Herder is still the Aristotelian virtue of the mean. The just man neither exceeds nor falls short. This is the message of the Confucian "Book of the Golden Mean," a fragment of which Herder included in his selections from Oriental literature in *Adrastea*: "Mean is the great foundation of the world; concord is the rule of the universe" (*Werke* XXIV, 11). The movement of history itself, as described in the fifteenth book of Herder's *Ideen zur Philosophie der Geschichte der Menschheit*, is a pendulumlike progression toward a midpoint where opposing forces are in balance and give a maximum of productive energy. Yet Herder recognizes that the result of such a process is always a compromise and always entails a loss. Herder's belief in the efficacy of the mean is therefore tinged with doubt and uncertainty: "Our earth has received the ambiguous golden lot of mediocrity, which we may at least dream of to our consolation as a *happy* mean" (*Ideen*, bk. I, chap. ii; in *Werke* XIII, 18). At best the mean is a standard only of optimal production, not of ultimate value. The straight line, according to the essay on Pygmalion ("Plastik"), symbolizes "solidity," but the circle, with its primal center, represents perfection: "The line of *perfection* is the *circle*, where everything shines out of one center and falls back into it" (*Werke* VIII, 64).

The circle, then, is the ideal. But it is the ideal of God, not of man, the ideal of the sun, not of the planets with their elliptical orbits. Man is incapable of self-contained perfection, of divine repose; he must try, says Herder, to content himself with the lesser ideal of maximum energy: "A round belly like a round head and round calf are overstuffed misgrowths; the germ of destruction is in them. Whence this last? I repeat, because the human vessel is capable of

4. Pope, who was greatly influential in Germany in the mid-eighteenth century, is the nearest English analogue. The aim of the *Essay on Man* is to convert man's image from that of a limited "middle state" or "isthmus" between God and beasts (II, 3) to an exuberant circular pond in the "centre" of the universe ("the Whole," IV, 361–72).

no *perfection* and therefore of no sign of the same; for perfection is *rest*, but they should *act, strive*" (VIII, 65). The ideal of human beauty is not the center of rest in the divine circle, but the other center, the center of balance, "the *juste milieu* between two extremes" (VIII, 66). In the late essay *Kalligone*, Herder elaborates even further on this notion of beauty; here he no longer speaks of circles at all but rather of a visible "symmetry" or "eurhythmy," defined as the "proportioning of a center to both its sides" (XXII, 47).

The circle of perfection, meanwhile, appears again where we might expect it, in a work of rational theology—the fifth of Herder's dialogues on Spinoza's system called *Gott*. These dialogues contain a notion of perfection different from that in the Pygmalion essay, perfection not as ultimate repose in God, but as the natural form of any object: "All perfection of a thing is its *reality*" (XVI, 552). Herder does not describe the circle here as a divine form unsuitable for natural objects, but on the contrary as the form that matter tends to adopt of its own accord. When matter is in the liquid state and thus free to choose its own shape, according to Herder, it naturally falls into round droplets. Yet when Herder describes a droplet, a curious thing happens. He is not content to depict the droplet, like the divine circle, as a region organized around a unique center; nor does he regard the center as the source and goal of the surrounding matter. Instead, the vocabulary of the *juste milieu* creeps in; the center is defined by the interplay of opposing forces: "The droplet is a sphere; in a sphere all parts move equally into harmony and order around one center. The sphere rests in itself; its center of gravity is in the middle; its form is thus the most beautiful subsistence of similar substances, which come into relation around this center *and with equal forces balance one another*" (XVI, 553, my emphasis).

A revealing ambiguity in the phrase "which come into relation around this center" shows Herder caught between two conceptions of the center. Even in this pantheistic context he is reluctant to attribute divine perfection to a terrestrial object. Rather than treat the center as a spiritual essence and the soul of the organism (as Carus later did, in the passage quoted on p. 19 above), Herder retreats to a mechanical and linear conception of the center as the point of balance between opposites. Then he substitutes a magnet for the droplet; organization around a unique center gives way to organization along an axis of polarity running between two extremes. Herder seems almost to be presenting a model for relating the transcendent circular standard of perfection to the more human scale of the balanced mean; as he says, "every sphere would in this way become a composite of two hemispheres with opposing poles" (XVI, 556).[5] Herder prefers symmetry to complex unity; where he has a circle, his tendency is to flatten it.

Nowhere is this flattening more striking than in Herder's discussion of vision in "Plastik." As the circle tends to become a line, so the sphere of vision becomes, for Herder, a plane. He denies all depth perception; all vision, he says, is flat: "The panorama which I see before me, what is it with all its manifestations but a picture, a surface? . . . Each object shows me exactly as much of itself as the mirror shows me of myself, that is, *figure, front side.*"[6] Only touch gives us a sense of substance, of body, of life; sight is as superficial and fleeting as light itself: "It is a proven truth that an undistracted blind man collects much more complete concepts of physical characteristics by feeling than does the sighted man who glides over the surface with a ray of light. . . . It thus remains true: 'The body which the eye sees is only surface, the surface which the hand feels, is body.'"[7] We need only compare a typical passage by Joseph Görres in order to see how the romantics reversed these priorities: the Idea, he says "looks outward into the depths of the universe to perceive the not-I and the rays of light adhere like soft tentacles to the most distant bodies in order to feel its forms with a tender touch and to cling to its outlines."[8] Herder subordinates sight to touch;

5. Herder changed "hemispheres" to "halves" in the second edition.
6. Herder, *Werke* VIII, 6. Novalis echoes this conception in his *Encyclopedia* (*Schriften* III, 458): "The eye is a surface sense." But the fragment in question belongs to the specialized context of Novalis's studies of Plotinus (see the editors' note, III, 975–77), and it does not have the same fundamental significance for Novalis that the basic generalization in "Plastik" has for Herder.
7. VIII, 8. The same ideas appear in Herder's *Journal meiner Reise, Werke* IV, 443–45.
8. "Glauben und Wissen," *Werke* III, 27.

for Görres sight takes over the role of touch even to the fullness of its erotic potential.[9] For any post-Kantian thinker the outer visual sphere, or horizon, is a constitutive part of our experience. For Herder the visual sphere and depth perception are products of analogical reasoning, rational illusions in a world whose exterior is essentially flat.

9. Novalis thought at one point of writing about "the primacy of the eye and the approach of all matter to light—of all actions to seeing—of all organs to the eye" (*Schriften* III, 571).

The Circle and the Organic World View

> Each being describes its curve: that of the spider, much less
> complex than that of the monkey, is much more so than
> that of the polyp. All these curves are but infinitely small
> portions of the prodigiously varied curve which comprises
> the universe. Only the supreme intelligence knows the
> equation of this curve.
>
> —Charles Bonnet, *Principes phi-*
> *losophiques*

Herder's vocabulary of centrality, which makes use of both the circle and the line, distorts to some extent the tendency of his thought,
which is to concentrate on axial polarities and to discount the circle, as a divine form unsuitable for man. A gap between forms of
expression and tendencies of thought likewise appears at times in
the romantics. Herder's vocabulary of linear organization and of
the balance of opposing forces with the center as the point of equilibrium (*Indifferenzpunkt*)[1] was by no means absent in the romantic period; but the romantics tended to reinterpret the vocabulary
and to assimilate it to the more characteristically romantic circle.
Just as Herder can be observed at times retreating from the incipient
romanticism of his imagery, so can certain key passages in the romantics be seen to advance beyond the mechanistic world view.

Centrality, as we have seen, was a quasi-Kantian perceptual category for Friedrich Schlegel. If we wish to find the category discussed
and the tendency to assimilate the line to the circle illustrated, the
natural place to look is in the philosophy of Schlegel's "romantic"
period. His lectures on transcendental philosophy delivered at Jena
in 1800–1801 do indeed furnish a typical example (*KA* XII, 6).
Schlegel locates philosophy along an axis leading from consciousness to the unconscious: "The elements of philosophy are *con-*
sciousness and the *infinite.*" Philosophy is a central science whose
goal is the elucidation of reality; reality is thus the midpoint of this

1. Carlyle's "centre of indifference" in *Sartor Resartus* is a punning mistranslation
   of this word. "Indifference" in German is *Gleichgültigkeit*.

axis, "the point of equilibrium between both." The linear image suggests that reality is a secondary product of these two forces, but Schlegel wishes to begin his philosophy with the real world, not with the process by which the real world is engendered. Consequently he immediately revises his image. Eschewing a line whose midpoint (reality) is the result of the interaction of its two extremes, he speaks of a circle in which Herder's mechanistic dualism remains only as an empty linguistic residuum: "Both elements make a closed sphere, in whose center is reality." The older vocabulary survives, but the conception is changing. The same is obviously true of a fragment in the philosophical notebooks: "In the ethical realm the extremes are nature, but the middle is art. . . . Harmony the midpoint of ethics" (*PhL* IV, 320). To Herder, "extremes" always meant contradictory forces. By making the extremes identical ("nature") Schlegel bends the line, as it were, into a circle, whose single extreme ("nature") is its perimeter and whose center is art. Whenever the romantics use an apparently dualistic vocabulary—in a pronouncement such as "Poetry as the primitive is the center of all rhetoric and history" (*LN* 1797)—we may reinterpret it in terms of a circle, which the two contraries somehow cooperate in forming and in which the center is the primary phenomenon ("the primitive").[2]

This reinterpretation was tantamount to a new way of seeing the world. The romantics, it cannot be repeated too frequently, were fully aware of the change and often used it as a vehicle of self-definition. Such is the case with the Jena lectures. Schlegel actually described his system as a "dualism," and he says that "all reality is

2. Wordsworth's tendency is to temper the eighteenth-century mechanistic conception, but not to revise it so thoroughly as the Germans. Instead of implying an actual cooperation of contraries, he merely softens the opposition, speaking, for example, of "feelings which, though they seem opposed to each other, have another and a finer connection than that of contrast." The "finer connection" suggests to him a bending of the axis of polarity around on itself, although he does not stress the image or use it "categorically": "It is a connection formed through the subtle progress by which, both in the natural and the moral world, qualities pass insensibly into their contraries, and things *revolve* upon each other" "Essay upon Epitaphs, I," in *Literary Criticism of William Wordsworth*, ed. Paul M. Zall (Lincoln, Neb., 1966), p. 95, my emphasis. In *The Borderers* it is the villain Oswald who claims: "So meet extremes in this mysterious world, / And opposites melt into each other" (ll. 1529–30). The hero Marmaduke also comes to speak of the identification of opposites, but only after he has fallen and his heart has become "frozen" (ll. 2185–86).

the product of contradictory elements" (*KA* XII, 8). But the opposition is not linear; we must learn, he says, how to convert the line
into a circle. Schlegel is careful to tell us how to do this:

> If anyone wants to know how a circle can be described out of two oppos-
> ing elements, let him imagine the matter approximately thus: The center of
> the circle is the positive factor, the radius the negative, and the periphery
> point the point of equilibrium. Now the positive factor in the equilibrium
> point [that is, the + in the ± point] has the urge to unite with the positive
> factor in the center, but because of the negative factor it cannot approach
> the center, but is merely driven around the center. [XII, 10]

Schlegel's model is easily recognizable. The "urge to unite" is the
force of gravity, and the circle is the path of planetary revolution.
The product of two linear forces, the positive centripetal force and
the negative centrifugal force, is a circular motion. The old mechanical center, the point of equilibrium, becomes the perimeter, making
way for a new center. The new romantic center is reality, but, as we
shall see, reality mystically understood, based, as these lectures say,
on "enthusiasm" (*Enthusiasmus*) and "yearning" (*Sehnsucht*).

Schlegel presents the derivation of the circle from linear forces
as a useful paradigm and guide to thought. He undoubtedly did not
intend to imply that he was describing facts and that circles actually
are derived from lines. On the contrary, the romantics always regarded the circle as the fundamental form. Romantic philosophers
tenaciously insist that circular orbits do not result from centrifugal
and centripetal forces, but precede them, and that the "central
forces" are mere secondary rationalizations. We find this attitude
as early as the influential mid-century Swabian pietist Friedrich
Christoph Oetinger, who distinguished between the "dead" central
forces and the "living force" of actual movement in a circle.[3] Again
in Kant, we find the late notebooks repeatedly attacking the reality
of the central forces in the course of speculations on the problem of

---

3. "Hence, too, there is a twofold force, the one elementary, which I also call dead
because motion is not yet in it, but only a solicitation to motion . . . ; the other
is ordinary force, joined to actual motion, which I call live. And of the dead
force one example is centrifugal force itself, and then the gravitational or centripetal force," Oetinger, *Inquisitio in Sensum Communem et Rationem* (Tübingen, 1753), reprint, ed. Hans-Georg Gadamer (Stuttgart, 1964), §20, p. 39.
In the same reprinted volume, see also *Theoriae Musicae Analysis*, pp. 39–40.

the deduction of natural laws from the laws of human reason.[4] Hegel expresses the same viewpoint with even more vigor in his *Habilitationsschrift*, "Dissertatio philosophica de Orbitis Planetarum":

> For geometry does not try to construct circles or other curves out of lines intersecting at a right angle or at any other angle whatsoever, but supposes the circle or other curve under discussion to be the given and determines from these data the ratios of the remaining lines; this method of positing the whole and determining the ratios of the parts from it—and not that of compounding the whole out of opposing forces, that is, out of its parts—is the true method, and physics ought to imitate it exactly.[5]

The geometric construction of the circle is a mere abstraction, a misleading representation of a more profound and more organic truth. Franz von Baader makes the distinction in his important early work "Über das Pythagoräische Quadrat in der Natur": "In using the sphere and its midpoint as symbol one customarily thinks of the latter only as the mathematical point, whereas one ought to think of the actual center of the periphery as the life-giving inner One, in comparison to the external, visible many (individual)" (*Werke* III, 257). Baader's contrast of midpoint and center is not a distinction between a realistic conception and an idealistic one, between an apparent circle and a true circle. The romantic conception embraces the visible as well as the mystical One, the periphery as well as the center, and indeed it recognizes the necessity of "comparing" the two; it rejects only the fleshless mathematical reduction of the circle to imaginary points and lines. Romantic philosophy embodies the natural propensity of the mind—as Kant had described it in the *Critique of Judgment*—away from analytical reasoning, which was felt to be destructive dissection, and toward a teleological, organic way of thinking. Center and periphery must be thought together; the whole, for the romantics, is greater than its parts. The opening of Schelling's essay "Von der Weltseele" illustrates this propensity:

4. See the *Opus Postumum* in Kant's *Gesammelte Schriften* (Akademieausgabe) XXI (Berlin, 1936), 165, 167, 170, 171, 286, and *passim* (additional references in the index in vol. 22 under "Zentralkräfte" and related terms).
5. G. W. F. Hegel, *Werke*, ed. D. Friedrich Förster and D. Ludwig Boumann (Berlin, 1834), p. 10.

Each motion that returns into itself presupposes a *positive* force that (as *impulse*) *fans* the movement (makes it as it were the start of a line), and a *negative* that (as *attraction*) *guides* the motion *back into itself* (or prevents it from being diverted into a straight line). . . . But an invisible power leads all phenomena back into the eternal cycle. . . . These warring forces, represented at once in unity and in conflict, lead to the idea of an *organizing principle* which forms the world into a *system*. Perhaps the ancients wanted to suggest such a principle with the *World-Soul*. [*Werke* II, 381]

Within the very first page Schelling has swiftly led his reader from the mechanistic notion of opposing forces to a holistic conception of a mystical system in which conflict is but one aspect of unity. As in Schlegel's description of the construction of a circle, our understanding is said to grasp the component forces first. But true ontological priority belongs to the "formative principle."

The Necessity of a Center

> We have a distinct antipathy to bifurcation. It is unorganic
> to let the thing in the middle disintegrate.
>
> —Heinrich Wölfflin, *Prolego-*
> *mena zu einer Psychologie der*
> *Architektur*

Everywhere the romantics see teleology and everywhere they look
for circular organization around a center, the symbol of teleology:
"In the human mind as in the universe nothing is above or below,
everything demands equal rights to a common center which manifests its secret existence through the harmonious relationship of all
parts to it."[1] The center is indispensable, for it is the formal cause
of the circle. The center is not the product of experience, to be
found by empirical search or to be deduced by abstract reasoning;
it is a prerequisite for experience even to be possible. The simple
formulation of this view is Franz von Baader's comment, "Middle
is spirit." A fuller statement, found in one of Baader's political
works, makes explicit the vitalistic assumptions and precludes too
idealistic an interpretation: "For the orient or rising of each sphere
is its center, from which it proceeds and into which, likewise, it
always again returns, and nothing can be more unsuitable than to
join the uncomprehending multitude in calling this central knowledge abstract, as if the center, which comprises the whole periphery
in itself, were an abstraction from it."[2]

This forms, for example, an important aspect of Goethe's doctrine of renunciation. "To renounce" means to concentrate on es-

1. Goethe, "Ernst Stiedenroths Psychologie," *Werke* XIX, 420. Cf. Joshua Rey-
   nolds's somewhat more static conception in his important essay in Johnson's
   Idler, no. 82: "Every species of the animal as well as of the vegetable creation
   may be said to have a fixed or determinate form, towards which nature is continually inclining, like various lines terminating in the centre."
2. Franz von Baader, *Werke* XIV, 385 (marginal annotation to C. J. H. Windisch-
   mann, *Über etwas, das der Heilkunst noth tut*); XIV, 96 (*Vorlesungen über die
   Philosophie der Societät*).

tablishing and defining the central self at the expense of the temptations of external pleasures; renunciation is the process of collecting
oneself in preparation for turning outward with purpose and understanding: "Man should hold on to every form of possession, he
should make himself the center from which the common good can
proceed, he must be an egoist so as not to become an egoist, hold
together so that he can give."[3] Once the center has been established, generosity becomes an orderly and significant movement,
not merely a wasteful dissipation of the self; it is therefore described
at one point in *Wilhelm Meisters Wanderjahre* as a "circular"
emanation from "a pure center" (*Werke* VII, 840–41). Without an
organizing center, on the other hand, there can only be fragmentation and chaos. This is true in the natural realm, where the "plant
entelechy" is the "ruling center" that holds the different parts together;[4] but it is equally true in the human realm. At a certain stage
in history, the unifying force of tradition becomes so weakened that
beliefs held in common are no longer sufficient to unite men. A
ferment results without creative potential: "Instead of teaching and
peacefully intervening, people throw seeds and weeds to all sides at
once; a center to look toward is no longer given, each individual
steps forth as teacher and leader and presents his consummate folly
as a consummate whole."[5]

Wilhelm von Humboldt thought that the attempt to grasp "the
form from its center, its necessary conditions" was a unique virtue
"characteristic of Goethe's poetic manner."[6] There is some justice
to this statement. The qualities of limitation and enclosure, and

3. *Wilhelm Meisters Wanderjahre*, Werke VII, 782. The analogy in the plant king-
    dom to renunciation is the expulsion of excess matter, a phenomenon which is
    described in Goethe's essay "Verstäubung, Verdunstung, Vertropfung." "Why
    should this last expulsion of pollen not also be just a freeing from burdensome
    matter, so that the fullness of the most genuine inside may make its way at last,
    from a living primal force, toward an infinite propagation" (*Werke* XIX, 253).
4. "Nacharbeiten und Sammlungen," *Werke* XIX, 132.
5. "Geistesepochen, nach Hermanns neuesten Mitteilungen," *Werke* XV, 367. Cf.
    Schiller, *Die Piccolomini*, 416–20: "Then / Well for the whole, if there be found
    a man, / Who makes himself what nature destined him, / The pause, the central
    point to thousand thousands— / Stands firm and stately like a firm-built column,
    / Where all may press with joy and confidence" (trans. Coleridge).
6. "Goethes zweiter römischer Aufenthalt," *Werke* VI, 539.

therefore of harmony and balance, suggested by the word "grasp" are indeed a special achievement of some of Goethe's works. But there is evidence that this was Schiller's intellectual ambition as well: the scholar's "noble impatience," according to his inaugural lecture in Jena, "cannot rest until all his concepts have arranged themselves in a harmonious whole, until he stands in the center of his art, his science, and from here surveys its realm with a satisfied glance."[7] And it takes only a slight shift of emphasis to think of the center, not as the unifying principle, but as the generating principle. At least this kind of center, productive if not controlling, is sought by all romantic authors. It became a pastime of Karl Philipp Moritz, for example, to pick out the central scene, character, or passage in a work of art, the point at which the basic conflicts and concerns are most clearly revealed.[8] Friedrich Schlegel, with his theories of romantic irony and progressive form, would seem less likely to have had such a "central" orientation; yet he constructed his own novel *Lucinde* as a series of arabesques surrounding a central narrative section, and he looked for a center in the works of the most romantic authors of previous generations: "As among those of Cervantes and Shakespeare, so too among the stories of Boccaccio there must be a *central story*."[9] In Schelling's transcendental idealism these various activities find their philosophical justification. The identity (or "indifference") of nature and consciousness, according to Schelling, is the central fact out of which all discrimination and development of individuals emerge. Without this original unity, a relationship between man and nature—and in particular man's knowledge of nature—would be inconceivable. As early as 1795, on the opening page of the essay "Vom Ich als Princip der Philosophie," Schelling defines his program in terms of the romantic metaphor of the circle and explains (though without using the word) the necessity of a center:

7. Schiller, "Was heißt und zu welchem Ende studiert man Universalgeschichte?" *Werke* IV, 752.
8. There are two descriptions of this pastime, by Caroline Herder and by K. F. Klischnig. Both are quoted in Moritz's *Schriften*, pp. 345–47.
9. *LN* 1997. In the "Nachricht von den poetischen Werken des Johannes Boccaccio," which followed this fragment by about one year, Schlegel finds the "center and common viewpoint" of Boccaccio's works in the *Fiammetta* (*KA* II, 393—not the *Ninfale fiesolano*, as Eichner says in his note to *LN* 1997).

Either our knowledge must be totally without reality—an eternal circling, a constant reciprocal flowing of all individual sentences into one another, a chaos, in which no element is distinct, or —

There must be a last point of reality, on which everything depends, from which all permanence and all form of our knowledge proceeds, which distinguishes elements and describes for each the circle of its continuing influence in the universe. [*Werke* I, 162]

Human Art and the Divine Center

> whate'er
> Full of mysterious import Nature weaves,
> And fashions in the depths—the spirit's ladder,
> That from this gross and visible world of dust
> Even to the starry world, with thousand rounds,
> Builds itself up; on which the unseen powers
> Move up and down on heavenly ministries—
> The circles in the circles, that approach
> The central sun with ever-narrowing orbit—
> These see the glance alone, the unsealed eye,
> Of Jupiter's glad children born in lustre.
>
> —Schiller, *Die Piccolomini* (trans.
> S. T. Coleridge)

What if no center can be found? The "last point of reality," the divine center organizing the external world and binding it together, is not always readily visible. An individual's limited perspective may not suffice to discover the structure of events and the relations among objects. Much remains inexplicable; much seems a linear mechanical procession to infinity, without purpose and without end. Some romantic authors, unable to perceive the ordering hand in the universe, yield to this appearance, striking the nihilistic note implicit in Schelling's first possibility, knowledge without reality. The best-known text of this type, the "Speech of the Dead Christ" in Jean Paul's *Siebenkäs*, describes the centrifugal chaotic tendencies of a world in which time is a circle without a center, represented by an empty watchface with neither figures nor hands.[1] The

---

1. For Wordsworth too a center is necessary to felicity; see for example *The Prelude* (1850) V, 252, and *The Recluse*, ll. 143–51. But for many later authors in English, such as De Quincey and Poe, the presence of a center can be the sign of a demonic fixation. Thus in "Dreaming," De Quincey writes, "Unless this colossal pace of advance can be retarded (a thing not to be expected), or, which is happily more probable, can be met by counter-forces of corresponding magnitude—forces in the direction of religion or profound philosophy that shall radiate centrifugally against this storm of life so perilously centripetal towards the vortex of the merely human—left to itself, the natural tendency of so chaotic a

echoes of Schelling's thought and even of his vocabulary are unmistakable: "The whole spiritual universe is exploded and shattered
by the hand of atheism into countless quicksilvery points of I's,
which shine, run, wander, fly together and apart, without unity and
permanence."[2]

The image of dissolution presented here by Jean Paul, and elsewhere in a few works of Wackenroder, Tieck, and E. T. A. Hoffmann, as well as in the anonymous novel *Die Nachtwachen des
Bonaventura*, is one to which the German romantics succumb only
on occasion. The divine plan is hidden, but most had confidence in
its existence. The natural order cannot always be understood, but it
can always be believed; faith, as Fichte taught, must always precede
knowledge. Where the human perspective fails, seeing only dis-
harmony and destruction, the romantics still believe in a higher
viewpoint from which all falls into place. Aberrations and injustices
are not symptoms of chaos, but challenges to rise above them and
discover their part in the universal scheme: "Seen from *this* height
the individual successions of causes and effects (which deceive us
with the appearance of mechanism) disappear as infinitely small
straight lines in the general organic circle in which the world itself
proceeds."[3]

The view from a height over a surrounding landscape is one of
the most characteristic situations found in German romantic literature. The landscapes are never realistic; they are marked by an
abundance and variety of objects and inhabitants, shapes and con-
tours symbolic of the plenitude of life itself. To see the unity in this
multiplicity, the form in this chaos, and to discover the universal
human experience are the observer's task, set by the central com-
manding prospect:

tumult must be to evil" *Collected Writings*, ed. David Masson (Edinburgh,
1889–1890), XIII, 334. De Quincey's comments on dreaming, especially the
notion of the "vortex of the merely human," should be contrasted with an
essay by Franz von Baader on the same subject, "Unterscheidung einer centralen
Sensation von einer bloss peripherischen und excentrischen . . . ," *Werke* IV,
133–40, and with Heinrich Werner's *Die Schutzgeister oder merkwürdige
Blicke zweier Seherinnen* (Stuttgart, 1839), pp. 548–59.

2. Jean Paul (Friedrich Richter), *Werke* II, ed. Gustav Lohmann (Munich, 1959),
266. See Walther Rehm's analysis of Jean Paul's various dream visions in
Experimentum Medietatis (Munich, 1947), pp. 20 ff.

3. Schelling, "Von der Weltseele," *Werke* II, 350.

We, the sons of this century, enjoy the advantage that we stand on the summit of a high mountain, and that many lands and many times lie revealed to our eyes, spread out round about us and at our feet. So let us then use this good fortune and roam with cheerful looks over all times and peoples and strive always to detect the *human* in all their manifold feelings and works of feeling.[4]

The goal is a selfless perfection of the self, not complete knowledge of mechanical or causal forces (for this is already implicit in the elevated perspective), but complete understanding of this knowledge, of human feelings and of the divine will. The goal is unreachable. No matter how high the perspective, it is still a personal one, and it still limits our understanding, according to Wackenroder: "Each sort of being strives for ideal beauty: but it cannot go outside of itself, and sees ideal beauty only in itself. . . . The general, original beauty . . . reveals itself to Him who made both the rainbow and the eye which sees it" (*Herzensergießungen*, pp. 49–50).

The Creator alone, we might say, understands the Creation. Wackenroder's formulation, however, is less simple, and to follow him we must make an additional distinction. His ideal is the revelation of beauty rather than understanding. The distant view from above is not the scientific view of Leibniz's mechanistic creator, but that of the disinterested aesthetic eye. For Wackenroder, as for Schelling, the highest viewpoint, from which all phenomena merge into a rounded, organic whole, is that of art. "The straight line belongs rather to science, the curve rather to art," as Görres was to say.[5] Therefore, Wackenroder makes the transition from the natural landscape through "feelings and works of feeling" to beauty. Beauty is the name of the understanding that the elevated central viewpoint is capable of conferring. Yet true beauty, in this view, is more than human, and an appreciation of it is reserved for the all-embracing divine eye. The divine circle is infinite; a finite horizon always surrounds the human observer. The romantic who does not yield to nihilism therefore still has no cause for rejoicing. Art pro-

4. Johann Heinrich Wackenroder, *Herzensergießungen eines kunstliebenden Klosterbruders*, p. 49.
5. "Exposition der Physiologie," *Werke* II², 3.

vides a center, but it is at best only a surrogate. True beauty and true art are beyond the grasp of mankind.[6]

Wackenroder's words are echoed in a text published a few years after the *Herzensergießungen* that also expresses the need to get outside oneself, to the elevated standpoint that is required, and the impossibility of actually reaching the goal:

> I surrender these leaves not as a sacrifice [to art], no, they are to feed the flame in which I will one day offer my pure sacrifice. Be well inclined toward me, dear reader, for I destroy myself as it were with this book, which is but too much more penetrated with me than with itself, in order to attain more quickly the power of objectivity and to do what I can from my standpoint. It is already an inner delight for me to look out over all the failings which I had two years ago; to correct all of them I should have to stand on the last height, which always flees before us.

This passage is remarkable not so much for its contents as for its location: in the preface to the most willful, most subjective, most romantic of all the romantic novels, Clemens Brentano's *Godwi*.[7] No book could be more ill designed as a tribute to the power of objectivity than this fountainhead of confusion and mistaken identities, supposedly narrated by a dying author whose informant refuses to reveal what has happened. The discrepancy is intentional, for the contradiction between the subjectivity of the finite work of art and the objectivity of the ideal of art lies at the heart of romantic aesthetics. Moritz could still speak of a basic similarity, in which the finite circle of art imitates—with the necessary adjustments and distortions and "on a smaller scale"—the infinite circle of nature.[8] Writing less than ten years later, Brentano envisions a totally new relationship in place of this unbridgeable gap. Ideal beauty being unreachable, to try to ape it would be futile. Indeed, human efforts

6. Gerhard Fricke analyzes Wackenroder's growing sense of the subjectivity, the fallibility, and eventually the deceitfulness of human art in his "Bemerkungen zu Wilhelm Heinrich Wackenroders Religion der Kunst," *Festschrift Paul Kluckhohn und Hermann Schneider* (Tübingen, 1948), pp. 345–71.
7. Brentano, *Werke* II, 15.
8. "Die metaphysische Schönheitslinie," *Schriften*, p. 156, and again in almost identical wording, in "Über die bildende Nachahmung des Schönen," *Schriften*, p. 76. Both essays discuss the question at length.

would be consumed by the intensity of the absolute. Instead, romantic art makes a virtue of its very shortcomings, parading the distance between its achievement and its goal in order to demonstrate the strength of its desire to reach that goal. Romantic art is measured by its energy rather than by its achievement. In Brentano's metaphor, it is the flame that nourishes the altar of beauty, not the object sacrificed on the altar. It is not perfection, but the striving for perfection. This explains the surprising reversal that seems to substitute a maximum of subjectivity for ideal objectivity. Romantic art begins by turning away from its ideal, for with increasing distance the strength of the desire to return is also increased. Even art's imperfections are a source of pleasure for the person who can contemplate them and who desires their correction. Actually to correct them, were such a thing possible, would mean eliminating the desire and with it the pleasure. The preface does close with a promise of future improvements: "But I will keep striding forward faster, with more artistry and more enthusiasm, so that the space that divides me from the goal may continue growing smaller and finally remain visible only to the seer." It is perfectly evident, however, that Brentano did not intend these pious, if not very clear lines to be taken literally. For the preface is attributed to the fictional author Maria and dated June 1800; by that time (according to the epilogue included with the novel) Maria was already mortally ill; hence the phrase "I destroy myself" in the preface. The preface by the dying Maria amounts to a guarantee by Brentano that no improvements would be made and to a statement of belief that the tension and striving aroused by its faults constitute the book's strength.

There is one German word that suggests both tension and striving, the one by similarity of etymology, the other by similarity of meaning: *Tendenz*. This is the essential quality of romantic literature; Brentano points to its necessity when he has Maria (in yet another example of romantic irony) open the preface with an apology for its absence: "This book has no *Tendenz*." Following Brentano's preface, we might define the fundamental condition of romantic literature as the expression of the striving of the subjective human center to regain the ineffable divine center. We would not be alone.

In Schlegel's *Gespräch über die Poesie* one character defines poetry in terms reminiscent of Wackenroder's as a "higher idealistic view of things." He is immediately corrected by another participant: the definition is too self-assured, not ironic enough. Romantic poetry (and all poetry, Schlegel's spokesman says, is romantic) does not possess an absolute viewpoint, but only strives for it. It is "the *Tendenz* toward a deep, infinite meaning" (*KA* II, 323). The concepts *Tendenz* and "striving" thus resolve a dilemma implicit in romantic centrality. The individual is caught between the intellectual hubris of claiming a divine central viewpoint and the psychological extravagance of the nihilists who deny the center. Only if he shuttles between these two extremes can he avoid the pitfalls of either one. Indeed, Schlegel's programmatic essay "Über die Unverständlichkeit" claims that *Tendenz* is not the means to some end, but is in itself the end of romanticism: "All is but mere tendency, the age is the age of tendencies" (*KA* II, 367). But *Tendenz* and striving are only a verbal resolution of the dilemma; they name the movement of the romantic individual, but in themselves they do not help us to describe it. Hence Fichte's *Grundlage der gesamten Wissenschaftslehre* of 1794–95 devotes many pages to an analysis of striving without by any means exhausting its significance. Therefore, we must begin a closer examination of some of the major "tendencies" of German romanticism, for which I will take as my guiding thread the shifting relations of center and periphery.

II. The Open Circle

Young man: A new thought of the greatest importance, whose consequences for literature are all but inestimable. For every new idea is like the first peep of dawn; first it gently reddens the mountains and treetops, then suddenly here, there, with a flaming glance it ignites a river, a tower in the distance; now the mists in the depth swirl and divide and coil, the circle expands far and farther, immeasurable blooming lands emerge—who can say where that will end! — Dear madam, I know you have long shared our conviction that those fantastic artificial inventions in poetry separate us from nature and little by little have created a wonderful, conventional, nowhere present, *written* life above life, I should say: have set a Bible above the tradition, so that we must hasten back to reality — —

Poetess: Brief! I beg of you, be brief, I am growing faint. —

Man in gray: In short, we are making a story.

> —Eichendorff, "Viel Lärmen um Nichts"

The Dialectic of Objectivity

> To be sure, these poetic airs which so love to spread their
> peacock's fan everywhere, what are they but that perfidious
> irony, suspended with equal indifference above all appear-
> ances, above good and evil; thin ice on which every high
> sentiment, virtue, and human dignity slip and make them-
> selves ridiculous; cold, cold, cold, 'til I shudder in my in-
> most soul! Oh, the impudent lie of divine objectivity! Out,
> poet, with thy true heartfelt opinion behind thy miserable
> objects! Speak out thy innermost with frankness!
>
> —Eichendorff, "Viel Lärmen um
> Nichts"

For the romantics experience begins with almost pure negativity.
Since the divine center in the (presumably) harmonious world-orga-
nism is hidden, striving can be directed only toward "a purely *imaginary* object."[1] Brentano's consumptive Maria, surrendering his
positive identity to encroaching disease, symbolizes the plight of romantic consciousness; in man's perpetual movement toward death,
"pain is life."[2] Experience comes through feeling, but feeling is a
passion (*Leidenschaft*) and therefore a kind of suffering (*Leiden*)
that continually attacks the domain of the self. Experience consists
of a loss of independence and a sacrifice of will: the loss results from
the impingement of the world on the citadel of the self and the sacrifice from submission to this impingement. It is not by chance that
Brentano's *Godwi* closes with a vision of Orpheus, who typifies the
pattern of loss followed by self-sacrifice.[3] Only this is Orpheus with
a difference; his Hades is life itself, and what he unsuccessfully at-

1. Fichte, *Grundlage der gesamten Wissenschaftslehre*, in *Werke* I, 267.
2. Schiller, *Wilhelm Tell*, l. 2382.
3. Compare Walther Rehm's discussion of Orpheus in relation to the centrality of
poetry in the opening sections of *Orpheus: Der Dichter und die Toten* (Düsseldorf, 1950). The pattern of a descent into darkness followed by a return that is
either unsuccessful, willful, or insincere is extremely common; see Jacques
Derrida, *Of Grammatology*, tr. Gayatri Chakravorty Spivak (Baltimore, 1976),
part 2, chap. 2, for a discussion of the guilt-ridden "supplement" that follows
blindness in Rousseau.

tempts to salvage from change and mortality is his own identity: "As now you descend into the darkness of errant life, [and] return with new spirit into the depths of the breast, there to find lost youth surrounded with shadows, boldly subduing death you bring poetry back. So did Thracian Orpheus once descend to Orkus, sought his beloved, found her entrusted to death" (*Werke* II, 459). Such a reference to Orpheus, whose quest was ultimately a failure, and the awareness that the presumed author of these lines is already dead ironically overshadow the hollow felicity of the couplets that follow this passage. The search for permanence and immortality can be only a perpetuation of error and a lesson in futility; as Schlegel pointedly wrote: "What does not annihilate itself is worthless" (*LN* 226). On the other hand, as the preface to *Godwi* shows, each loss is also a gain, in energy, in validity, and in universality. In self-submission the soul feeds the altar of objectivity; it moves closer to God and to His world: "A mediator is he who perceives divinity in himself and yields up and destroys himself in order to proclaim, communicate, and represent this divinity to all men in behavior and action, in words and works" (Schlegel, *Ideen* 44).

This cosmic modesty differs from the cosmic nihilism of Jean Paul's dead Christ. In the speech the latter adopts a doctrinaire stance and an assertive tone that can become as oppressive in their way as any other dogma. The nihilist affirms the nothingness of the universe. The romantic, in contrast, initially risks no affirmation at all. For most German authors Byronic nihilism is no more accessible an alternative than the empty sublimity of Byronic heroism. Instead of these heady extremes, we find a confused intermediate state, beset by nagging feelings of inadequacy and defeat. "Each self-destruction destroys itself. Much more painful [*viel empfind-licher*] when one shows somebody *how little* he is, than that he is nothing at all" (*LN* 254). Yet all this destruction leaves a residue; some "little" knowledge or insight is produced. For though the romantic, like Orpheus, proceeds through ignorance, in darkness, and with eyes averted, his goal is positive. His negativity is a calculated method of continual evasion and withdrawal rather than the vacuous state of the nihilist.[4]

4. See further Dieter Arendt's compendious and readable survey, *Der "Poetische Nihilismus" in der Romantik* (Tübingen, 1972), where, however, some false

The romantic, in short, would like to begin with the world; "the beginning," as Hegel's *Science of Logic* codifies this view, lies in "pure being," not in self-consciousness.[5] The romantic attempts to transfer the center of his existence away from the self—where it is vulnerable both morally (to pride) and metaphysically (to solipsism)—to the not-self of objective reality. He wants, that is, to surrender the initiative to nature, to substitute a natural order for the more fragile order imposed by his ego. This is a precarious undertaking. The suppression of the self permits the discovery of the natural order, but does not guarantee it; it is, in Fichte's phrase, "not knowledge, but a decision of the will to abide by our knowledge."[6] Indeed, the selfless, unprejudiced observer confronts at first a chaos of undigested sense impressions, and for the romantic (though not for the Kantian) the task of reducing these to order is long and wearisome.[7] We easily recognize this initial meaningless objectivity or, as we might call it, scrupulous incomprehension, as the mode of the first half of *Godwi*; the fictional author tries to present as authentically as possible a series of documents that he does not understand. In this respect, too, Maria symbolizes the status of mankind in the romantic world view, compelled to accept a chaos of appearances in order that a pattern may eventually be discovered. Once he has placed himself, by a decision of the will, out of

---

judgments result from the failure to distinguish between the methodological *via negativa* and true nihilism.

5. Hegel, *Wissenschaft der Logik* I, 69. See also Dieter Henrich's discussion of the negativity of beginning with being, "Anfang und Methode der Logik," *Hegel im Kontext* (Frankfurt, 1967), pp. 73–94.

6. *Die Bestimmung des Menschen*, *Werke* II, 254.

7. See in particular Friedrich Schleiermacher's *Dialektik*, ed. Rudolf Odebrecht (Leipzig, 1942), pp. 143 ff. Here the characteristic romantic departures from Kant are particularly evident: (1) whereas Kant uses only words like "confusion" (*Verwirrung*), and those not very often, the romantics substitute the more poetic and emotive term "chaos" to describe "the absolute beginning of thought from the organic side" (p. 147); (2) whereas Kant believes in the spontaneity of judgment, of knowledge of objects, and of "intuition," for the romantics these are the goal of a slow and difficult intellectual effort; (3) whereas Kant posits the uniformity of the human intellect, the romantics, like the American pragmatists, assume that we live in different "spheres" or "circles" (in the *Dialektik*, as in many later romantic works, it is the language of each group that circumscribes and unites it) and that to attain a single center of consciousness is an "infinite task," which can never be "solved" except by the "asymptotic approximation" of a "constant approach" (pp. 169–71).

the center—or, to use Runge's phrase, his spirit has moved away from the sunrise[8]—the romantic is ready to turn and examine the world, to try to fill the void. We may now consider the nature of this endeavor.

Goethe was its methodologist. He readily recognized his own penchant for "object-oriented thought" ("gegenständliches Denken"), directed toward the object of perception rather than the remote noumenal "thing-in-itself."[9] Goethe, in other words, was a phenomenologist; he believed that reality is inherent in appearances, not in unknowable entities. This belief he registered as a guiding principle at the opening of his massive treatise on optics: "For actually we undertake in vain to express the essence of a thing. We perceive effects, and a complete history of these effects would undoubtedly embrace the essence of that thing."[10] These effects, however, are much more fragile than the impenetrable substances of other philosophies, and a headstrong investigator can easily distort or disfigure them to suit his preconceptions. The most difficult and important task for the scientific investigator in Goethe's view is to respect phenomena and to exclude his personality from impinging on them; the most serious error is to substitute analysis and abstraction—that is, one's own thoughts—for the description of real observed phenomena. This concern for disinterested observation or "pure intuition" was closely allied to Goethe's passionate involvement in optics.[11] His quarrel with Newton was based on the conviction that Newton had imposed a false order and an arbitrary center on his observations: "Newton had based his hypothesis on a complicated and derivative experiment, to which the throngs of other phenomena, if they could not be passed over in silence and brushed aside, were artificially related and placed around in uneasy situations; much as an astronomer would have to proceed who for

8. "One who wished to hold on externally to the sunrise would be foolish to go east; he must needs travel due west whenever the sun rose" Philipp Otto Runge, *Schriften* I, 189.
9. "Bedeutende Fördernis durch ein einziges geistreiches Wort," *Werke* XIX, 361–65.
10. *Zur Farbenlehre: Didaktischer Teil*, "Vorwort," *Werke* XXI, 13.
11. The common phrase "pure intuition" ("reine Anschauung") can be found, for example, in *MuR* 533.

a whim wanted to put the moon in the center of our system." [12] For this reason—and with the excuse that "we theorize with each attentive look at the world" (*Werke* XXI, 15)—Goethe's own scientific writings consist of careful accounts of his (sometimes quite telling) experimental observations together with moralizing generalizations, but with very little of the analytical and theoretical reasoning that would ordinarily be expected to bridge the gap between the specific and the general.

Goethe's resistance to theory was very great. [13] Theorists prescribe their reasoning to others; they adopt, in other words, a stance of intellectual superiority, like that of a teacher toward his students, which impedes the inevitable process of revision and correction: "Hypotheses are lullabies with which the teacher soothes his pupils; the thoughtful, upright observer recognizes his limitations more and more" (*MuR* 579). Intricate systems and overeager syntheses blind the experimenter to the very facts he is out to discover. One of the most memorable of Goethe's many statements of this tenet is telling: "What is half-known hinders knowledge. Since all our knowledge is only by halves, so our knowledge always hinders knowledge" (*Werke* XVIII, 174).

In view of these considerations Goethe's prescription is almost self-evident. The object of investigation should have the leading, primary, central role; it should be an end in itself and not merely a means for the scientist to confirm and buttress his own self-importance. For this offense Goethe attacked a book by a French physicist named César Mansuète Despretz in an uncharacteristically harsh and sarcastic review. "It lies in each man," Goethe writes with heavy irony, "to regard himself as the center of the world since, after all, all rays proceed from his consciousness and return there again. Might one therefore resent in capital spirits a certain imperialism, a yen for acquisition?" Instead of this spurious centrality, Goethe emphasizes the advantages of a more flexible attitude, ca-

---

12. *Zur Farbenlehre: Didaktischer Teil*, "Einleitung," *Werke* XXI, 25–26.
13. For an example of the way Goethe evades abstraction, answering a theoretical criticism (that he had neglected to study root systems) with a metaphorical and moralizing response (that one ought to be more concerned with what is above ground), see the page entitled "Unbillige Forderung," *Werke* XVIII, 190–91.

pable of moving from one subject to another and of seeing the same object in various lights and in manifold relationships, "as indeed every new viewpoint enables new perspectives, and on the periphery of every circle infinitely many perspectives are conceivable, standing in many different relations to one another" (*Werke* XVIII, 282, 283).

A brief essay entitled "Der Versuch als Vermittler zwischen Subjekt und Objekt" develops the positive consequences for scientific method and practice of this belief. The ultimate aim of scientific investigation is the complete description of one or more phenomena. A complete description is one that, both literally and metaphorically, views the phenomenon from all angles, taking into account all of its effects and interactions with allied phenomena.[14] The investigator will therefore proceed slowly, even pedantically, from each step to its nearest conceivable neighbor in order to weave as tight and continuous a fabric of observation around the object as possible:

> It can be said of every phenomenon that it is related to countless others, as we say of a free-floating shining point that it sends its rays out to all sides. So that if we have made such an experiment, then we cannot investigate too carefully, what borders *directly* on it? what follows *next* from it? This is what we have to pay more attention to than to what is *related* to it. *The multiplication of each and every experiment* is thus the actual duty of the scientist. He . . . must work unceasingly, as if he wanted to leave nothing for his successors to do, even though the disproportion of our understanding to the nature of things early enough reminds him that no man has capacity enough to conclude anything. [*Werke* XVIII, 85]

In typical romantic fashion Goethe here names the goal only to remove it from the realm of possible attainment. Nature always defeats man's attempts at mastery; hence objectivity for Goethe is always a discipline, never a secure possession. At the same time the discipline must never become an end in itself, for that would mean

---

14. Cf. Goethe on himself: "Goethe's works are products of a talent that does not develop progressively and also does not flutter about, but tries itself out from a certain center toward all sides simultaneously and attempts to work at close range as well as at a distance" "Summarische Jahresfolge Goethescher Schriften," *Werke* XV, 509—10.

shifting the center of attention back from the object to the scientist. Nothing could be more foreign to Goethe's nature than the single-mindedness of the self-denying researcher, determined to discover all the answers unaided. To avoid this sublimated, but still perilous, form of self-centered pride, the scientist must recognize practically as well as theoretically the inevitable shortcomings of his perspective, through a willing acceptance of the insights and viewpoints of others. Cooperation and tolerance are the watchword, not competition; each individual has an equally great—or an equally slight—claim to knowledge. Only by submerging individualities and combining viewpoints can additional progress be made: "What is true of so many other human undertakings is true here too, that only the interest of many directed to a single point is capable of producing something excellent" (*Werke* XVIII, 79).

The romantic doctrine of objectivity, in sum, has two fundamenmental principles. The first, governing the relationships between the self and the world, states that the world should be made central and primary and that to this end the self should endeavor to suppress its inevitably biased subjectivity. The second, which concerns the relationships among subjects, states that all peripheral or "eccentric" viewpoints are of similar value and complement one another, so that individuals should practice an active tolerance toward strange and unfamiliar attitudes. Considering now the various forms of this second principle, we will see how it tends to absorb and supersede the first, undermining the object-orientation of romantic objectivity and making room for a new kind of positivity.

In his earlier statements of the principle of tolerance, Friedrich Schlegel keeps its two poles in balance; passive subordination of the self to the world seems to go hand in hand with active support of the work of other individuals: "I have expressed some ideas that point toward the center, I have greeted the dawn in my fashion, from my standpoint. Whoever knows the way, may he do likewise in his fashion, from his standpoint" (*Ideen* 155). Only in subtle ways does this fragment betray the instability of the concept of tolerance. In its position at the end of a very provocative collection and in its implicitly evaluative stance—extending tolerance only to those fellow geniuses who "know the way"—the fragment begins to privilege subjective will over objective discipline. In a later work, "Lessings Geist aus seinen Schriften," Schlegel fluctuates more visibly between discipline and will as competing principles of tolerance, until he finally comes down on the side of the earlier and more balanced conception: "Tolerance is the virtue of the as yet militant, warring church"—the stage of the younger, polemical Schlegel; "in the religion of peace, in the church triumphant"—the Catholicism to which Schlegel was soon to convert—"it will be no longer necessary and no longer possible. True tolerance, however, cannot proceed from indifference, but rather from the universal view, which is chiefly provided by the historical attitude toward human development and the construction of its epochs." The complacent historicism of this last clause—though the German is actually quite awkward and thus not fully self-assured—begins to sound like Schlegel's later dogmatism, but the following paragraph restores the balance with an uncharacteristic skepticism: "Enlightenment, or suppression of all prejudices, would be a fine undertaking in itself. . . . But how deeply the inauthentic settles in man's being, attaches itself everywhere, to the little good, and occupies the latter's place, until all remnant of the authentic is lost" (KA III, 90– 91). The shiftiness of Schlegel's expression here is good evidence for the dialectical pressures inherent in the concept. Ultimately, man's peripheral position and limited vision come to seem a desirable end and not a weakness, and at that point tolerance begins to sound much like its opposite. The philosopher Friedrich Heinrich Jacobi leaves no room for doubt in the matter: "He alone is *truly* tolerant who concedes to each of his fellow men—as to himself—*the right of intolerance*; and no one *should* be tolerant in any other way; for a real indifference in respect of all opinions, since it can only arise out of radical unbelief, is the most frightful degeneracy of human nature." [15]

15. F. H. Jacobi, *Von den göttlichen Dingen und ihrer Offenbarung*, in his *Werke* III (Leipzig, 1816), 315. In an even later stage tolerance is extended only toward like-thinking men, and "the relaxed demands for natural human commonness" become confounded "with the hard insistencies of ethical universality," as Murray Krieger has said about Wordsworth in *The Classic Vision* (Baltimore, 1971), pp. 186–87. Thus, in his very late lectures on the *Philosophy of Life*, Schlegel pays lip-service to tolerance—"it is, I should say, almost indifferent

Typically, then, even the romantic who rejects all claims to intellectual authority actively encourages novelty of vision for its own sake. The "characteristic," highly individual pose, which for the eighteenth century was generally a sign of comic or tragic deformity, now becomes desirable; as Schlegel says, "Perspective is dignity, power." [16] There is no durable foundation located in a common center of reality; instead there is a hope of continual progress in common, based on self-expression and the development of unique characteristics: "No artist should be the sole and only artist of artists, central artist, director of all the rest; but all should be it equally, each from his own standpoint. . . . Like the Roman senators, the true artists are a nation of kings" (*Ideen* 114).

The notion of a nation of kings strikes precisely that balance between individuality of outlook and unity of purpose sought by the romantics. But objectivity is, as we have seen, a process, not a product: the continuing adumbration of man's common goal of revealing the truth (or God) in nature. The balance between individuality and unity therefore expresses itself as a procedural form, not as a content. It is a framework for ideas but not an idea itself. It is, for Schlegel, the dialectical form of irony or of the philosophical conversation, "consisting of eternal seeking and never quite finding" and yielding "an indefinite prospect into infinity." [17] Schlegel explains the advantage of this form most succinctly in his essay on *Wilhelm Meister*:

For this purpose conversations about the characters in Meister could be very interesting . . .; but they must be *conversations* in order to banish one-

---

from which point of the circumference or the periphery one sets out in order to reach the center and to develop this further as a foundation" (*KA* X, 13)— but this is only a pretext for launching an intemperate attack on his ideological enemies, the Rousseauists and atheists.

16. *LN* 1582. Schlegel is speaking about painting in this fragment. Contrast Herder in "Plastik": "As soon as a *perspective* becomes rooted in, the living features become a surface and the beautiful round *form* disintegrates into a pitiful *polygon*" (*Werke* VIII, 12). A transitional, "value-free" attitude appears in *LN* 67 (from which *Ath. Fr.* 244 derives): "Aristophanes' works which can be viewed from all sides: Gozzi's works need a viewpoint."

17. "Über die Form der Philosophie," in "Lessings Geist aus seinen Schriften," *KA* III, 100.

sidedness through the form itself. For if an individual reasoned only from his own peculiar standpoint about each of these characters and delivered a moral judgment, that would likely be the least fruitful of all possible ways to consider *Wilhelm Meister*; and at the end no more would be learned than that the speaker thought about these objects as he now stated. [*KA* II, 143]

Objectivity, then, was inextricably bound to a form of activity, and the doctrine of objectivity was consequently the source of a great deal of productive energy. It gave the impetus to the tremendous—I hesitate to say fruitful—development of romantic science and led to the exploration of new fields as well as to the reawakening of interest in others nearly forgotten. Romantic science was attuned to the expansion, rather than the deepening, of awareness. It concentrated on discovering new truths and on classification (as a means both of gaining a perspective on its discoveries and of recognizing the truly strange and novel), and it neglected abstract analysis and conceptualization. These tendencies are present in Goethean morphology, in the study of the occult sciences (including, of course, electricity and magnetism), and, indeed, in the heart of romantic "philosophy of nature" itself.[18] Their most lasting product, however, was the science of linguistics. Linguistics, from the point of view of the theory of objectivity, was the romantic science par excellence. It was the study of otherness in its purest form, not merely the discovery of new facts and objects, but the discovery of new attitudes and ways of seeing, in fact of whole new worlds. The very purity of linguistics helped its greatest exponent, Wilhelm von Humboldt, to a deepened awareness of the difficulties of achieving true objectivity.

18. On Goethe, see Carl Gustav Carus, *Göthe* (Leipzig, 1843), p. 88: "Not an original analytical tendency of his mind, not a striving to bring himself notice and fame through the most exact possible analyses of natural life, nor even less any need to enter the investigation of nature for purposes of practical life brought him closer to natural science, but rather—as Plato says that philosophy in general must begin with admiration—it was admiring love and living in deeper union with nature that obliged him earnestly to devote and dedicate himself to a scientific inquiry into nature." Typically elaborate and unwieldy systems of classification, sometimes with attendant schematic diagrams, can easily be found in Görres's work of philosophical astronomy, psychology, and physiology. See also Hegel's invective against formalistic philosophy of nature in the preface to the *Phänomenologie des Geistes*, pp. 42–43.

Humboldt, like Schlegel, began as a disciple of the Enlightenment. An early essay, "Über Religion," makes a plea for tolerance (in the conventional sense) on the basis of man's perfectibility. Humboldt first describes his conception of perfect spiritual beings; these would not necessarily be universal, but they would be unprejudiced and capable of perceiving the universal ideal center that unites them:

They would not remain with themselves and the limitation of their horizon, they would pass over to all similar beings around them, appropriate what they found in them, give them what they still lacked. So the idea of a harmony of all spirits would gradually develop in them, so they would gradually create an ideal of all spiritual perfection and come to consider themselves and all other beings as but so many copies of individual parts of this idea. [Schriften I, 55]

So much for pure spirits. But men are partly spiritual; they are therefore capable of participating in this development. Humboldt envisions an unending progress of humanity by means of education toward a state of many-sided culture. Man's spiritual nature "teaches him to concentrate all of his viewpoints on himself and his inner being, and so each situation—painful or joyful—is an occasion for providing his soul with a heightened degree or a new side of culture" (I, 60). This optimism never entirely deserted Humboldt. He never developed the theology of the loss of the divine center, which weighed so heavily on the other romantics, because he himself was free of mystical influences.[19] His use of imagery is likewise unique among his contemporaries; he tends to place the human observer at the center rather than on the periphery. He came, nevertheless, to recognize the centrifugal tendencies of human nature and the inevitability of individual variations. He expressed these with a striking metaphor in a letter of 1803 to his friend Karl Gustav von Brinkmann: "It is only as if each facet of an artfully polished mirror considered itself a separate mirror."[20] To counteract this tendency to fragmentation and to move toward a universal viewpoint require an active effort of the will. The passages from

19. Humboldt himself noted as much in 1796 in the course of an unflattering account of Franz von Baader in his diaries (Schriften XIV, 342–44).
20. Wilhelm von Humboldts Briefe an Karl Gustav von Brinkmann, ed. Albert Leitzmann (Leipzig, 1939), October 22, 1803, p. 155.

"Über Religion" leave us at best with only a confused impression of the initial source of the energy: is it man's spiritual nature, his soul, or external circumstances? By 1806 Humboldt clearly felt that man must strive from within himself to overcome his own inertia and to open ever new viewpoints: "One can never seize the world from enough sides, and it is such a pity when man sinks into eternal monotony."[21]

Also in 1806 Humboldt published, in the closing pages of the essay "Latium und Hellas," his first important contribution to the philosophy of language. Here, he defines language as "a world between the external phenomenal world and the practical world in us"; then he directs his eager intellectual energy to seizing the different worlds contained in mankind's many languages. Indeed, the eagerness is so great that it outstrips its object, and instead of resting content with mere discovery, Humboldt speaks of actually producing more languages in order to increase the variety of perceptions: "Since the spirit which reveals itself in the world cannot be exhaustively known through any given quantity of perspectives, but rather each new view always discovers something new, so it would be good to multiply the various languages as much as the number of men inhabiting the earth's surface permits" (III, 167–68). What the young Humboldt, in other words, regarded as a natural process of gradual development, the mature thinker came to see as essentially an aspect of the human will. Totality remained the goal, but it was an unattainable goal, a "regulative ideal" in the philosophical language of the time—something to be felt and ardently desired, not a concrete possibility. By the same sort of reversal that we saw in the preface to *Godwi* Humboldt makes of this feeling an end in itself, concluding that the strength of the desire is proportionate to its apparent distance from fulfillment. The further we pursue and recognize individuality—so Humboldt explains the purpose of linguistic study—the more conscious we become of the fundamental unity of humanity: "For the awareness of a totality and the striving after it is directly given with the feeling of individuality and strengthens itself to the same degree that the latter is sharpened,

21. Humboldt to Karoline von Wolzogen, July 23, 1806, in *Briefe*, ed. Wilhelm Rößle (Munich, 1952), pp. 273–74.

since each individual carries in him the whole essence of mankind, only along a particular path of development."[22]

There are, then, two apparently contradictory emotions associated with romantic objectivity. The first requirement is a modest self-abnegation: the observer submerges his personality in the observed so that the world may manifest its organization and its essence. This asceticism is a deliberate choice that must be continually reinforced; it is a discipline endowed by Goethe with a methodology, by Schlegel with a theory, and by Humboldt with a fitting subject. The more rigorously a person submits to the discipline, the more completely and willingly he devotes himself to illuminating his chosen subject, the more successful he will be. The object itself may be insignificant—we can never know in advance, since the true order of the universe is hidden. The intense seeker can, nevertheless, always hope to find his way through it to God and the divine plan, and to confer on it the central importance of a mediator. Or, as Novalis wrote, "Every beloved object is the center of a paradise" (*Blütenstaub*, 51). This presupposes of course that the object receive the love, the overflowing emotion, of the seeker. Romantic objectivity is thus not merely a discipline—and here is where the second emotion comes into play—it is an expansive discipline, an exuberant asceticism, of which Humboldt's call for more languages is a characteristic example. The observer's abundant emotional participation imbues his object with the vitality and significance which he then finds in it; the scientific investigator's choice of a field is rewarded with insight whenever he brings with him a committed determination. Objectivity begins with a contribution from the subject.

This is the well-known principle of the hermeneutic circle, which Schleiermacher elaborated in the early decades of the nineteenth century. Understanding, he claimed, must always begin with an anticipatory guess, which subsequent experience then modifies and refines. But Schleiermacher was only articulating a concept widespread among his contemporaries; they too recognized, though often with an affective justification rather than Schleiermacher's

---

22. *Über die Verschiedenheit des menschlichen Sprachbaues*, in *Schriften* VII, 37.

intellectual one, that the initial movement toward knowledge, the constitutive impulse, must come from the subject. Even the Olympian Goethe, the great enemy of system and hypothesis, fought his way back to this recognition: "In the meantime everything that is called hypothesis reasserts its old rights, if it only moves the problem from the spot, so to speak, especially if it seems quite incapable of solution, and places it where observation is made easier."[23] This realization is a late one for Goethe; it marks a partial and unwilling retreat from his ideal of objectivity. Thus, in one aphorism (*MuR* 1222) he compared hypotheses to scaffolding; it must be dismantled when a building is completed, but also must be erected before construction can begin. Ultimately, as Goethe eventually conceded, in his "Versuch einer Witterungslehre," the possibility of scientific investigation rests on the initiative of the scientist, on his free or even arbitrary resolution to begin research and to focus on a particular phenomenon: "Nothing remains now for the serious observer but to decide to place the center somewhere and then to look and to see how he can treat the rest peripherally" (*Werke* XX, 913).

For Goethe then, and even more for the other romantics, the intention comes to substitute for the fact. With sufficient devotion and exuberance any object can be decreed the center and made to point the way toward the truth. In this new transformation of the principle of tolerance the material world itself becomes a matter of indifference; the critical factor is the subjective one. The observer of genius can transform any object whatsoever into a mediator that reveals the world's order; every point is equally divine to the inspired eye.

Novalis in particular constantly returned to this fundamental belief, developing his ideas as a series of "philosophical additions and corollaries" to his favorite quotation from *Wilhelm Meister*, "Here or nowhere is America."[24] He invokes Socrates as his model, for

23. "Versuch einer Witterungslehre," *Werke* XX, 937.
24. "Hier ist *Amerika oder Nirgends. philosophische* Zusätze und Corollarien zu diesem Text" (Novalis, *Schriften* II, 543). See also *Schriften* I, 89 ("hier oder nirgends"); I, 301, II, 564, and III, 423 ("überall und nirgends"); II, 131 and 545, ("überall oder nirgends"); III, 649 ("Hier ist Amerika, etc."); also Schlegel, *PhL* V, 169 and 470 ("überall und nirgends"), and aphorism 582 in the *Fragmente aus dem Nachlasse eines jungen Physikers* (Heidelberg, 1810) by

Socrates was the great master of irony, the fearlessly energetic seeker after wisdom, and above all the intellectual magician who specialized in extracting knowledge even from ignorance, truth even
from error: "The meaning of Socratics is that philosophy is *everywhere* or nowhere—and that we can orient ourselves everywhere
with little effort on whatever happens along and can find what we
seek. Socratics is the art of finding the location of truth from every
given position and so determining the relationship of the given to
the truth" (*Schriften* II, 545). Truth is a function of the subject; it
results from the process that his exuberant energy initiates and
maintains. Time and again Novalis reasserts the notion that "everything is a seed" (II, 563) and depends only upon the creative power
of the mind to fructify. The important thing is to be sufficiently
"spiritual": "All contingencies of our life are materials from which
we can make what we want. He who has much spirit makes much
out of life. Every acquaintance, every occurrence would be, for the
thoroughly spiritual person, the first member of an infinite series"
(*Blütenstaub*, 66).

Objectivity and tolerance may be considered two poles of the
same epistemology, the former standing in the sphere of matter, the
latter in the perceiving subject. The two are complementary; while
one waxes, the other wanes. I have tried to analyze the emergence
of tolerance, first as a principle of action, then as a process or form
of action, next as an energy or impulse to action, and finally as a
power of almost creative force. There is yet one more stage, in
which tolerance becomes an inundation, completely overwhelming
the object pole. The logic of this is not far to seek. The treatment of
tolerance as a power, as the ability to produce truth from any object, leaves a residual ambiguity. This ambiguity is the unsettled
question of priority: all the initiative seems to come from the subject, yet there must first be an object, as a kind of catalyst. We make
an infinite series, as Novalis says in the last quotation above, but

---

Novalis's close friend and mentor, J. W. Ritter: "The central sum of nature=
Spinoza's God—nowhere and everywhere—the last true nature-ego. She [the
sun] exists without a body. Her body is the universe. Everything *always* circles
her. [*Alles kreißt* immer *ihr*; evidently a corrupt text.] Suns . . . are sprouts from
an infinite root. In love man sees the central sun. He looks at her then as she is,
without form, clear as the ether."

the series proceeds from the material circumstance and not from the spirit. The center still lies, albeit precariously, in the object.

The ambiguity surfaces in an aphorism included in the *Vermischte Bemerkungen*, the collection from which the *Blütenstaub* fragments were drawn: "Every individual is the center of an emanation system" (*VB* 109). This skirts the question of the location of the center, for "individual" refers ambiguously either to a single object or to a single productive intelligence. The former, "objective" interpretation is suggested, though not required, by the adjacent fragment (*VB* 108): "If the spirit sanctifies, then every true book is a Bible."[25] Like an "individual," a book too is of course intermediate, partaking of both spirit and matter, but at this point Novalis emphasizes the materiality of the true book, comparing it (in *VB* 110) to a lump of gold, in contrast to false books, which are insubstantial, like paper money.[26] But opposed to this interpretation, which places the center in a material object, is a subjective one, which makes a person the center of emanation. Novalis's next work, the collection of political aphorisms called *Glauben and Liebe*, inclines to this view. The decrees of society may look, in a democracy, like the product of the countless individuals to whom they apply. But, says Novalis, laws are not in fact the product of those who are (in political terms) their objects; instead they are "emanations" of a "pure spirit," a spirit that is "realized" in the person of the monarch (*Glauben und Liebe*, 66). Democracy and monarchy are really just two faces of the identical reality, depending upon whether its laws are seen as object-centered (democracy) or as subject-centered (monarchy). And Novalis is a monarchist. He consequently closes *Glauben und Liebe* with a theory of tolerance that in its higher or "sublime" form is not a theory of tolerance at all, but a theory of power: "This tolerance leads gradually, as it seems to me, to the sublime conviction of the relativity of every positive form—and the true independence of a mature spirit from every individual form, which to him is no more than a necessary tool."[27]

25. Cf. Schlegel, *PhL* IV, 516: "Infinitely many Bibles must be possible."
26. I follow the ordering of these three fragments (*VB* 109, 108, 110) proposed by Novalis's editors; see *Schriften* II, 746.
27. *Glauben und Liebe*, 68. Recent criticism, inspired by earlier work of Richard

Glauben und Liebe rightly had the impact of a revolutionary document, for it highlights a dramatic reversal in romanticism. Its expression, however, still hedges; the aphorisms still cautiously speak of democracy as well as of monarchy, of tolerance rather than power, and of subjectivity that needs objcts as tools instead of pure subjectivity. Later notebooks acknowledge Novalis's reversal more openly; they abandon the veiled language of the political work and allow the full energy and exuberance of the romantic spirit to assert themselves:

The fate that oppresses us is the inertia of our spirit. Through expansion and education of our activity we will transform ourselves into fate.
Everything seems to stream in on us because we do not stream out. We are negative because we want to be—the more positive we become, the more negative the world around us becomes—until at last there will be no more negation—but we are all in all.
God wants gods.
Isn't our body itself nothing but a common central operation of our senses—if we have power over our senses—if we are able to set them into activity at will—to center them in common, then it depends only on ourselves—to give ourselves a body such as we want.
Yes, if our senses are nothing other than the modifications of the organ of thought—of the *absolute element*—then with the power over this element we will also be able to modify and direct our senses at will. [*Schriften* II, 583–84]

Having now traced the dialectic to its conclusion as a doctrine of power, I should like to present it briefly from a different perspective. The romantic notion of tolerance arose from the partial failure of an earlier Enlightenment ideal. What had once seemed a possible goal came to be recognized as an idea that could be approximated but never fully realized. Karl Philipp Moritz was among the first to express this recognition in terms of the category of centrality: "Now a contest can arise among all the various rational forces on

---

Samuel, has tried to reclaim Novalis as a liberal; see Wilfried Malsch, *"Europa"*: *Poetische Rede des Novalis* (Stuttgart, 1965); Helmut Schanze, *Romantik und Aufklärung* (Nuremberg, 1966), pp. 151–60, and "Romantik und Rhetorik," in *Rhetorik*, ed. H. Schanze (Frankfurt, 1974), pp. 136–39. The label we apply depends on where we stop the dialectical wheels from turning; my aim has been to emphasize the historical end-point of the dialectic.

earth—each man will find a better perspective than his neighbor's for looking at things, and the actual center or actual goal of all human thought will be ever more closely approached, though perhaps without ever being reached."²⁸ From the very beginning, a crucial shift of the center is made—from the world of experience to the world of ideas, and consequently from the realm of the senses to the realm of sensibility, and from knowledge to art. This is evident in the undertone of irrationality and the hostility to analysis in all the romantics, but it is most explicit in the chapter "Einige Worte über Allgemeinheit, Toleranz und Menschenliebe in der Kunst" in Wackenroder's *Herzensergießungen*:

Stupid men do not comprehend that there are antipodes on our globe and that they themselves are antipodes. They always imagine the place where they are standing as the center of gravity of the whole,—and their spirit lacks the pinions to fly round the whole sphere of earth and to play with *one* glance over the self-sufficient whole.

And they likewise regard *their* feeling as the center of all beauty in art, and proclaim the definitive judgment on everything as though from the judge's bench, without considering that no one named them judges and that those who are condemned by them could pretend to equal authority. [P. 47]

The disproportion between the two halves of this comparison is striking; indeed, it makes altogether a strange argument for tolerance. The first paragraph, in fact, has nothing to do with tolerance. Tolerance, as has been said, governs only the relationships between subjects; it would make no sense to speak of tolerance or brotherly love toward "the sphere of earth." The first part presents instead a theory of objectivity, describing the relation of the subject to the world. It is not the traditional theory of objectivity, however, with its submergence of the self in the service of reality. This version has been partly assimilated to a fully developed principle of tolerance. Already anticipating Novalis, Wackenroder attributes objectivity, not to a passive observer, but to an exuberantly active subject, hyperbolically exceeding human capabilities; and already the source of unity is in the "one glance" of the subject rather than in the object.

28. "Der letzte Zweck menschlichen Denkens: Gesichtspunkt," *Schriften*, p. 11.

The notion of tolerance, then, exerts a pressure that tends to restrict the scope and value attributed to the object-center. The object finds some protection in the ideal realm of art. But even there a similar pressure toward subjectivity exists. A description of the creative artist by Novalis is a good example: "The poet must have the capacity to imagine other thoughts, also to represent thoughts in all kinds of sequence and in the most manifold expressions. . . . He must invent conversations, letters, speeches, tales, descriptions, passionate utterances of a thousand different men, filled with all possible objects and a variety of circumstances, and he must be able to put them on paper in appropriate words" (*Schriften* III, 689). The superficial resemblance to Keats's "negative capability" only underscores the enormous differences. Novalis is concerned only with the poet's response to the ideas and utterances of thinking subjects.[29] His poet is more than a chameleon; he is a magician whose universality manifests itself as creativity. The German even more than the English translation (because the German postpones the verb *erfinden* to the very end of the clause) gives the impression of a gradual but inevitable progression from empathy through sympathetic response to independent creation as the definition of the poet's nature unfolds.

This progression, finally, is also found in an essay by Brentano and Achim von Arnim, "Verschiedene Empfindungen vor einer Seelandschaft von Friedrich, worauf ein Kapuziner," which contains, in a single brief work, a synoptic presentation of the whole dialectic.[30] Although naturally details vary between Brentano's version of the dialectic and the version I have just given, the principal features (sense of loss, passionate objectivity, dialogue as a source of truth, and ultimate transcendence and destruction of the

29. A typical eighteenth-century argument for tolerance, by way of contrast, addresses itself to the intellectual as well as the perceptual level, to objects as well as persons: "We each see not merely a different rainbow, but each a different object and each a different sentence from the next man," Lichtenberg, *Aphorismen* F760. See also the account of the concept of tolerance in Ernst Cassirer, *The Philosophy of the Enlightenment*, trans. Fritz C. A. Koelln and James P. Pettegrove (Boston, 1955), pp. 160–82.
30. Brentano, *Werke* II, 1034–38. The appendix contains a complete translation of the essay. Another translation, with an introduction by Philip Miller, appeared in the *Quarterly Review of Literature* 18 (1973), 345–54.

object) are all in evidence. The essay in dramatic form, originally published by Kleist in the *Berliner Abendblätter* in a drastically altered version entitled "Empfindungen vor Friedrichs Seelandschaft," consists of a series of imaginary conversations about a well-known painting of a vast seashore with the small figure of a monk in the center, looking away from the viewer toward the sea. Brentano's largely satirical portraits of typical museum visitors are framed by an introduction and epilogue describing his own reaction and that of "a gentle tall man" representing Arnim. In spite of the polemical high spirits the essay is carefully constructed and merits detailed attention.

In the introduction the effect of the real landscape is contrasted with that of Friedrich's painting. The terms of the contrast initially seem vague and arbitrary: in nature a "claim" by the heart is "broken off" by the landscape, whereas the picture makes a "claim" on the spectator, which it then fails to fulfill. Evidently both nature and art cause a fundamental dissatisfaction, but the personal involvement and frustration are greater in the confrontation with nature. Observation of nature begins with a sense of identification; one's voice, as Brentano says, is echoed all around, by the waters, the breeze, the clouds, the birds. Yet this is illusion; there is no vital sympathy and nothing "pertaining to life." The opening sentence is a triumph of periodic rhetoric that parodies a full-blown Ciceronian tricolon crescendo and re-creates the impression of fond expectations deceived by a lifeless, inorganic "object"-nature: after an initial expansive clause full of relational prepositions comes a set of three starchily balanced antitheses that grow (following the classical pattern) toward a petrified climax that contains three substantivized infinitives and then a fourth, longer phrase pivoting around yet another nominal form ("Geschrei"); the third colon subsides into a still more artificial and abstract antithesis. The finite verbs, except in the first clause of hopeful anticipation, are of the most colorless variety. Nature responds to the call of humanity with a profound stasis.

A powerful sense of loss attends the painting as well. But the loss is a product of an interaction between the spectator and the canvas. A metamorphosis takes place; Brentano says that he becomes the monk, the picture becomes the shore, and the sea disappears. The emptiness felt before nature is thus temporalized by art as a process of vanishing. In contrast to the static rigidity of nature, art "affords no rest," but induces constant activity. Although it appears in the introduction of the essay, this description of the effect produced by art is proleptic. Brentano waits by the picture to observe the same feeling develop among the museum visitors and, as I hope to show, breaks off the dialogue when it emerges. Incitement to action—in this case a mental action, the attentive listening of the essayist—is the ultimate gift of the work of art.[31] The energizing property of art is, as Brentano hints, the product of a true dialectic, whose stages are not discarded, but all implicitly preserved in its conclusion; what Brentano says is that the conversations he notates, trivial though some of them appear, all belong "to the picture."

The first to pass, a couple, are certainly the most empty-headed, a lady who looks at her catalogue instead of at the picture and a gentleman ("perhaps very ingenious") who seems more seriously interested in his own genius than in the painter's. The lady is a literalist; all emotion is purged from her concrete factual orientation. She is a person to whom "deep" can mean only "not shallow" and who can conceive of no other Friedrich but the one her husband the general has told her about. Hers is an objectivity that exceeds all sense; in its analytic tendency (distributing the epithets "deep" and "sublime" to different parts of the picture) and its concentration on particular facts at the expense of their associations, it collapses into incomprehension. The man sins similarly through an excess of subjectivity. Concerned only with "feeling" and with an "ingenious" but uninformative allusion to Ossian, he speaks in generalities that bear no relation to the painting in front of him.

Brentano's dialectic begins, not coincidentally, at precisely the same point as Hegel's in the *Phenomenology of Mind*, with an objectivity that sees only elements and no unities and with its attendant subjectivity that sees nothing at all. (The verbal linkages between the first three conversations establish the swift dramatic pace

31. It is significant that the effect of grace proceeds specifically from a work of art; the "central" role of the painting in this essay is comparable to that of poems in romantic novels, to which I will return in the last chapter. For the significance of Brentano's characterization of the painting as "pure decoration," that is, as an arabesque, see the chapter "Arabesque, Allegory, and Irony."

and thus the forward momentum of the dialectic.) The next three parties, in reaction to this, attempt to do justice at least to the superficies of the object, to describe the painting's evident contents, if not its deeper meaning and organization. Two young ladies, the first of these three succeeding groups, make a negative contribution. Lacking the luxuriant imagination of the first man, they correct his reference to Ossian and his harp. Their emotional reaction, that the picture is "gruesome" (*graulich*), is shallow, but it has one advantage over that of the first man: it refers to an effect produced by the picture rather than to the "sentiment" of the painter. The young ladies are followed by "two connoisseurs" (*zwei Kunstverständige*) who display the inadequacy of *Verstand* as the first man displayed that of *Geist*. Contenting themselves with a determination that the landscape is "gray," they become involved in a quickly stagnating discussion about the quality of the picture. They are followed by three philistines, a governess with her two charges. The governess, more concrete than the preceding viewers, identifies the landscape as the sea off the island of Rügen. Her precision, however, only leads away from the object, serving as a springboard for the reminiscences and wishes of the girls. As their attention wanders, art is overcome by reality, the unique present by the general past and future. This episode, like the previous ones, is soon over; none of the characters so far has been able to "get much" out of the painting. Their failure is reflected in their inability to maintain a normal discussion. The first couple's conversation consists of nothing but misunderstandings and contradiction; the next two pairs sustain theirs only with the help of awkward word play (Ossian-*Ozean*, *graulich-grau*) and verbal quibbling. The philistines manage little better; the two girls echo rather than answer each other; most of the sentences are exclamatory fragments; and the whole trails off irresolutely.

The next group—a woman, two children, and two men—is larger and also remains longer in front of the picture. It represents a clear advance, for the children in this group have reached the same level as the governess in the preceding group: the first child thinks the monk is a weathervane he has seen, as the governess had identified the landscape with one familiar to her, and the second child, again like the governess, wonders why Friedrich painted the way he did and not better. The adults, meanwhile, are much more sophisticated. One man stresses both the individuality and the emotional depth of the painting, and in response to a question from one of the children he gives the first reasonably serious description of its contents. The second man, with the concurrence of the other, makes the first attempt to explain the meaning and structure of the painting as a whole. When he speaks of the monk, he uses the standard romantic metaphor for an organism: he is "the unity in the totality, the lonely center in the lonely circle." [32] Not content with these generalizations, he proceeds to an imposing allegorical interpretation of each of the principal features in the landscape as they mirror "his own isolation": "the enclosing sea, free of ships, which limits him like his vow, and the barren sand shore that is cheerless, like his life, seems again to force him forth symbolically like a lonely shore plant prophesying itself."

This is another piece of virtuoso rhetoric; especially noteworthy is the balanced second half of the long sentence, containing a clause describing the appearance of the monk in the landscape followed by a responding clause describing the aspect of the landscape, with the point of juncture marked by the bold repetition of "scheint," and displaying remarkable consonant harmonies with a particularly high incidence of sibilants.[33] So climactic a sentence could well make a fitting conclusion to an essay in praise of Friedrich's painting. Yet Brentano goes beyond it, and to an episode that can easily seem like the ridiculous after the sublime. The reason for continuing is not easy to see. The lady of the party, who has not spoken previously, now expresses dissatisfaction; she claims that the interpretation obscures the pleasure she received and alienates her from a picture in front of which she feels "at home." She wishes for more life and complains that the man has left her only with "nightmares

32. Typical occurrences of "die Einheit in der Allheit" are Schelling, *Werke* II, 368, and Görres, *Schriften* III, 23.
33. "Wie göttlich ist diese Staffage gewählt, sie ist nicht wie bei den ordinären Herrn Malern ein bloßer Maßstab für die Höhe der Gegenstände, er ist die Sache selbst, er ist das Bild, und indem er diese Gegend wie in einen traurigen Spiegel seiner eigenen Abgeschlossenheit hinein zu träumen scheint, scheint das schifflose einschließende Meer, das ihn wie sein Gelübde beschränkt, und das öde Sandufer, das freudenlos wie sein Leben ist, ihn wieder wie eine einsame, von sich selbst weissagende Uferpflanze symbolisch hervorzutreiben."

and dream yearnings for the fatherland." One can understand her reaction to the somewhat soporific balance and harmony of the long sentence (whose only conjugated verb forms are "ist" and "scheint," a uniformity produced, in the case of the last "scheint," in defiance of grammar). But this is only the symptom of a deeper dissatisfaction with allegorical interpretation in general, as well as with the one under discussion. The reasons will become clear if we consider Brentano's definitions of allegory.

The most interesting occurs in an essay, published a few years after "Verschiedene Empfindungen," which explains the figures decorating the jacket of *Hesperus*, a new periodical: "The symbol should be just a hint, which also explains itself at the same time, it is, so to speak, a metamorphosis of the thing into a picture of its meaning, taking place before our eyes. There is a movement, a becoming in the symbol, not an imitation, a will to representation, or an animated reflection, which latter properties belong more to allegory, which has something of the dramatic, just as in the symbol the epic predominates." [34] The contrast, though intricate in appearance, is actually close to Goethe's and relatively straightforward. Symbol is active; allegory is, if not completely static, at least self-contained (imitation, representation, reflection). Or, more precisely, symbol is dynamic, allegory relational. The relational aspect is foremost in the description of Friedrich's landscape; the man describes the monk's reaction to the sea and in return ("wieder") the response of the sea and the sand. He dramatizes the whole; and by slightly personifying the sea and the shore and slightly reducing the monk in status (with the comparison to a plant), he makes of them three equipollent actors in what could well be called an "animated reflection" of the painting.

Although the essay "Erklärung der Sinnbilder" helps to identify the allegorical traits in the interpretation of Friedrich's landscape, it does not account for the woman's dissatisfaction. A passage in *Godwi* will bring us further:

It is remarkable and always renders me useless for my fellow men in the present that I never observe a thing in itself, but always in reference to

34. Brentano, "Erklärung der Sinnbilder auf dem Umschlage dieser Zeitschrift," *Werke* II, 1051.

something unknown, eternal; and indeed I cannot observe anything at all, but I must go round in it, for I would like to live and die at every point that I value, and so I never come to rest, because with every step that I take forward the end point of the perspective takes a step forward. Only that man can be happy and calm who can look at something and who feels no urge for all distance to be close to him. [*Werke* II, 148–49]

That Godwi is describing an allegorizing tendency is confirmed for us by the paragraphs that follow.[35] His attitude, Godwi proceeds to say, makes him incapable of playing chess or even billiards; he cannot take the games seriously in themselves, but imaginatively dramatizes them and concerns himself with the constellation of figures rather than with the progress of the game.[36] Godwi's self-accusations also apply to the last man in "Verschiedene Empfindungen" analyzed above. In a more subtle form he falls into the same error as the lady in the first sketch. In his attempt to do justice to each element of·the painting he fragments it and misses the meaning of the whole. Although clever, his interpretation is readily felt to be speculative, slightly outrageous, and therefore "useless." In spite of continual reference to "something unknown, eternal," it is really too concrete, for instance in its specification of the sea as the monk's vow. Its virtuosity and dramatic quality do not keep it from frigidity; it covers "every point" but gets nowhere. The horizon, to remain with Godwi's metaphor, comes no closer; there is no transcendence, and indeed no real motion. The man converts Friedrich's landscape into a dream world whose lack of direction is reflected in the circularity of his description, which moves from the monk to the landscape and back ("wieder") to the monk. Even the mode of prophecy is unable to project out of this confined, lonely, lifeless world; the monk prophesies only himself. Allegory

35. Another confirmation is provided by a later passage in the novel, which explicitly associates allegory and "ubiquity," though with positive connotation: "The picture was warm and full of allegory, the whole expression gently importunate and radiating equally from all points" (II, 317).
36. A good player, by contrast, would presumably have a symbolic attitude. In this connection it is worth noting the resemblance of Brentano's theory of symbolism to Hans-Georg Gadamer's analysis of play in *Truth and Method*, tr. Garrett Barden and John Cumming (New York, 1975). Gadamer, like Brentano, stresses dynamism in his definition, "Play is the performance of the movement as such" (p. 93), as well as in his concept of "transformation into structure" (pp. 99–108).

appears here as an attempt to give a fully adequate interpretation of an object from all sides, to be respectfully "tolerant" of its otherness, in sum, to be objective. But precisely its many-sidedness turns out to be a stifling vicious circle. Conversation is halted because the other man can only indicate full agreement. Even so, this episode does not simply peter out like the previous ones; the incipient energy of the group's objectivity manifests itself to the woman's "yearning" and more precisely in her desire to move on to another painting.

The last sketch, which presents a woman and her guide, seems disastrously flippant, but it is best regarded as an example of high irony. If the preceding episode is marked by ponderously serious objectivity, this one is characterized by capricious high spirits. If one wished to describe the tone of this sketch more precisely, one would have to speak of willfulness rather than flightiness; the two participants harp obtrusively on a few themes and expressions. This manner is set from the beginning when the lady refuses to be reasoned out of her extravagant description of the painting, "It is as if the sea had Young's night thoughts." These are one-sided individuals, "characters" in the then current sense of the word. The conversation, though mostly sexual badinage of no aesthetic significance, is much livelier than in the other episodes, with the partners eventually finishing each other's sentences.

The men of the previous group began by praising all the qualities of a painter—intelligence, sentiment, and technique.[37] But their initial equality of emphasis eventuates in the lady's complaint that her emotion has been obscured. The last woman begins with an exclusive emphasis on feeling—her feeling and that expressed by the painting (the painter is not mentioned in this episode). Her guide responds by experiencing "yearning," a real yearning rather than the dream yearning of the preceding woman. Emotion shades into action as the affair reaches its successful conclusion. But there is no discontinuity between emotion and action, between art and reality; the same yearning is felt in both:

37. "FIRST MAN: He really knows what he paints. SECOND MAN: And also paints what he knows, and feels it, and thinks it, and paints it." Notice the circularity of the second man's sentence.

GENTLEMAN: Oh, I wish I were the Capuchin who in his eternal loneliness looks out over the dark portentous sea that lies before him like the apocalypse, so would I eternally yearn for you, dear Julie, and miss you eternally, for this yearning is in truth the sole splendid feeling in love.
LADY: No, no, my darling, in this picture too.

The picture induces a yearning that goes beyond it into real life. This is a true transcendence, which does not need to touch on every point—the man does not mention the shore in the landscape, for example—which "feels no urge for every distance to be close," but is "happy and calm" in its deprivation—and which therefore gets somewhere. Symbols of transcendence, the expectant look of the monk and the apocalyptic sea, dominate an interpretation that is itself only a springboard to a further goal.

Although—or perhaps because—it is by no means disinterested and therefore violates all principles of aesthetic distance and objectivity, this partisan interpretation evidently seemed to Brentano far more satisfactory than the allegorical interpretation. It is the last of the episodes and must contain the "wonderful sensation" that Brentano said in the introduction he was waiting to hear. And in fact, the yearning and the account of the monk looking out over a boundless sea recapitulate details of Brentano's own introductory descriptions of the natural and poetic landscapes.[38] In other words, in appropriating the picture to his own ends and wishing ultimately to be rid of it, the guide has also done it justice and been a good guide. What he says of others could thus well be applied to himself: "In the end she [woman] destroys what she feels, from sheer lying she speaks the truth."

The energy—one might well say, the life force—produced in this last episode prepares the way for the final reversal, in which the object is, in fact, "destroyed," or at least forcefully rejected and not just abandoned. The reversal is marked by a change in external form from dramatic to narrative, although dialogue remains the mode. The criticism now leveled at the painting is sweepingly gen-

38. There remains the significant difference that the real sea as Brentano describes it is spatially limitless but temporally static, whereas the painted sea in the guide's energized version is temporally infinite. In the allegorical version, it will be remembered, the sea stood for pure limitation and vacuity.

eral: "It would not be difficult to name a dozen pictures where sea
and shore and Capuchin are better painted." The speaker continues
with more specific and constructive criticism to substantiate his dis-
approval of the Capuchin, but the conclusion of the essay still seems
a harsh and ungenerous attack on a fellow romantic. Or rather, it
would seem so out of the context of the romantic dialectic. For we
can recognize the attack as something positive, something that allows Brentano, in contrast to the lady of the allegorical party, to
"go home" and remain there, to found a normal life. The criticism
of the painting does not reflect on the painter's achievement; it is
an integral part of the dialectic. The painting's vital contribution to
the development is clearly defined in the introductory portion of the
essay: it makes a claim that it does not fulfill. The picture is there in
order to be surpassed and to make a hyperbolic movement possible.
It is not sensational, as the spokesman in the epilogue says, like a
criminal "in the pillory"; its natural propensity is to vanish away
and in vanishing to energize life.

If we consider Brentano's essay as a whole, we can observe a
peculiar circularity of structure. Beginning with a movement from
nature to art, he concludes by returning from the picture into life.
Indeed, the return, though it does eventually proceed to an entirely
new setting (Arnim's house), moves via the natural landscape behind the picture, when Brentano's speaker makes a reference to the
"coastal dwellers" whom Friedrich did not paint. Brentano's dialectic—given the proleptic character of the introduction—thus
flows backward, toward its starting point. It illustrates the retro-
grade movement of *Zugrundegehen*, which bends the forward impulse of a dialectic back into a curve; as Hegel wrote: "It must be
confessed . . . that progress is a *return* into the *ground*, to the *original* and *true*. . . . The essential thing for science is not so much that
something pure and unmediated is the beginning, but that in its
totality it is a self-contained circle in which the first also becomes
the last and the last the first" (*Wissenschaft der Logik*, I, 70). In
contrast to Kant's synthetic a priori, this is an analytic a posteriori,
contingent because historical, but nevertheless moving from the
particular and limited toward the general and fundamental.

The romantics began by trying to discover in concrete terms the
order and form of the world. They were gradually led back to an

inquiry into the source of order and of the knowledge of order and thus ultimately to a belief that objective order is established through the activity of the subject. In each of its stages and as a whole, the dialectic of objectivity transmutes form into energy, inert matter into life, knowledge into experience. And so, after taking Orpheus as its initial embodiment, we may take Faust as its final paradigm. For like a more persistent Orpheus, Faust descends repeatedly into the "darkness of errant life"—into Auerbach's Cellar, into dreams, into the mysterious realm of the Mothers, and at last into blindness. But unlike Orpheus, Faust does not abandon his quest; instead the quest becomes an end in itself, and the passion for activity remains even after the passion for the object of the activity has disappeared. "Man errs so long as he strives," says the Lord (line 317). In *Faust*, as also in *Wilhelm Meister*, man's course is errant, he wanders on the periphery, his mode is circulation.[39] Instead of trying to correct his deficiency, Faust learns to affirm it, to accept his limitations and his (Orphic) blindness. In this perpetuation of striving, rather than in the repose of the center, lies his salvation: "Who exerts himself ever striving / Him can we redeem" (lines 11936—37). Energy is its own reward; the periphery stands in for the unreachable center.

39. "Zirkulation" in *Wilhelm Meister*, *Werke* VII, 43 and 159; in *Faust*, see especially the angels' chorus at the beginning of the Prologue in Heaven. On Orphic elements in *Faust II*, see further Harold Jantz, *The Mothers in "Faust"* (Baltimore, 1969).

Poetry and Philosophy

Allegory is the philosophical concept of poetry.
—Schlegel, *Literary Notebooks*

For the romantic, the movement of thought is retrospective: "Philosophy should absolutely be studied *backward*, not genetically like poetry, but *palingenetically*. —Palingenesis of all systems is the spirit of historical philosophy. —Leibniz gave, so to speak, an ideal of the best chaos" (*LN* 1935). Leibniz's monads, according to a nearby fragment, are the origins or "principles of thought" (*LN* 1937), for they represent a formless "chaos" of pure energy. But the discovery of origins requires a transcendence of experience. The ultimate truths are inaccessible to formal logical reasoning; they can only be intuited, never demonstrated. Leibniz's intuitive methods were, as Schlegel once said, the source of his great superiority over his followers: "Leibniz asserted, and Wolff proved. Enough said" (*Ath. Fr.* 82). Novalis characteristically proceeded to a more emphatic formulation of the same truism: "Philosophy is the science of the general *divinatory* sense" (*Schriften* III, 464). Only genius, in other words, can discover the foundations of experience; fundamentally, as Schlegel repeatedly said, philosophy is no more than a form of mysticism: "Indeed, nothing positive can be learned from philosophy" (*LN* 256).

As we saw in connection with the dialectic of objectivity, the discovery of the meaning of existence was thought to depend upon a violent and essentially inimitable private act of will. This romantic belief differed from the Kantian system. Kant had also presupposed a chaos of immediate sense impressions, but he had proposed a much more optimistic solution to the problem of finding meaning in experience: he attributed to *all* human minds the power to organize raw sense data spontaneously into objective and universally valid meanings. But Kant's accounts of spontaneity and of the deduction of universal categories of experience remained obscure and confusing, and romantic inquiries into the nature of experience continued to be haunted by the specters of invalidity and solipsism. The failure of Kant's supposed solution defined the central problem. How could the discovery of the foundations of experience—compounded, as it was thought to be, out of assertion of the self and negation of the material world—be generalized? How could the access to the center of experience be made available? How could the possibility of truth and meaning in life be recovered for all?

Two examples can briefly illustrate the urgency of this problem. The first is that of the poet Heinrich von Kleist, who was driven to despair and suicide precisely by the impossibility of communicating an inner emotional truth: "If in writing I could reach into my breast, seize my thought, and with my hands place it with no further addition in your breast: then, to confess the truth, the whole inner demand of my soul would be satisfied."[1] Schiller's robber hero Karl Moor is a second example. His insanity, according to Hegel's profound analysis, results from the related impossibility of converting the inner truth of moral righteousness into a truth of external social reality.[2] Indeed, as Hegel says, for a figure like Karl Moor the accomplishment of his goals can only throw suspicion on their purity. The outer world can not only fail to express the prior inner world, it can actually contaminate it. The problem of extroverting the self—of sharing intuited values—thus becomes a formidable one for the romantics.

This problem defined the role attributed to art. Art was to communicate the discoveries of men of genius and to infuse the constitutive energy of creation into everyday life. "Poetry," so goes a famous maxim by Novalis, is a "mind-stirring art" (*Schriften* III, 639). Art mediates between the truths of philosophy and the realities of experience. In part this mediation was seen as the product of an alliance between poetry and philosophy; the Heideggerian phrase "dichten und denken" was a commonplace that appears, for example, on the first page of *Heinrich von Ofterdingen*. But another prevalent conception described poetry as the opposite of philosophy. Philosophy moves inward to intuit the hidden center;[3] poetry moves outward to expand and disseminate this discovery; philoso-

1. Heinrich von Kleist, "Brief eines Dichters an einen anderen," *Werke* II, 347.
2. *Phänomenologie des Geistes*, pp. 266–74.
3. "The tendency of philosophy should be centripetal . . . , *to seek religion* and to find it" (*PhL* IV, 1167).

phy regresses toward origins, poetry is, in Schlegel's well-known phrase, "progressive"; philosophy discovers, poetry creates; philosophy is "esoteric poetry," poetry is "exoteric philosophy."[4] In one fragment Novalis used a Fichtean myth of the fission of an originally unitary art in order to suggest this opposition between poetry and philosophy: "The first art is hieroglyphistics. The art of communication and reflection, or language, and the art of representation and formation, or poetry, are as yet One. Only later does this raw mass divide—then arises the art of naming, language in the proper sense—philosophy—and fine art, creative art, poetry in general" (*Schriften* II, 571–72). Another long fragment consists only of a series of antitheses distinguishing philosophy from poetry. The meaning of these antitheses is seldom clear, but the very fact of Novalis's insistent groping demonstrates the intent to contrast the two disciplines. I quote a few sentences: "[The poet] is the imaginative prophet of nature, just as the philosopher is the natural prophet of the imagination. To the former objectivity is everything, to the latter subjectivity. The former is the voice of the universe, the latter the voice of the simplest One, of the principle, the former song, the latter speech" (*Schriften* III, 693).

Despite Novalis's evident desire, this fragment fails to define with any clarity the relationship between poetry and philosophy. It is certain only that poetry was considered to be as necessary as philosophy, and furthermore that the function of poetry is to confirm the explanation of experience that philosophy adumbrates. As Schlegel says, "Where philosophy stops poetry must begin" (*Ideen* 48). Philosophy comes first, but poetry is more universal and therefore superior; it is not the handmaid of philosophy but the queen of the sciences. Even the philosophers Schelling and Hegel saw philosophy as a propaedeutic for the religion of art in which the Spirit is made objective and visible to all: "It is art alone which can succeed with universal validity in making objective what philosophy

4. A. W. Schlegel, *Vorlesungen über schöne Literatur und Kunst*, in *Schriften* III, 244. In Friedrich Schlegel's somewhat atypical essay of 1799, "Über die Philosophie. An Dorothea," philosophy and poetry are contrasted not as center and periphery, but as opposing extremes that should coalesce "in the middle." But here too the ideal middle seems unreachable: "Poetry and philosophy are an indivisible whole, eternally linked, although seldom together, like Castor and Pollux" (*KA* VIII, 52).

can only portray subjectively." [5] Philosophical activity is necessary in order to break the barrier of form that restrains the sources of living energy, but after a point art must assume the initiative in order to redeem this energy from the hermetic recesses of the philosophical aphorism.

Poetry, in other words, operates on the central chaos that philosophy intuits. It expands this hidden center and gives it substance; less figuratively, it converts the abstract ideals of the philosophers into manifest and communicable experience. As Heidegger later said, poetry gives voice to silence. Its essential contribution is to transform insight about life into lifelike discourse, to move philosophy out into the open. It is in terms of this metaphoric description of poetry as a movement away from the philosophic center into the natural distance that Novalis justifies the romantic landscape. Notice the immediate association of poetry, distant (noncentral) landscape, and the temporal flow of real event in the following passage:

The unknown, secret . . . should gradually be made conceptual. The concept or knowledge is prose—the [point of] equilibrium. On both sides is + and −. Knowledge is a means to arrive again at the *absence of knowledge*. (*Viz.* instinct.) Nature is per se inconceivable. Rest and ordered inconceivability. / Philosophy is prose. Its consonants. *Distant* philosophy sounds like poetry—because every call into the distance becomes a vowel. On both sides or surrounding lies + and minus poetry. So everything in the distance becomes *poetry—poem. Actio in distans*. Distant mountains, distant men, distant events, etc., everything becomes romantic, quod idem est [that is, romantic "is the same" as, or synonymous with, poetry]—thence results our arch-poetic nature. Poetry of night and twilight. [*Schriften* III, 302]

Novalis's diction in this passage should not be passed over in embarrassed silence. It is outlandish because it attempts to put into practice a complex and difficult ideal of poetry. It makes a relatively familiar statement (the same as Kleist's essay on the marionette theater, for example), that conceptual knowledge is not an end in itself, but a means to a higher, organized innocence. If Novalis had made this statement in straightforward conceptual terms, the style

5. Schelling, *System des transzendentalen Idealismus*, in *Werke* III, 629. For details see Luigi Pareyson, "Un problema schellinghiano: arte e philosophia," *Conversazioni di Estetica* (Milan, 1966), pp. 169–79.

would have belied the content of the statement (this is equally true of Kleist's essay). So he expresses himself not conceptually but poetically, using a metaphor—a rather farfetched and *distant* metaphor, since poetry works "at a distance"—in order to relate the philosophic idea to a fact of experience (that consonant articulation is much more difficult to perceive clearly than vowel articulation). The doctrine that art leads from mental concepts to concrete experience, that it anchors ideas in the realities of nature, became such a commonplace that Bettina von Arnim, rewriting her correspondence for publication in the 1830s, could attribute the notion even to Beethoven. She reports him as having said,

I must discharge the melody from the focus of enthusiasm to all sides, I pursue it, catch it up again with passion, I see it flee away, disappear in the mass of various excitements, soon I seize it with renewed passion, I cannot separate myself from it, I must multiply it with rapid delight in all modulations, and at the last instant I triumph over the first musical thought, you see, *that* is a symphony; yes, music is the bridge [*die Vermittlung*] from intellectual to physical life.[6]

In the sense of a movement via metaphor from the hidden to the revealed, from the ideal center to the natural circumference, and from the abstract to the concrete, it becomes possible to speak of poetry as an essentially "translated" form of expression. (The Greek μεταφορά lies directly behind the Latin *trans-latio* and the German *Über-setzung*.) "Every translation is poetic," says Schlegel (*PhL* IV, 61), and "an original work is a translation to the second power" (*PhL* IV, 501). Or as Godwi says, "The romantic itself is a translation."[7] Similarly, though often in a less positive vein, the romantics speak of poetry as allegory, an indirect way of speaking the

6. *Goethes Briefwechsel mit einem Kinde*, ed. Heinz Amelung (Berlin, 1914), pp. 345–46. The diction and imagery of this passage probably reflect the fashions of Bettina's circle rather than any authentic utterance of Beethoven's; see *Bettinas Briefwechsel mit Goethe*, ed. Reinhold Steig (Leipzig, 1922), pp. 345–46. For Goethe's version of the mission of poetry as a bridge from the ideal to the real, symbolized by the circle of the rainbow, see the poem "Phänomen" in the *West-östlicher Divan* and Konrad Burdach's note in the *Jubiläumsausgabe* V (Stuttgart, n.d.), pp. 328–29.
7. Brentano, *Werke* II, 262. In the context "das Romantische" is clearly a synonym for poetry (as it is for Novalis in the quotation on p. 83). See also Novalis's fragment on translation, *Blütenstaub*, 68.

truth. Thus, in Ludwig Tieck's novel *Franz Sternbalds Wanderungen* the old painter Anselm bases his (and presumably Tieck's own) theory of art on the premise that "all art is allegorical" (p. 300). And Ludoviko echoes him, in the discussion following the "Rede über die Mythologie" in Schlegel's *Gespräch über die Poesie*: "All beauty is allegory. The highest, just because it is inexpressible, can only be spoken allegorically" (*KA* II, 324). An entry in Schlegel's notebooks, finally, glosses and slightly tempers Ludoviko's rather pessimistic formulation: "Everything that I write is an allegory whose actual meaning it must be left to the mythologer to find" (*PhL* V, 246).[8]

Poetry is allegorical; it moves from the abstract center to the "other" world (other: ἄλλος) of concrete nature. It translates intuitions into metaphors of experience. What is the result of this allegory, the product of this translation? Intuition, for the romantics, is formless, chaotic, instantaneous, and energetic; which of these properties are preserved in poetic communication and which are necessarily transformed into something else? In particular, is a representation of chaos merely a chaotic representation, or do the romantics have a conception of artistic form?

The answer is by no means as clear as it would seem from a rapid reading of the early romantics. The romantic tendency to generate fragmentary or apparently shapeless, sprawling works is indeed amply supported by a subjectivist and anticlassical aesthetic. Poetry, Schlegel says many times, produces chaos: "*Understanding* and *caprice* must be chaoticized in poetry precisely because they are the agents of philosophy."[9] Poetry, as brought to its perfection in the romantic novel, would therefore be a chaotic representation of chaos; it was to compound the formless discoveries of speculative thinkers with the labyrinthine complexities of real existence: "Such a theory of the novel would itself have to be a novel that reproduced fancifully every eternal note of fancy and once again threw into

8. Two entries in Franz Grillparzer's diaries express the same conception: "All of poetry is but a simile, a figure, a trope of the infinite" (3312), and "Poetry is like the bright cloud in Orion's sword, a huge sea of light seems to indicate the center of the galaxy, but nothing can be proved" (828), *Werke* III, 285 and 284. For Schlegel, see also the Jena lectures, *KA* XII, 19 and 39–41.
9. *LN* 1672. *LN* 1958 also uses the verb *chaotisieren*.

confusion the chaos of the world of chivalry" (*Gespräch über die Poesie, KA* II, 337). It is true that in Schlegel's own novel Julius expounds in a letter to Lucinde a contrary intention: to recount their history "in clear and true periods" and "to develop from step to step the progressive, naturally ordered enlightenment of the misunderstandings infecting the hidden center of our finest existence" (*Lucinde, KA* V, 9). The heroic complexity of the diction at this point, however, is a sufficient commentary on the foolhardiness of Julius's search for a simple order. When a chance interruption spoils his direct approach to the meaning of his life, he fixes on a new indirect approach, exploiting the virtues of contingency itself and using his "undoubted right to a charming confusion" in order to loosen up the "irresistibly progressive and inflexibly systematic" material. Through this reversal he acquires a clear conception of "what [this letter] wants and ought to do: to reproduce and complete the most beautiful chaos of sublime harmonies and interesting pleasures."

But the decisiveness of these and other similar statements did not prevent Schlegel from asserting their contrary with equal emphasis. The number of passages describing poetry as central is immense; and since a center stands metaphorically for an organizing principle, the implication is that poetry is well organized. The whole of Schlegel's famous analysis of *Wilhelm Meister*, for example, rests on the conviction that Goethe's novel is not chaotic but is on the contrary a work in which "no pause is accidental and insignificant, and . . . everything is means and end at once."[10] Schlegel here, characteristically, outdoes his brother. Where August Wilhelm was fond of comparing works of art to natural organisms, Friedrich attributes to *Wilhelm Meister* a superlative and more than natural

10. *KA* II, 131. Schlegel's hermeneutic theory is influenced by Herder's philosophy of history: "See the whole *universe from heaven to earth*—what is means? what is end? is not everything means to *millions of ends*? not everything end of *millions of means*?" But Herder here and elsewhere stresses that the center or organizing principle is transcendent and never revealed to a human observer: "Each [link] is deluded into feeling itself as the *center*, into feeling everything *around it only so far* as it pours rays on this point or waves—beautiful illusion! But the great curve of *all* these waves, rays and apparent centers—*where? who? whereto?*" Herder, *Auch eine Philosophie zur Geschichte der Bildung der Menschheit, Werke* V, 559.

organization: it is premeditated throughout, "thoroughly organized and organizing" (*KA* II, 131). Similarly, one fragment defines poetry as "the midpoint between reason and unreason" and hence as "organized organization" (*PhL* III, 474). Poetry repeats and even intensifies philosophical chaos; poetry gives shape and form to our intuitions. Poetry is peripheral; poetry is central. Schlegel seems to stand everywhere and nowhere. At times like this the critic is tempted to hasten onward with a passing allusion to the "inexhaustible richness of romantic theory." Yet it is my conviction that more attentive reading will make sense of these contradictions; there is a plan to the mighty maze.

Let us reexamine some of the affirmations of poetic chaos. Narrative, says Julius, reproduces and completes "the most beautiful chaos of sublime harmonies and interesting pleasures." The two verbs, it may be supposed, correspond to two actions: "reproduces" to the retracing of the philosophical discovery of the chaotic life force, and "completes" to the poetic "translation" of this discovery into organized, communicable terms. For what does the expression "to *complete* the chaos" suggest, if not that the poetic work is limited, circumscribed, and, at least to that extent, disciplined and organized?[11] The work of art achieves a perilous synthesis of chaos and order greater than either of its parts; it fuses the sublime and the beautiful, the objective ("sublime harmonies") and the subjective ("interesting pleasures") into a triumphant totality. The phrase "the most beautiful chaos" has in itself the character of a mystic oxymoron that pervades Julius's whole definition, for chaos is intrinsically a sublime phenomenon, not a beautiful one. A fragment in Greek in the notebooks, $\pi\hat{\alpha}\nu = \chi\alpha o \varsigma + \kappa o \sigma \mu o \varsigma$, restates this complementary relationship between the sublime energy of chaos and the beautiful order of nature.[12]

Poetry is thus chaotic, but it conceives a new function and situation for chaos. "Beauty," according to one fragment, is "the whole,

11. See also Florestan's remark in the discussion of poetic closure in Part II, Book I, chap. 3 of *Franz Sternbalds Wanderungen*: "Without a conclusion, without an ending, pleasure, delight is completely impossible. . . . In art indeed the conclusion is nothing more than a completion of the beginning" (pp. 279–80).

12. *PhL* IV, 1427. Notice how all the associations of the Greek "cosmos" are relevant and the fragment consequently untranslatable.

the surrounding chaos." [13] The adjective here is the novel and informative word. The chaos of poetry is not the ideal punctual chaos
of the philosophers, but a chaos with spatial extension and thus
grounded in reality. It is not a chaos (or energy) of mind, but a
chaos (or energy) of nature. One of the entries in the *Literary Notebooks* captures in a colorful image this spatial quality of the romantic (that is, poetic) chaos: "There is a patriarchal romantic chaos
where there is no rising and no falling, everything is equal and
motley like a carpet and could be continued on all sides to infinity.
So in Amadis, Bojardo; it's also basic in Ariosto" (*LN* 1690). The
theory of allegory presented at the end of the central section of
Lucinde is an elaborate, although intentionally obscure, explanation of the need for a synthesis of chaotic energy with spatially conceived reality. The central chaos is incommunicable, and poetic narrative must use a concrete story to suggest it:

In that deepest center of life creative caprice conducts its magic game.
There are the beginnings and ends where all the threads in the web of intellectual development lose themselves. Only what gradually progresses in
time and spreads out in space, only what happens is an object of history
[or, of the story]. The secret of a momentary birth or transformation can
only be guessed and communicated allegorically for others to guess. [*KA*
V, 59]

Schlegel's theory of allegory forbids him to speak too directly here,
and he seems to leave open the possibility that narrative and allegory are alternative forms of poetry. But he then makes clear what
he has in mind—a fusion, a realistic story, which will still incorpo-
rate the central chaotic energy: "Even in what seems pure representation and fact allegory has crept in, and mixed meaningful lies
among the truth. But allegory just floats inspiringly as a spiritual
breath across the whole mass, like humor, which plays invisibly
with its work and just laughs quietly" (ibid.).

There are, in sum, two forms of chaos, one hidden, the other perceived in and through the temporal and spatial order of nature.

13. *PhL* IV, 136. This phrase was evidently highly significant to Schlegel, for he
    repeated it years later in his theory of creation in the Cologne lectures of 1804–
    5: "The playful struggling, the ether, is the surrounding celestial chaos" (*KA*
    XIII, 38).

Poetry translates from the one into the other; that is, it takes the revealed truths of philosophy and welds them to an expansive narrative context. Thus Brentano's essay on Friedrich's landscape communicates an ideal history of consciousness through what seems a superficial, merely anecdotal narrative. Poetry aims to produce what Moritz, in an interpretation of Werther's May 10 letter, called the interweaving or "intimate attachment" ("innige Anschließung") of the subject to the landscape.[14] In an entry in his *Encyclopedia* headed "Romantik" and dealing with fairy tales, Novalis defines the second-order chaos of poetry in precisely these terms, as a totality that synthesizes nature and mind and a chaos that has taken on the features of historical reality:

All of nature must be mixed in a wonderful way with the whole spirit world. The time of general anarchy—lawlessness—freedom—*nature's* STATE OF NATURE—the time before the *world* (state). This time before the world furnishes as it were the scattered traits of the *time after the world*—as the state of nature is a *strange image* of the eternal realm. The world of the fairy tale is the world *exactly opposite* to the world of truth (history) —and precisely for that reason so *thoroughly similar* to it—as *chaos* is to the *accomplished creation*. (About *the idyll.*)

In the *coming* world everything is as in the *former* world—and *yet everything is entirely different*. The *coming* world is the chaos of *reason*— the chaos which has penetrated itself—is in itself and outside itself—chaos² or infinity. [*Schriften* III, 280–81]

The purpose of poetry thus seems to be adequately defined in theory. Philosophy discovers a chaotic energy at the source of experience.[15] Poetry interprets this central truth as the guiding principle of a natural space. Poetry produces a spatial rather than a punctual chaos, surrounding rather than central (Novalis calls it "in and outside itself," both central and surrounding), natural rather than ideal (Novalis calls it "thoroughly similar" to nature), a chaos expressed through events and objects. Poetry, in other words, is to show the substance of philosophical truths.

14. Moritz, "Über ein Gemählde von Goethe," *Schriften*, p. 147.
15. "Only that confusion is a chaos from which a world can arise" (Schlegel, *Ideen* 71).

Arabesque, Allegory, and Irony

All active wit is allegory = mythological irony.
—Schlegel, *Philosophische
Lehrjahre*

A theory of poetry has meaning only in terms of poetic practice. As Schlegel says in a passage previously quoted, "Such a theory of the novel would itself have to be a novel" (*KA* II, 337). The fusion of the ideal and the real, or, according to Novalis, of the spirit world with nature, dictated that a natural subject matter be chosen to express the ideas. Such fusion demanded also that in return art shape and animate its material so as to reflect the ideas adequately. Corresponding to the search for a viable subject matter, in other words, was the search for a vital form.[1]

The form that exemplifies precisely Schlegel's "surrounding chaos" would seem to be the arabesque, as defined by the romantics. It was Goethe who had made the word fashionable, in an essay of 1789 entitled "Von Arabesken."[2] Goethe defined the arabesque as "a capricious and tasteful pictorial composition of the most varied objects, in order to decorate the inner walls of a building." Such arabesques, as Goethe points out, were used in Pompeii as an attractive and inexpensive way to finish off a wall that had a small picture in the middle of it. Goethe considered the arabesque, in other words, a framing device and therefore a "subordinated art."[3] The distinguishing characteristic seems to have been the arrange-

1. Herbert Schrade, "Die romantische Idee von der Landschaft als höchstem Gegenstande christlicher Kunst," *Neue Heidelberger Jahrbücher*, N.F. (1931), 1–94, is a valuable, though overly polemical, discussion of the equivalent double task in painting: first the natural landscape was emancipated as a legitimate and serious subject, then techniques had to be developed for expressing serious ideas in landscape painting.
2. Karl Konrad Polheim gives proof of the influence of Goethe's essay on Schlegel in *Die Arabeske: Ansichten und Ideen aus Friedrich Schlegels Poetik* (Munich, 1966), pp. 39–40. Schlegel also continued to use the better established term "grotesque" as a virtual synonym for "arabesque"; see *Die Arabeske*, pp. 110–12 and *passim*.
3. *Werke* XVII, 74 and 77.

ment surrounding a more significant center; thus in 1827 Goethe wrote about some illustrations by the young Moritz von Schwind to *The Thousand and One Nights*: "They are to be regarded as vignettes that adorn the title with a little historical picture, but then go up and down on both sides like arabesques so as to make a charming frame for the title."[4] This visual image of the surrounding chaos could undoubtedly be suggestive as a concrete (though not strictly literary) exemplification of what was at best a fragmentary and highly abstract aesthetic. And the fate of the arabesque, consequently, provides an instructive commentary on the practical meaning of that aesthetic. In the light of the foregoing it is not surprising that Schlegel gave the arabesque a prominent place in his major theoretical work, the *Gespräch über die Poesie*, and it is interesting to study the role attributed to the arabesque in that work. But what is surprising and even more interesting is the fact that Schlegel apparently felt the concept to be inadequate and virtually abandoned both the word (except in its technical sense) and the medley (the corresponding literary form) after the *Gespräch*.[5] The reasons can indeed only be surmised; but a few years later the arabesque (as Schlegel had understood it) was explicitly rejected by the painter Philipp Otto Runge and others associated with him. A close friend of Tieck's and through him of many other early romantics, Runge attempted perhaps more successfully than anyone else to put the romantic ideal of allegorical art into practice. His paintings and etchings depicting the times of day became well known as examples of the romantic arabesque. Yet his works do not conform to the accepted pattern

4. *Werke* XVII, 569. See also Goethe's review of *Albrecht Dürers christlich-mythologische Handzeichnungen* by N. Strixner (1808), XVII, 253–61, and the section "Ganze Wände" in Goethe's review of *Die schönsten Ornamente und merkwürdigsten Gemälde aus Pompeji, Herkulanum und Stabiae*, by Wilhelm Zahn (1830), XVII, 120–22.
5. Polheim, *Die Arabeske*, p. 22, provides the following data. Schlegel used the word "Arabeske" 119 times in his extant writings: 98 times between 1797 and 1801, and only 21 times thereafter. Of these, 14 instances occur in published works: 3 in the *Athenäum* fragments, 8 in the *Gespräch über die Poesie*, an additional one in the late revision of the *Gespräch*, and 2 in the *Briefe einer Reise durch die Niederlande*. The remainder occur in notebooks, and many of these, according to Polheim, are cryptic references to a projected work called *Arabesken*.

of a merely decorative and playful "surrounding chaos." He and his friends felt it necessary to restate the goal and to "educate the fancifully playful arabesque to be a philosophic, religious form of artistic expression." [6] Runge's uneasiness with the accepted notion of the arabesque confirms the conclusions about the goals of romantic art suggested by Schlegel's abandonment of the term.

The arabesque (or its synonym, the grotesque) at times suggested to Schlegel the euphoria of philosophical discovery, of pure formless intuition. At times, in other words, he seems to hold to the simple equation "chaos equals arabesque." [7] Thus, one of his most famous fragments describes the apocalyptic event of the times, the French Revolution, as a grotesque of "central" significance: "But one can also consider [the Revolution] the center and summit of the French national character, where all the paradoxes of the latter are crowded together; as the most fearful grotesque of the age, whose profoundest prejudices and most powerful forebodings are mixed into a grim chaos, are woven as bizarrely as possible into a gigantic tragicomedy of humanity" (*Ath. Fr.* 424). The grotesque, according to this fragment, is the product of a destructive "nearly universal earthquake, an immeasurable inundation," which suspends history and sets civilization onto a new path. In literature, too, Schlegel sometimes appears to characterize the arabesque simply as a concrete equivalent of the philosophical chaos: "The most important thing in the novel is chaotic form—arabesque, fairy tale" (*LN* 1804). (Even in this fragment, however, it is uncertain whether Schlegel is simply identifying arabesque with chaos, or whether the phrase "chaotic form" should be taken as an oxymoron referring to the circular "surrounding chaos" in contrast to the formless central chaos.) His longest and most influential definition of the literary arabesque treats it as a revolution in the mind—a return to the "original chaos of human nature" from which meaningful experience springs:

The arabesque is certainly the oldest and original form of the human fancy. Neither the humor of arabesque nor a mythology can exist without some-

6. This is the intention ascribed to the character Runge in Ludwig Tieck's semi-autobiographical story, "Eine Sommerreise," *Schriften* XXIII, 18.
7. Unpublished fragment (Ms III, 79) quoted by Polheim, *Die Arabeske*, p. 124.

thing primary, something original and inimitable, something which is completely indissoluble, which after all transformations still lets the old nature and energy shine through, where naive profundity lets the appearance of perversity and insanity or of simplicity and ignorance shine through. For that is the beginning of all poetry, to suspend the progress and the laws of reasonably thinking reason and to place us in the beautiful confusion of fancy, in the original chaos of human nature, for which I know at present no finer symbol than the colorful tumult of the old gods. [*Gespräch über die Poesie, KA* II, 319]

This passage, however, is less unequivocal than it seems. Like fragment 1804 in the *Literary Notebooks*, it conceals a potential disjunction. For the arabesque is only a propaedeutic, only the "beginning" of what a notebook entry calls the "eternal revolution" of "active chaos" (*PhL* IV, 730). Rather than possessing any definitive value, the arabesque, according to the *Gespräch*, has only an analogical function; it is "an *indirect* mythology" (*KA* II, 319, my emphasis). The conception toward which Schlegel was tending has, I think, been perfectly formulated in one of the famous lapidary sentences of the essay "Crise de vers" by Mallarmé, a latter-day romantic whose deft irony surpasses even Schlegel's own. In speaking of the relationships between art and what he elsewhere called the "virginal central palace" of experience, Mallarmé writes of the way art participates in the energy of life, vicariously and almost surreptitiously: "The reimmersion, ordinarily hidden, displays itself publicly by recourse to delicious almosts." [8] This Mallarméan notion of strategic approximation to a truly perfect chaos is rarely absent from Schlegel's conception of the arabesque; as he says in the *Gespräch über die Poesie*, "All the holy games of art are but distant imitations of the infinite game of the world, the eternally self-forming work of art" (*KA* II, 324).

For Schlegel, as for Goethe, the arabesque (the "holy games of

8. Stéphane Mallarmé, *Oeuvres complètes*, ed. Henri Mondor and G.-Jean Aubry (Paris, 1945), p. 361. The phrase "virginal palais central" comes from the essay, "L'action restreinte," p. 372. The conception of strategic approximation to an origin, which Blake ridiculed as the "limit of contraction," is also present, though less obvious, in Rousseau. See the various passages in Derrida, *Of Grammatology*, trans. Gayatri Chakravorty Spivak (Baltimore, 1976) on "the ungraspable limit of the *almost*," pp. 174, 184–85, 197, 249 (the quotation comes from p. 253). In both Rousseau and Schlegel the origin seems now infinitesimally close (as in *KA* II, 319), now infinitely distant (as in *KA* II, 324).

art" in this passage) is a subordinate art. Schlegel never seems to have regarded arabesque form as something good in itself: it is of value only in so far as it implies the existence of a higher, unlimited truth. Thus, in the case of Jean Paul, Schlegel was capable of condemning the arabesque character of his writings: "His decoration consists in leaden arabesques in the Nürnberg style" (*Ath. Fr.* 421). Even in *Wilhelm Meister* Schlegel expressed doubt about the playful and polemical aspects of the work and the arabesque intricacies of the plot. He admired without reserve only the three tragically romantic characters and the "architectonic" principal figures:

The others, which measured by the copiousness of the portrayal may seem the most important, are only the small pictures and adornments in the temple. They interest the mind infinitely, and it is well worth discussing whether they can and should be respected or loved, but for the heart itself they remain marionettes, allegorical byplay. Not so Mignon, Sperata, and Augustino, the holy family of nature poetry.[9]

Schlegel's account of *Wilhelm Meister* emphasizes pattern and structure rather than "romantic" praise of the arabesque. In its diction and its architectural imagery it looks forward to Schlegel's classicizing analysis of the apparent disorder of Gothic architecture in the essay "Grundzüge der gotischen Baukunst" (1806). Here, for example, is the latter essay's definition of what Schlegel regarded as the typical and best Gothic architecture: "Together with the greatest wealth of decorations a strict symmetry, and a persistent uniformity in the wealth."[10]

In his descriptions both of Goethe's novel and of Gothic archi-

---

9. "Über Goethes Meister," *KA* II, 146.
10. *KA* IV, 167. Similarly, *Ath. Fr.* 389, which speaks of "grotesques" in philosophy, praises them not because they are chaotic, but paradoxically because they have Gothic stability: philosophy "has works . . . where the confusion is orderly in construction and symmetrical. Many a philosopher's artificial chaos of the sort has had enough solidity to outlive a Gothic church." See also Eberhard Huge, *Poesie und Reflexion in der Ästhetik des frühen Friedrich Schlegel* (Stuttgart, 1971), which brings out clearly Schlegel's formalistic tendencies, though Huge then has problems with the status of irony: "As the transcendental mode of action of beauty that has taken on form, allegory thus possesses in irony its general condition, but also an initial particular embodiment of this form" (p. 122).

tecture Schlegel slights the opportunity to single out the arabesque decorative features, the "adornments in the temple," and subsumes the variety of the phenomenon under the unity of the idea. Only in the intervening *Gespräch über die Poesie* is there any apparently unqualified praise of the arabesque.[11] The *Gespräch* clearly represents a new direction in Schlegel's thought, a new prescription for reinvigorating modern literature. But like all of Schlegel's writings, the *Gespräch* is a polemic rather than an abstractly theoretical work. It is the constructive side of the effort that began with the vehement critique of modern literature in the essay on the study of Greek poetry. Far from being an aberration in Schlegel's career, the *Gespräch* should be seen as the consistent application of classicizing principles of form and hierarchical balance to the literature of an unclassical age. Everywhere the emphasis is on modernity, and the arabesque is praised, not as a universal good, but as an allopathic remedy for the stiffness of recent writing. Romantic energy is only one part of literature. It is "an element of poetry, which can predominate or withdraw to a greater or lesser extent, but which must never be entirely lacking" (*KA* II, 335). It has been lacking, the reader has been told a few pages earlier, in most of the learned pedants of "our unfanciful age" (*KA* II, 331). Consequently, "we also have an external reason for developing this sense for the grotesque *in ourselves* and for keeping *ourselves* in this mood. It is impossible *in this age* not to have to leaf through and even to read many, very many bad books" (*KA* II, 332, my emphasis). "Arabesques, ... together with confessions," according to another passage, "are the only romantic natural products of our age" (*KA* II, 337). The qualifying "only" in this sentence is significant. This limitation to a few literary types is not a proud statement and reflects no credit on the age, as a contemporaneous and less polemical entry in Schlegel's notebooks shows: "*Confessions*, arabesques, and that women write novels is the entire gain from the so-called

11. My discussion follows closely that of Ingrid Strohschneider-Kohrs in *Die romantische Ironie in Theorie und Gestaltung* (Tübingen, 1960), pp. 64–71. Strohschneider-Kohrs, however, emphasizes the self-limitation and "unrest" of romantic literature—this is particularly true of her discussion of Schlegel's essay "Über die Unverständlichkeit," pp. 273–82—whereas I am trying to reassert the positive (transcendent and utopian) aspects.

novel of the age." [12] In the notebooks from this period Schlegel repeatedly classifies the arabesque and the grotesque with the minor genres; indeed, the only categorical praise is the very earliest entry of all.[13] And so, after describing the arabesque as "the beginning of all poetry," the *Gespräch* proceeds immediately to emphasize the plurality of paths toward the "tolerance" and "eternal revolution" for which the arabesque is only preparatory (*KA* II, 319–22).

The value of the arabesque, then, lies in the results toward which it leads. Its contribution is entirely negative and preparatory: it "suspends reason" and returns the mind to its "original" state.[14] This explains one apparent contradiction in Schlegel's judgments. For while arabesque is indirectly mythology because poetry springs from it, it is in itself empty of poetry, "without mythology," "philosophical painting," in the phrases of a later fragment (*LN* 2117). The arabesque landscape is not merely a dehumanized landscape, as Schlegel says in another fragment, but (and the parenthetical addition makes this perfectly clear) an entirely imaginary, empty landscape of the mind: "*Landscape* without any figures, Idyllic, Romantic in the great style,—*arabesques* are absolute (absolutely fanciful) painting" (*LN* 977).

Eventually the arabesque would need correction if modern art was to communicate an organic, lifelike quality; it would have to be related, allegorically, to a central idea, it would have to be made "systematic." Systematic organization becomes the standard that some of the fragments set for the literary work: "The more organic, the more systematic.—System is not so much a *kind* of form as the

12. *LN* 1743. See also *PhL* IV, 266: "Bad mistake to write *confessions* rather than to modestly romanticize one's life."
13. *LN* 1653: "Courtly poems have so far all been just arabesques." *LN* 1867: "*Myth, fairy tale, novella* reflect real *life*; *arabesque, pastoral, legend* are all just poetical poetry." *LN* 1890: "There is an arabesque, an idyllic, a legendlike (antiquely noble) and a novelistic prose; the last is the highest." The one exception, a marginal addition and therefore difficult to date, but undoubtedly much earlier, is *LN* 407: "Arabesque humor is the highest." *LN* 1804, "the most important thing in the novel is chaotic form—arabesque fairy tale," is a second apparent exception, but it refers only to the novel, that is, to the contemporary situation, in contrast to the neighboring fragments, which are largely concerned with ancient poetry.
14. A negative contribution can still be a necessary and by no means insignificant one, of course. See the long entry *PhL* II, 592, distinguishing among negativity, neutrality, and nullity.

essence of the work itself" (*LN* 931). Schlegel's published *Athenaeum* fragments express this in an only superficially different way. As the rigidly logical forms prescribed by Leibniz's followers had lacked vitality, so the infinite caprice of the modern arabesque, he suggests, lacks permanent significance. He calls therefore for a fusion of free form with a systematic, essential meaning: "It is equally deadly for the spirit to have a system and to have none. So it will just have to resolve to unite both" (*Ath. Fr.* 53).

Philipp Otto Runge's arabesque art, so far as his intentions can be recognized through the obscurity of his writings, attempted to produce just such a fusion. His best-known paintings and sketches, particularly the various versions of the times of day, are highly fanciful, yet the figures are placed in a complexly symmetrical arrangement and are intended as allegorical representations of serious ideas. They are not "a mere arabesque," as Brentano said in a letter requesting Runge to illustrate the *Romanzen vom Rosenkranz*; on the contrary they "develop by necessary metamorphoses out of the spirit of the whole" in order to portray "the meaning or the highest aspect of the phenomenon."[15] Seen as abstract spatial compositions Runge's works do appear to be chaotic arabesques, but understood as dynamic temporal structures they unfold in a strict order the implications of a single central conception. They are play, but also display; Runge's arabesques are arabesques in Schlegel's more restrictive sense, but they are systematic and significant as well. Runge's reply to Brentano describes this double character of the arabesque; it is meaningful, and yet it seems exactly the opposite of its meaning: "If the poem is individual, then the arabesque will be symbolic—if it is sad, then let the latter be joyful and exuberant, so the frame also gives a nice opportunity to show from above and in a higher perspective what happens below."[16]

Runge's works thus do not have the revolutionary quality attributed by Schlegel to the arabesque; they do not "suspend reason."

---

15. Letter of January 21, 1810, Brentano, *Briefe*, ed. Friedrich Seebass (Nuremberg, 1951) II, 6 and 9. Brentano later substantially revised the letter for publication; the two versions are printed parallel to each other by Wilhelm Schellberg in "Clemens Brentano und Philipp Otto Runge," *Literaturwissenschaftliches Jahrbuch der Görres-Gesellschaft* VIII (1936), 166–215.

16. *Philipp Otto Runges Briefe in der Urfassung*, ed. Karl Friedrich Seebass (Berlin, 1940), p. 381. The letter was dated January 9, 1810.

Rather, they are organic; they attempt to show the development of a real meaning out of the perceptual chaos—the confused jumble of sensations, emotions, and fantasies—with which we live. This is the program that Runge had already communicated to Tieck much earlier, in a letter of January 12, 1802; there must be arabesque, but the arabesque must in turn engender a truth of nature:

I wanted to reproduce in images how I arrived at the concepts of flowers and of all nature; not what I imagine and what I must feel, and what is to be seen as true and consistent in it, but, how I have come upon it and still am coming to see, to think and to feel it, thus the way which I have traveled. . . . For now the thing would seem to lead much more to arabesque and hieroglyphic, but the landscape must emerge from these.[17]

Görres, in his review of Runge's *Tageszeiten*, took this manifesto one step further; since the works lead beyond arabesque, he denied that they are arabesques at all:

And what should we name the manner in which these pictures seem to be thought? Should we call them arabesques? We should be unjust to them in wishing to compare what deep seriousness and meaning has formed with that which has proceeded from the merely playful jesting of a jovial fancy, which, surrendering itself alone to a motley succession of forms, hops in willful exuberance from figure to figure as though from branch to branch, and seeks meaning only in free play and which like humor scorns deeper meaning. . . . Therefore let us call them rather *hieroglyphics* of art, *plastic symbolism*.[18]

Runge's reaction thus illustrates the consequences of Schlegel's refusal to take the arabesque as his ultimate goal and of his desire for a fusion of freedom and system. Romantic art was to combine play with deep meaning; or, in the more formal vocabulary of the theorists, it was to be not solely ironic, but ironic and allegorical at once.[19] The alternation between high-spirited satire and deep, al-

17. *Schriften/Fragmente/Briefe*, ed. Ernst Forsthoff (Berlin, 1938), p. 38.
18. "Die Zeiten: Vier Blätter nach Zeichnungen von Philipp Otto Runge," in *Kunstanschauung der jüngeren Romantik*, ed. Andreas Müller, Deutsche Literatur in Entwicklungsreihen, Reihe Romantik, XII, 189.
19. Görres's phrase "plastic symbolism" admittedly points toward a somewhat different conception of art; Walter Benjamin discusses the phrase (popularized by Creuzer) in *Ursprung des deutschen Trauerspiels* (Frankfurt, 1963), pp. 179–84. As Benjamin demonstrates, the term symbolism was used to refer to imme-

most mystical meditation is the defining characteristic of nearly all German romantic novels, and even in *Wilhelm Meister*, where the fusion may be less apparent to a modern reader, Schlegel finds both that irony "hovers over the whole work" (*KA* II, 137) and that "the characters . . . are in their essence more or less general and allegorical" (*KA* II, 143). Irony and allegory are superficially anti- thetical, but from a deeper perspective they are virtually identical: both serve to express the belief that the world of appearances is disjoined from the world of significance, with only the secondary difference that allegory points toward the higher meaning and irony does not. Allegory is irony with a purpose; irony is allegory freed of the melancholy inherent in the inability to express its meaning directly. Several of Schlegel's fragments refer to this fundamental similarity; thus, "all active wit is allegory = mythological irony" (*PhL* IV, 466), and "*wit* is the force of allegory" (*LN* 1813).

The aim of romantic art was development of a form to unite the advantages of allegory with those of irony. It was to develop a mode of expression that would point the way to the hidden truths intuited by the philosophers without creating the impression that these truths are inaccessible to ordinary understanding. If allegory looks toward the past out of nostalgia for a meaning that it is striv- ing to re-create, and if irony remains caught in an eternally repeated

diate, momentary significance, allegory to the sort of emergent temporal sig- nificance that Runge sought. See also Ernst Bloch's distinction—almost an echo of Runge's letter to Tieck—between allegory as "determination of the way" and symbolism as "determination of the goal," *Das Prinzip Hoffnung* (Frankfurt, 1959), p. 951. In what follows I am indebted to the persuasive analysis of allegory and irony given by Paul de Man in "The Rhetoric of Temporality," in *Interpretation: Theory and Practice*, ed. Charles S. Singleton (Baltimore, 1969), pp. 173–209. De Man, however, is in error when he claims that "the connection and the distinction between allegory and irony never become, at that time, inde- pendent subjects for reflection" (p. 192). De Man finds such a connection in Stendhal and, in a subsequent essay, in Nietzsche; only lately and in passing has he acknowledged its presence in the romantics: see "Nietzsche's Theory of Rhetoric," *Symposium* 28 (1973), 43, on Nietzsche's "ironic allegory" and "The Purloined Ribbon," *Glyph*, no. 1 (1977), 46, on Schlegel. On the relation- ship between allegory and irony, see also Beda Allemann, *Ironie und Dichtung* (Pfullingen, 1969), pp. 77–82; the essays, both called "Zur Poetik der deutschen Romantik," by Wolfgang Preisendanz and Ingrid Strohschneider-Kohrs in *Die deutsche Romantik*, ed. Hans Steffen (Göttingen, 1967), pp. 54–74 and 75–97; and, for more general speculation, Angus Fletcher, *Allegory: The Theory of a Symbolic Mode* (Ithaca, N.Y., 1964), pp. 229–33.

present, the romantic fusion turns toward the future in hopeful anticipation of a never fully realized meaning: in "a preliminary feeling of a great splendid meaning which I'll understand someday," as Matthias Claudius had already said (*Werke*, p. 19). Like all ironic modes this fusion has its destructive side: the sentimental yearning for a harmonious lost ideal must be rejected if art is to contain a constructive effort toward developing new meanings. But it must be recognized that ironic destruction and allegorical anticipation are always meant to accompany each other. The reason is given by A. W. Schlegel in one of his contributions to the *Athenaeum* fragments: "The mirage of a past golden age is one of the greatest hindrances to the approach of the golden age which is to come. If the golden age is past, then it was not really golden. Gold does not rust or erode" (*Ath. Fr.* 243). The irony that demystifies a mythical past prepares the way for future fulfillment.

This utopian expectation underlies even the apparently most destructive forms of Schlegel's irony. I will give two examples.[20] The first is the climax of *Athenaeum Fragment* 116: "The romantic genre is still developing, indeed that is its essence, that it can only develop eternally, never reach perfection. . . . Only a divinatory critique might dare to want to characterize its ideal." Far from denying "a reconciliation between the ideal and the real," Schlegel here posits just such a coalescence of real romantic poetry with "its ideal," although he relegates this coalescence to a utopian "divined" future. That such a positive hope for reconciliation lurks behind the concessive sentence "Only a divinatory critique . . ." becomes unmistakable when one reads the closely parallel conclusion of the "Rede über die Mythologie" in the *Gespräch über die Poesie*: "All thinking is a divining, but man is just now beginning to become aware of his divinatory power. . . . Methinks, he who understood the age, that is, that great process of general rejuvenation, those principles of eternal revolution, must succeed in seizing the pole of humanity and understanding and knowing the activity of the first men and likewise the character of the golden age which is yet to come" (*KA* II, 322). Irony ("eternal revolution") com-

---

20. These are the two principal passages cited by de Man in his argument that irony denies any "belief in a reconciliation between the ideal and the real," "The Rhetoric of Temporality," p. 202.

bined with reflective self-awareness produces Novalis's "chaos that has penetrated itself," a utopian future that is unrealizable in fact, but toward which irony nonetheless tends. This tendency is only implied in *Athenaeum Fragment* 116, but it is fully explicit—perhaps even ironically overly explicit—in Schlegel's essay "Über die Unverständlichkeit." This essay's conclusion, in fact, explodes into two long paragraphs of apocalyptic rhetoric:

> The new age announces itself as fleet of foot and winged of sole; the dawn has put on seven-league boots. . . . Soon it will no longer be a question of a single storm, but the whole sky will burn in one flame and then all your small lightning rods will help no longer. Then the nineteenth century begins in truth, and then too that small riddle of the incomprehensibility of the *Athenäum* will be solved. . . . Here too will be confirmed what I set out in a prophetic spirit as a maxim in the first fragments. . . . Nothing is more beautiful on earth than when poetry and music act in noble concord for the ennoblement of mankind. [*KA* II, 370–71]

Subsequent developments in romantic poetics confirm that Schlegel's rhetorical extravaganza is fundamentally serious. Romanticism is often thought to be disposed to arabesque or irony or symbolism and to be hostile to allegorical idealization, but this is far from the case. Even Novalis recognized the desirability of a centering, structural sense and conceded the necessity of allegory: "Poems . . . like mere fragments from the most diverse things. At most true poetry can have an *allegorical* sense in the whole and an indirect effect like music, etc." (*Schriften* III, 572). To be sure, mechanical allegory was scorned, but there is a second, true allegory. Tieck draws the distinction in the introduction to *Phantasus* (*Schriften* IV, 129). Allegory, he says, is "good and bad," but properly understood it "serves as a support to the whole." "There is perhaps no invention that does not have allegory, albeit unconscious, as the ground and basis of its being." In this passage Tieck does not use the vocabulary of center and periphery. But it does appear in a preceding discussion of Ariosto, who is both criticized and defended as a mere entertainer, a poet of "arabesques" who "lacks a center and true coherence" (pp. 122, 120). The ideal of poetry throughout this section of Tieck's introduction is Novalis's fairy tale, which unites Ariosto's arabesque playfulness with Dante's allegorical depth: romantic poetry combines the peripheral luxuriance of arabesque or irony with the central stability of true allegory. These ideas are further elaborated in the lectures on aesthetics by Tieck's friend Karl Wilhelm Ferdinand Solger. Here we find the distinction between good and bad allegory.[21] Here we find analyzed at length the tendency of modern literature toward allegory and toward irony. And here we find as the high point of modern literature, in *Hamlet*, a fusion of allegory and irony, an "*allegorical* conscious irony" (p. 248, Solger's emphasis).

In the most recent contribution to the symbol-allegory debate Tzvetan Todorov has expressed surprise that Solger associated allegory with modern and romantic art.[22] In fact, this supposed anomaly is none. Solger is in the mainstream of romantic theory. The vocabulary may change because of the negative associations of the word allegory, but the combination of play and deep meaning remains the utopian goal. As Lothar says in the frame of E. T. A. Hoffmann's *Serapionsbrüder*, referring to the *Phantasus* for support, "To no work . . . belongs a clear, calm mind more than to such a one as, discharging its lightning from all sides into the blue in unruly, playful caprice, still should and must bear a firm kernel within" (p. 254). Irony is the St. Vitus's dance of the arch-romantic artist Kreisler in Hoffmann's novel *Kater Murr*—"in diesen Kreisen kreiselt sich der Kreisler" reads the famous, untranslatable text— yet this same ironically whirling dervish "stood in the center of these very events."[23] The German painter Reinhold in "Prinzessin Brambilla" rails against "the stupidity of admitting irony only allegorically,"[24] but here we need to emphasize the adverb. Irony is valid in its own right, according to Reinhold, and not "only" when it serves an obvious didactic intent. Nevertheless, the irony that he praises itself embodies what we would call true allegory: its superficial circles express a solid, central, and hidden meaning: "Our playfulness is the speech of that archetype itself, resounding from within us and necessarily conditioning the gesture by means of that principle of irony which lies within, just as a rock lying in the

21. *Vorlesungen zur Ästhetik*, Leipzig, 1829, pp. 133–35.
22. *Théories du symbole* (Paris, 1977), p. 256.
23. *Lebensansichten des Katers Murr*, pp. 352, 497.
24. "Die Ironie nur allegorisch gelten zu lassen," Hoffmann, *Späte Werke*, p. 247.

depths forces the brook rushing above it to form circling ripples on the surface" (*Späte Werke*, p. 247).

Allegory and irony, then, are only secondarily opposites; they are cognate and often inseparable outgrowths of man's temporal predicament. Allegory, as de Man says, expresses the lack of cohesion between subject and object, or more properly between sign and significance; its center is hidden.[25] But in mating with irony, which is self-centered, it expresses the determination to recover this cohesion.[26] The metaphor for the lack of it is the hidden center of allegory, as the metaphor for the ambition to recover cohesion is the self-centeredness of irony. All through the work of the romantics, though hidden away in unlikely places, runs a fascination with the power of an Archimedean point, or self-centered "hypomochlion" (a word meaning "fulcrum" and whose source for the romantics I have been unable to find).[27] And it is, appropriately, in the

25. "The Rhetoric of Temporality," p. 190.
26. Allegory, when it functions as an anticipation of meaning, is the narrative embodiment of a system and is a virtual synonym for structure as used by the structuralists. Both allegory and structure imply that form is a ritual enactment, in contrast to a delusory historicism that attempts to present the past "as it really was" without the imposition of an arbitrary form. De Man's critique of the symbol is thus almost perfectly congruent with Lévi-Strauss's critique of Sartre in *The Savage Mind* (Chicago, 1966). Compare, for example, de Man's analysis of allegory's renunciation of an idealized past with Lévi-Strauss's description (p. 236) of the "'disjoined' past of myth." In *PhL* IV, 118, Schlegel uses the word *allegorical* to refer to a principle of "construction," where we should certainly say *structural*: "*Metaphor* and *epithet* refer to single words, parisosis and *antithesis* to cola, *hyperbaton* and anacoluthon, hysteron proteron to the whole period. All these figures should be allegorical. Not only the period, but the paragraph as well should be constructed." In other words, allegory is what structures plot, as rhetoric is what structures diction; to adopt a Schlegelian phrase, which is also a recent title, allegory is the "poetry of prose."
27. Archimedes: Novalis, *Blütenstaub*, 94; Goethe, *MuR* 221; Humboldt, II, 137 (*Über Goethes Hermann und Dorothea*, chap. 9); humorously in Brentano's essay on philistines in *Werke* II, 968; and later in, for example, Jakob Burckhardt, *Weltgeschichtliche Betrachtungen* (Darmstadt, 1956), p. 5. Burckhardt here echoes a leading idea of Humboldt's essay, "Über die Aufgabe des Geschichtsschreibers" (*Schriften* IV, 50). Hypomochlion: Novalis, *Schriften* III, 64 and 574; Schlegel, *LN* 1934, *PhL* III, 550, 558, and 560, V, 844, 845, 864, 869, and 1002; Schelling, *Werke* III, 400 (*System des transzendentalen Idealismus*), and humorously in the "Visum Repertum" by Görres in "BOGS der Uhrmacher," most readily accessible in Brentano's *Werke* II, 898. In English the Archimedean reverie is found in Wordsworth's introduction to the "Ode:

most self-centeredly ironic of all his works, the essay "Über die Unverständlichkeit," that Schlegel makes his most direct attempt to elucidate the inexplicable, to define the hidden center of experience, and thus to justify veiled, allegorical language:

Yes, the finest thing that man possesses, peace of mind itself, hangs, as anyone can easily learn, ultimately somewhere on such a point, which must be left in the dark, but in return it carries and holds the whole and would lose this power in the same instant that someone tried to dissolve it into reason. Verily, it would grieve ye if the world were ever, as ye demand, thoroughly comprehensible in earnest. And is not even the infinite world itself formed by reason out of incomprehensibility or chaos? [KA II, 370]

Intimations of Immortality"; the word *hypomochlion* was used by Coleridge in the "Theory of Life," *Works* I, 393. See also Peter Szondi, "Friedrich Schlegel und die romantische Ironie," *Satz und Gegensatz* (Frankfurt, 1964), pp. 5–24.

Open Nature

> The primal matter from which all heavenly bodies have sprung occupies all the space in the universe; thus geometrically speaking it is an infinite sphere. But the sphere is generated by the procession of the point out of itself, whence it decomposes into center and periphery. The primal divison which comes into the primal matter, or actually through and with which the primal matter is created, is the process through which the previously identical center divides into center and periphery, but without becoming absolutely twofold, for the periphery is the center itself, placed everywhere.
>
> —Oken, *Über Licht und Wärme*

A particular conception of nature corresponds to the romantic conception of poetic communication:

> Thus is the soul of the artist often captured by wondrous reveries, for every object in nature, every moving flower, every drifting cloud is a memory for him or a hint of the future. Armies of airy figures which find no reception from other men wander back and forth through his mind; particularly the spirit of the poet is an eternally moving river, whose murmuring melody is silent at no instant, every breath touches him and leaves a trace, every ray of light is reflected, he has the least need of wearisome matter and depends the most on himself.[1]

The allegorical perspective of poetry produces a new, more authentic, temporal understanding in which the fixities and definites of nature yield to a dynamic sense of flow. Tieck's poet "hängt am meisten von sich ab"; he is his own center of gravity, his own fulcrum. It is apparent that this Archimedean self-reliance is both less transcendent and more dialectical than its nearest analogue in English, that of Emerson. Tieck's poet neither dissipates his ego in order to become "part or parcel of God" nor does he risk scholarly disengagement from practical *effects* in order to "sit at home with

1. Ludwig Tieck, *Franz Sternbalds Wanderungen*, p. 160.

the cause." [2] Nature is highly important for him, and it is also highly seductive; as communication requires a fusion of allegory and irony, so a proper perspective depends upon maintaining a difficult balance between self-surrender and self-possession.

Most, if not all, romantic landscape descriptions reflect this double aspect of nature: spiritual and physical, temporal and spatial, organized and chaotic, saving and damning. The metaphor that resolves each of these paradoxes into a dialectically unified whole is that of the infinite circle. With this conception the German romantics reforged in a new way the circle whose breaking Marjorie Nicolson described in her well-known study of macrocosm and microcosm in the seventeenth century. [3] Nature for the romantics is organized and therefore circular; from a high enough observation point the landscape appears to spread out and surround the observer. But the organization is infinitely ramified and can truly be comprehended only *sub specie aeternitatis*. Moritz's essay "Die metaphysische Schönheitslinie" gives the basic version of this fertile doctrine. Taken as a whole, Moritz says, nature is an immense organism, but considered in any of its parts it seems to be fragmented and disorderly: "If we imagine nature as a great circle whose parts together have a leaning toward one another, then the bends are almost unnoticeable on account of the immeasurable size of the perimeter, and we believe we see everywhere nothing but

2. Quotations from the essays *Nature* and "Self-Reliance," Emerson's *Works* I, 16 and II, 70. The epigraph to the necrologue on Carlyle (X, 453) supports my attribution of an ontological rather than simply a political meaning to "cause": "Hold with the Maker, not the Made. / Sit with the Cause, or grim or glad." See also Kenneth Burke's essay on Emerson's "soft-hearted dialectic," as he calls it, "I, Eye, Ay— Concerning Emerson's Early Essay on 'Nature' and the Machinery of Transcendence," in *Language as Symbolic Action* (Berkeley, 1968), pp. 186–200. For the question of engagement in *Franz Sternbald*, see my analysis of the plot below.
3. *The Breaking of the Circle* (New York, 1962). For summaries of romantic views, see Helmut Rehder, *Die Philosophie der unendlichen Landschaft* (Halle, 1932), to be supplemented by Rehder's essay, "Ursprünge dichterischer Emblematik in Eichendorffs Prosawerken," JEGP 57 (1956), 528–41. The older conception of nature as a finite circle (a limited sphere) may be illustrated by a passage from Matthias Claudius: "Man . . . is bound to the imperfect, to time and place. . . . He can make discoveries round about in his circle, find many and various things, beautiful and useful, clever and profound, but left to himself he can never arrive at perfection; for he . . . cannot go beyond himself " (*Werke*, pp. 541–42).

straight lines, or merely *purposive means* [*abzweckende Mittel*], where there is yet an enduring leaning toward the goal" (*Schriften*, p. 154). Nature is a circle, but one that is closed only at an infinite distance, one that does not restrain, an open circle. And so, Moritz could write an essay on "domestic felicity," describing the fulfilled elemental relation of man to nature in such terms: "Even if all else around the *single house* fell away, still round about there remains beautiful open nature" ("Häusliche Glückseligkeit," *Schriften*, p. 34).

"Beautiful open nature" round about is not the carefully ordered landscape of the neoclassical age. But except for moments of utopian reverie—Tieck's ecstatic evocation of the poet virtually freed of "wearisome matter" is another such moment—it is not quite the romantic landscape either. For while the romantic landscape is an "open," infinite circle, it is also a "surrounding chaos"; its infinitude is one of infinite variety, constantly changing and developing. Here is how Görres, to begin with the weightiest example, comments on Schelling's analysis of space as "infinite circumference" in contrast to the "infinite center" of time:

Space will not appear [to mortal beings] in its whole infinite expansion, as the nowhere present and yet everywhere penetrating totality, as the ethereal and therefore resting energy, as the shining glassy sea that lies around the throne of the godhead, but it will pass into this [mortal] region as a conditioned energy that constantly expands the sphere of its activity with a force that is measured but not limited in its effectiveness; which therefore does not fill the whole circle in motionless quiet, but evolves through the whole sphere with uniform velocity and therefore strives for infinity through continual action, without ever enclosing infinity in itself.[4]

The dynamic plenitude about which Görres is speaking will be readily recognized as the stereotyped and almost universal mode of romantic landscape descriptions. They are impossible anthology landscapes in which whole spectra of natural phenomena, often preternaturally active, are interwoven, while at the same time a distant mist mutes the restrictiveness and restores the open feeling of the circle of the horizon. One such description, in which as it hap-

---

4. Görres, "Glauben und Wissen," *Werke* III, 25–26. For Schelling's analysis see "Von der Weltseele," *Werke* II, 363–65.

pens the word "chaos" actually appears, will call to mind countless others: "[The castle] stood like an enchantment high above a broad, indescribable chaos of gardens, vineyards, trees, and rivers, the castle hill itself was a large garden where countless artificial fountains sprang up out of the green. The sun was just descending behind the hill and covered the splendid picture with brightness and shimmer, so that nothing could be clearly distinguished." [5]

It should be emphasized that this is not vague romantic enthusiasm, but intentional poetic effect. In the course of an elaboration on one of A. W. Schlegel's discussions of organic form, Eichendorff explained the necessity for this effect as one aspect of what he calls the "organic unity" of art: "Only a landscape with all the apparently confused wealth of forests, mountains, and rivers yields the full expression of concealed beauty." [6] This passage has not received the attention it deserves as a testimonial to the conscious workmanship of Eichendorff and the best of his fellow romantics. The wording is precise: the beauty is hidden by the confusion, but the confusion is only apparent, and the beauty is real. Beneath their chaotic surface most romantic landscapes are designed to suggest an ordering principle. It is, as the following examples show, the order of the infinite circle. Romantic landscape descriptions teach the reader by force of example to see nature as a series of concentric circles protectively enveloping the observer and also opening out toward a horizon of

5. Joseph von Eichendorff, *Ahnung und Gegenwart*, chap. 13, *Werke*, p. 686. In a masterful analysis of this passage Oskar Seidlin discovers in it a special, demonic character ("Eichendorffs symbolische Landschaft," *Versuche über Eichendorff*, Göttingen, 1965, p. 40–41). Far from denying this particularity in what I have called a typical landscape, I would argue that every such description of any significance employs the generic features of the romantic landscape to carry an individualized message. On the dynamism of Eichendorff's landscapes, see Richard Alewyn, "Eine Landschaft Eichendorffs," in *Eichendorff Heute*, ed. Paul Stöcklein (Munich, 1960), pp. 19–43.
6. *Zur Geschichte des Dramas*, HKA VIII², 315. The parallel passages in A. W. Schlegel's *Vorlesungen über dramatische Kunst und Literatur*, chap. 25, are also interesting. "Romantic [art] is the expression of the secret drift toward a chaos, ever struggling for new and wonderful births, hidden under the order of creation, nay in its very bosom." "Romantic drama should be thought of as a great painting where, in addition to figure and movement in more substantial groups, the surroundings of the persons are also depicted, not merely the nearest, but also a significant perspective into the distance, and all of this under a magical illumination which fixes the impression thus or otherwise" *Schriften* VI, 112.

infinite potentiality.[7] I have chosen my examples from Novalis, Eichendorff, and Tieck, whose landscapes to me represent best the inherent tendencies of the romantic dialectic.

The most famous of those strange systematic allegories called fairy tales by the romantics begins with the paradigm for all such landscapes—a progression outward to an indefinite horizon and to the mysterious workshop of the Creator, concluding with a fusion of classical symmetry and radiantly dynamic plenitude. This is the first paragraph of the fairy tale in the ninth chapter of Novalis's *Heinrich von Ofterdingen*, which I will quote in full, emphasizing the relevant features:

The long night had just begun. The old hero rapped on his shield so that it resounded *round about far into* the deserted streets of the city. Then the high colorful windows of the palace bgan to brighten from the inside and their figures moved. They moved ever more actively as the reddish light increased, beginning to illuminate the alleys. The huge pillars and walls were also gradually seen to grow brighter; at last they stood in the purest milky blue glow, and played with the gentlest colors. The whole region now grew visible, and the reflection of the figures, the din of lances, of swords, of shields, and of helmets, which bent *from all sides* toward crowns appearing here and there, and finally, as these faded and made room for a plain green *ring*, closed a large *circle* around it: all this was re-

7. In what follows the parallels to James Thomson are noteworthy. See the analysis of Thomson's *Seasons* as a "translation" and of his world as "a maze made up of concentric circles" in chap. 3, "The Development of Blank-Verse Poetry from Milton to Wordsworth," by Donald G. Marshall (Ph.D. dissertation, Yale University, 1971) (the quotations are from pp. 188 and 160). Thomson's dialectic —somewhat like Wordsworth's and Emerson's—differs from that of the German romantics only in being less pointedly dualistic and more dependent upon an externally transcendent grace. The action of grace provides, among other things, the unfounded (and thus in a sense transcendent), optimistic Newtonian belief in the reality and infinity of space: the circle of nature never threatens for Thomson to become a demonic enclosure as it does for Eichendorff, and he possesses a firm assurance that the chaotic labyrinth of matter leads to the infinity of God. (Marjorie Nicolson's book, *Newton Demands the Muse*, Princeton, N.J., 1946, puts Thomson into his Newtonian context.) Compare lines 626–27 of "Autumn"—"In cheerful error let us tread the maze / Of Autumn unconfined"—with the following passage from *Franz Sternbald* (p. 297), which is discussed below: "'We all err,' said the old man, 'we must err and beyond error there certainly lies no truth, both are also certainly not opposed, but are mere words, which man composed in his helplessness to designate something which he in no wise meant.'"

flected in the rigid sea which *surrounded* the hill on which the city lay, and even the *distant* high *belt* of mountains which *enclosed* the sea *all around* was covered up to the middle with a *soft reflection*. *Nothing could be clearly distinguished*; but a wonderful rumbling was heard nearing, as from a *distant immense* workshop. The city on the other hand appeared bright and clear. Its smooth, transparent walls *reflected* the beautiful rays, and the surpassing *symmetry*, the noble style of the buildings, and their *beautiful arrangement* became visible. Before all the windows stood charming clay pots full of the *most varied* ice and snow flowers, which *sparkled* most agreeably. [*Schriften* I, 290–91]

Novalis, as so often, speaks for himself and his contemporaries so distinctly as to render any commentary superfluous. But he speaks only schematically; the relentlessly circular landscape almost defies visualization, whereas the beautiful city is described only in vague, general terms. I should like to consider in some detail the more complex case of Eichendorff, whose works contain in substance a version of what Novalis's works contain only in powerful outline. Countless passages in Eichendorff's poems and stories, like Novalis's fairy tale, describe a circular and open landscape— though often these characteristics appear only in unobtrusive epithets such as "rings," "umher," "weit," and "die Runde." Here, as one example from Eichendorff, is the landscape seen by Florio looking out a window, in "Das Marmobild" (*Werke*, p. 1156). So far as we are told, incidentally, the window itself is not round, but, as so often in Eichendorff, it is the symbol of a pure constitutive "betweenness" (in Heidegger's sense): light seen through a window appears to be illumination entering this world as a translucence of central spiritual energy: "The house lay at the exit from the city, he surveyed a broad, still circle of hills, gardens, and valleys, clearly illuminated by the moon. Out there also there still was, as it were, a subsiding and reechoing of past joy everywhere in the trees and rivers, as if the whole region sang quietly like the sirens whom he heard in his sleep." [8] Florio walks outside and sings a song, and the

8. In "Ein Wort über Eichendorff," in *Eichendorff Heute*, pp. 7–18, Richard Alewyn describes windows somewhat differently, as "the boundary and crossing point between a [dangerous] interior space and open space" (p. 15). But one can be lost in the (chaotic) open as well as confined in an interior, and in that case the light coming from a lighted interior can be a protective guide issuing from

song again evokes the infinite, all-inclusive roundness of nature: "Vom Hügel grüß ich in die Runde / Den Himmel und das stille Land" (From the hill I greet around / The sky and the quiet land). For Eichendorff, as for the other romantics, these landscapes embody an ideology. The full, rounded openness of nature expresses the multeity in unity of life—*organic* life—itself. And conversely, organic unity, says Eichendorff, in arguing against the mechanical unities of neoclassic drama, can normally exist only in the open freedom of nature: "For only in a few peculiar cases can here in the drama, as also outside in real life, that organic growth of a plot of any stature at all with its natural multiplicity of ramifications be locked up like a hothouse flower in one salon, one street or arbor."[9] Any enclosure is arbitrary and thus evil, but the openness of nature is a window opening onto the infinite, that is, onto God and heaven. "Heaven is open, O Father, take me up!" says Eichendorff at the end of the first poem in the section of his poems called "Geistliche Gedichte," and the last poem of the section concludes, "Mußt' höher, immer höher fliegen, / Ob nicht der Himmel offen wär."[10] Eichendorff's reverie of an encircling world stretching out to infinity and permeated by the mysterious voice of God thus parallels the paradigmatic opening of Novalis's fairy tale: "There is so deep, secret, blissful a solitude that one imagines catching sight of the dark circle of the hills and woods far beneath one, glimpsing realms of wonder on the sides, distances gently covered over by night, hearing the voice of the hermit, bright and pious through the

---

a central anchor point. In stanza 15 of "Der armen Schönheit Lebenslauf," for example, the lighted windows came to replace the absent stars as signs to the wanderer of the watchfulness of God, who will bring her home safe. In a line such as "Gott Vater aus dem Fenster schaut" in "Seemanns Abschied" windows lose all physical significance—and therefore all potential for expressing a boundary between two alternative realms of existence—and retain only the connotation of constitutive translucence.
9. *Zur Geschichte des Dramas, HKA* VIII², 315.
10. The eagle, that is, barely able to see the earth below, nevertheless had to "fly ever higher to see whether heaven be not open." The connection between these two poems was pointed out by Hilda Schulhof in "Die Textgeschichte von Eichendorff's Gedichten," *Zeitschrift für deutsche Philologie* 47 (1916–18), 48. On openness in Eichendorff, see Oskar Seidlin, "Eichendorff und das Problem der Innerlichkeit," in *Festschrift für Bernhard Blume*, ed. Egon Schwarz et al. (Göttingen, 1967), pp. 126–45.

boundless stillness." [11] Alternatively, as in the following passage from the story "Viel Lärmen um Nichts," the expansive power of the observing intellect may be emphasized in terms strongly reminiscent of Thomson:

For every new idea is like the first peep of dawn; first it gently reddens the mountains and treetops, then suddenly here, there, with a flaming glance it ignites a river, a tower in the distance; now the mists in the depth swirl and divide and coil, the circle expands far and farther, immeasurable blooming lands emerge—who can say where that will end! [*Werke*, p. 1199]

Whatever the emotion, such passages characteristically combine an idealizing diction with a mood of hopeful potential ("one believes," "who can say where that will end"). They are not confined to the present or past of literal description, but look ahead expectantly toward corroboration and fulfillment. Thus they are designed to stir the mind (in Novalis's phrase) and to inculcate an attitude; not merely ideological, they are also didactic. As required by the allegorical conception that poetry is a surrounding chaos, they make their ideal communicable by projecting it onto nature.

The content of this message is inseparable from its form. Romantic poetry opens up the exoteric truths of philosophy, romantic allegory is open to the future, and the corresponding romantic ethical prescriptions emphasize openness to opportunity, challenge, and danger. In the infinite circle of the created universe, as this chapter's motto suggests, every instant is critical because every point at every time is a center caught in the act of engendering a living sphere. There is no "objective" order in which such a universe could rest, no fixed center around which it rotates. Only the individual subject can beget order, and that order is constantly endangered by the dynamism of the world that is begotten. "Be on thy guard" is the watchword of all such landscapes, as Eichendorff makes explicit at numerous points in his poetry and prose alike: "Hüte dich, sei wach und munter!" (Be ever watchful and alert.)

In chapter ten of the novel *Ahnung und Gegenwart* the didactic

11. Letter to Heinrich Otto Graf von Loeben, December 27, 1812, published in the Eichendorff yearbook *Aurora* 1 (1929), 58.

intention of romantic landscapes becomes explicit. Eichendorff speaks of two ways of reading: the wooden, unsympathetic way of adults and the fresh and vivid way of youth. The latter leads to imaginative participation in the infinite circle, that is, in the consummated life of nature. To read properly—and the youthful way, says Eichendorff, is the proper way—means to find a central perspective, to see and join in the organized fullness of the world. Nor is Eichendorff merely speaking here of a way of reading; he is trying to teach a way of life as well, for nature too is a book to be read. The youth's book, with its rustling leaves (*Blätter*) for pages, is but one facet of nature:

With such lively, artistic child's eyes Friedrich flew through these books as well. When between times he looked up from the page [*vom Blatte*], the beautiful circle of the landscape shone from all sides into the story, the figures, as the wind rustled through the leaves of the book, raised themselves up before him in the boundless green quietude and stepped out alive into the shimmering distance; and thus actually no book was so badly conceived that he would have laid it untaught and unrefreshed out of his hands. And those are the right readers, who compose with and over the book. For no poet gives a finished heaven; he only raises up the ladder from earth to heaven. To him who, too lazy and unwilling, feels not the courage to climb the golden, loose rungs the secret letter remains eternally dead. And he would do better to dig or plow than thus with worthless reading to go idle. [*Werke*, p. 629]

Seize the opportunity is the moral of this passage. Poets offer a ladder to spiritual truth—an open, "loose" ladder—not a closed, "finished" world; find out the ladder and use it. Read creatively and meaningfully and your existence will begin to make sense. Thus, the passage is a lesson for living as well as for reading. Nature presents the same ladder and the same opportunities to climb it and to gain the correct—for Eichendorff, the Christian—perspective:

That is Jacob's dream ladder, he said cheerfully, as God sometimes lets it down on such spring nights, quick now! We are climbing to heaven. I already see the stars flicker through the treetops. — Now they had reached the last steps, all at once they walked out of the dark foliage, like miners out of a shaft, into the open. There they saw on the right the old castle and in front of it the broad, airy flower beds, still arbors, and bushes, a fountain splashed sleepily among them, farther off an immeasurable prospect in the moon's gleam shone up at them through the wonderful solitude.[12]

Occasionally, on special nights, grace descends, and if you act you will find yourself in a beautiful central situation. Learn to read, learn to see, learn to live: in all of Eichendorff's landscape descriptions this is the message. And the message is implicit even in the active suspension of disbelief necessary in order to imagine a circular prospect out of a flat window; for this active empathy of the reader's is both an act of will and an act of faith, the very combination of will and faith needed to live a Christian life.

Once both will and faith are mentioned, however, it becomes necessary to add that for Eichendorff, as for the other romantics, will is the primary ingredient. His ethic, and that of his central landscapes, is one of self-reliance. Although the character in *Dichter und ihre Gesellen* can speak—in what is really an amorous conceit—of the rarity of grace, the narrator of *Ahnung und Gegenwart* echoes Novalis's maxim that "everything is a seed" (*Schriften* II, 563) when he says that every book, no matter how bad, can be a source of inspiration. Grace is ever present in each mote of what Tieck called "wearisome matter"; it remains now only to respond, to act, to develop inner resources. Thus it is not surprising that even the Archimedean dreams of the other romantics find their echo in Eichendorff, though a satirical echo and one from which as a Catholic he would willingly distance himself:

Dumb stuff! answered the Fat Man, climbing with difficulty and half turned to the other: You always have such preposterous tricks in your head and think, that is poetic, just because it is queer. I need no such good-for-nothing fence, I carry Jacob's ladder itself on me at all times, I just set it up, right into the air, wherever I like, and I scramble right up it quicker than all of you put together. ["Viel Lärmen um Nichts," *Werke*, p. 1191]

The setting here is not the labyrinth of nature but the labyrinth of a formal garden, and the speaker is a bad poet, Faber, a revenant from *Ahnung und Gegenwart*. Eichendorff's self-parody serves to remind him and his readers of the potential excesses of his own beliefs. Self-reliance is essential, but not too much self-reliance. Our

12. *Dichter und ihre Gesellen*, chap. 24, *Werke*, p. 1026.

independence must be tempered by guidance; Jacob's ladder can be placed only on God's earth. Eichendorff's works are full of such reminders: along with the exemplary landscapes are many that function as warning examples, false perspectives symbolizing false ways of life. Thus, from *Ahnung und Gegenwart* I have already given the description of a chaotic landscape lacking organic (circular) unity and belonging to an equally chaotic mistress. Such warning landscapes are possible because nature is a purely material world and not inherently divine or infinite. When it is full and alive, it can be a hieroglyph or allegorical sign pointing to God, but it always needs an alert observer capable of "reading" its message sympathetically. Both the natural and human poles are complex. Thus it is misleading when one commentator on the mythology of Eichendorff's landscape writes, "The creative immediacy, the *nunc* of the observational experience, is given with the elevated position." [13] Such easy and immediate transcendence characterizes the trivia of romanticism, but not the major authors. [14]

Indeed, we find in Eichendorff's works various perversions of nature's open circle that illustrate the need for sensitive cooperation between man and nature. One such occurs in "Erwartung," a poem of despair in which a lover thinks of his absent beloved. Release comes finally in this poem, but only as the result of a double epiphany of nature and man. First the moon enters to illuminate the "eery" (*schaurig*) surroundings: "Des Mondes hohe Leuchte / Tritt in die stille Welt" (The moon's high lamp / Steps into the quiet world). But in spite of the mythological associations of the moon's processional entry with its "high lamp," [15] the moon only intensifies the stasis and causes the lover to join in the eeriness of the landscape: "Wie schauert nun im Grunde / Der tiefsten Seele mich! / Wie öde ist die Runde / Und einsam ohne dich!" (How I shudder

13. Gerhard Schmidt-Henkel, *Mythos und Dichtung* (Bad Homburg, 1967), p. 62. On mythology in Eichendorff, see Leo Spitzer's unjustly neglected essay, "Zu einer Landschaft Eichendorffs," *Euphorion* 52 (1958), 142–52.

14. Here, for instance, is one minor author's clichéd description of the great circle of nature: "So through every change of appearances you breathe immortal existence; for the circulation [*Kreislauf*] of beauty that once seized you is the stage of eternal spirits for the heavenly uniting of their being" (A. L. Hülsen, "Naturbetrachtungen aus einer Reise durch die Schweiz," Schlegel's *Athenäum*, vol. 3, p. 51).

15. Compare the Greek Artemis Selasphoros and Horace *Odes* IV. vi. 38.

now at the bottom / Of my deepest soul! / How desolate it is around / And lonesome without thee!) Only when the beloved herself appears do the objects in the landscape (the forest and the personified night itself with its moon and stars) regain their vital life force and motion. Without both heavenly illumination and human love the "round" of nature remains dead. [16] The perils lurking in the romantic "observational experience" come from both sides; they arise (in the terms of Brentano's essay on Friedrich) from a claim made by the heart and ruptured by the landscape, or from a claim that the landscape makes without eliciting a response from within.

Another of Eichendorff's warning landscapes expands to infinity, but disperses the idealizing perspective into the wealth of what becomes a purely material and purely sensual nature. Such a landscape is "preternatural"; it has too many centers and preys on the mind:

> Leis wächst durchs dunkle Schweigen
> Ein Flüstern rings und Neigen
> Wie ein geheimes Singen,
> In immer weitern Ringen
> Ziehts alle, die da lauschen,
> In seine duftge Rund,
> Wo kühl im stillen Grund
> Die Wasserkünste rauschen. [17]

The perils here, as so often, seem to be erotic; the landscape mirrors the disintegrating personality of an insanely melancholy lover (line 3 of the second poem in the cycle speaks of his apparent insanity). The ideal beloved, if, indeed, there is one, is never mentioned by the poet, whose power of focusing—that is, unifying and idealizing —has been lost. Instead, the erotic potential is projected onto the objects surrounding him and, as if the objects were not enough

16. It goes without saying that only a critic for whom Eichendorff's landscape is intrinsically infinite independently of any human society could identify the moon with the beloved in this poem and think that there is only one epiphany: Lawrence Radner, *Eichendorff: The Spiritual Geometer* (Lafayette, Ind., 1970), p. 361.
17. "Der Sänger I," stanza 3: "Softly through the dark silence there grows / A whispering round about and bending / Like a secret singing, / In ever larger rings / It draws all who listen / Into its fragrant round, / Where waterworks rustle / Cool in the quiet dale."

in themselves, onto a whole series of hypostasized actions ("ein Flüstern," "Neigen," "Singen," in this stanza). The whole poem is overly sensory, and the sensuous landscape is overly full. The first stanza begins by drawing the attention of the chief sense, sight, to a drunken Dionysian landscape. Complex reflections and, later, echoes, add to the already heavy sensory demands made by the landscape (for instance in line 7, "Es weht *und* rauscht *und* ruft," my emphasis). Even the sunset is not a sign for sensory relaxation and contemplation. Rather, the senses of feeling ("zieht," "kühl") and smell now begin to do their part in attracting what could have been a central consciousness into the growing ("leis wächst") centrifugal force of the landscape. Even the pious close of the first poem is only a temporary respite on the way to the poet's total collapse in the second poem; significantly enough, it speaks of the Lord leading the protective stars *out* from home—"Führt doch aus stillem Hause." This landscape does not lack either objective reality or the potential implied by openness. But the animation conferred by a central organizing spirit is missing.

Answering to this landscape of subjective "desolation" ("Öde," in the last poem) is another type, the enveloping landscape that is closed in, and therefore not whole but limited and fragmented. This is the landscape of objective death:

> Du kanntest die Wellen
> Des Sees, sie schwellen
> In magischen Ringen.
> Ein wehmütig Singen
> Tief unter den Quellen
> In Schlummer dort hält
> Verzaubert die Welt.
> Wohl kennst du die Wellen.[18]

This is the fifth stanza of a poem originally entitled "Abendland-schaft," but published as "Nachruf an meinen Bruder";[19] the

18. "You knew the waves / Of the lake, they swell / In magical rings. / A melancholy singing / Deep under the springs / There keeps the world / Enchanted in slumber. / You knew the waves well."
19. The other famous poem to his brother, "Die Heimat," contains the same image in its last two lines: "Ach dieses Bannes zauberischen Ringen / Entfliehn wir nimmer, ich und du!" ("Alas, you and I will never / Escape this curse's magical rings!")

change in title illustrates the essential equivalence of landscape and lifescape throughout Eichendorff. And the formal contour of the poem repeats the image on yet another level; the rondeaulike closure of each stanza with a return of the first line isolates the stanzas from one another, while halting rhythms and broken syntax in various parts of the poem reinforce the impressions of fragmentation, entrapment, and, particularly in the almost indecipherable third stanza, a meaningless world.

Finally, a third type of warning example is the seraphic false centrality, which we have already seen in the Faber of "Viel Lärmen um Nichts," but which for later readers is preeminently the perspective of another artist in a different satiric story. He is not even a productive artist but a reproductive one, a performer, with an unobjective, empty comic perspective. The Taugenichts, as Herman Meyer has decisively shown, lives in an impossible fairy-tale world in which "things are valued not in their objective thusness, but only in relation to the immediate feeling of the hero." [20] What is impossible about this perspective, as Meyer implies but does not state, is that while the Taugenichts is fabulously lazy and passive, he nevertheless thinks that the world revolves around him: "Behind me the village, gardens, and church towers set, before me new villages, castles, and hills rose; beneath me seedlings, bushes, and meadows merrily flying past, above me countless larks in the clear blue air." [21] Both temporally and spatially the Taugenichts exhibits a limited naiveté bordering on the ridiculous. It is "like an eternal Sunday" in his mind, so that even Saturday brings him no pleasures of its own, but only the "anticipatory joy of the coming Sunday"; but of course in the real world there are work days as well, and rather than acknowledge them the Taugenichts gives up telling the days after a few more Sundays. And while he travels to Italy in body, he remains in Austria in spirit and is quickly surrounded by fellow countrymen speaking German and performing charades out of a Berlin

20. "Raumgestaltung und Raumsymbolik in der Erzählkunst," *Zarte Empirie* (Stuttgart, 1963), p. 48.
21. "Aus dem Leben eines Taugenichts," *Werke*, p. 1063. Leo Spitzer cites this passage as an example of spurious centrality in an aside in "Zu einer Landschaft Eichendorffs," *Euphorion* 52 (1958), 147. See also the burlesque picture of the Taugenichts standing motionless and playing his violin in the midst of a revolving swarm of dancers, children, and dogs, in chap. 3, p. 1085.

Frauentaschenbuch.[22] His naiveté spares him any real danger among the perils of the south, but it also prevents him from withstanding any real challenge or experiencing any real growth. Consequently, when he returns he finds himself, in a mixture of disappointment and relief, engaged not to a dashing countess but to a maid who is the porter's niece. And still the Taugenichts remains a "good-for-nothing"; instead of settling down he dreams of returning to Italy—in the company of his Austrian student friends of course. The Taugenichts's lifescape is a far cry from the great circle of nature; it is a very small circle indeed, or rather a point on which he stands while the scenery flickers past him.

The idea of a lifescape helped to determine the structure of the German romantic novel. Nearly all are picaresque novels, novels of wandering in which the hero traces a path on the map. And the path that he follows defines what sort of person he is: "He wants each of us to pursue his own path, because each new path goes through new lands, and each leads back at last to these dwellings, to this sacred homeland. So I too wish to describe my figure." [23] The characteristic path of Eichendorff's heroes, though each has his own particular stamp, is a circle, often opening at the end onto an infinite prospect into the future. With Friedrich's career in Eichendorff's first novel the metaphor is made explicit, and subsequently it lies unmistakable, even though unexpressed, behind nearly all the other narratives: "Now he stood in the same place where he had begun, as though after a circle described with difficulty, prematurely at the other, more solemn, and quiet end of his journey, and had no more yearning for the stuff over the mountains and beyond." [24] Friedrich's career is in fact a great circle, which ends in the stillness and serenity of God; the rest of his mortal career is devoted to preserving from dissipation the experience he has acquired, to remaining secure, though not inactive, in the bosom of Christ. This is the subject of his great valediction in the last chapter:

He who, tempestuous of heart, feels himself called to join directly in engaging the *circling* machinery of the world, he may *fly from here*, as far as he

22. *Werke*, pp. 1061, 1065, 1067, 1081, 1082, 1119.
23. Novalis, "Die Lehrlinge zu Sais," *Schriften* I, 82.
24. *Ahnung und Gegenwart*, chap. 20, *Werke*, pp. 756–57.

is able. The time is not yet come to build, so long as the bricks, still soft and unseasoned, melt in one's hands. In this misery, as always, there seems to me no other help than religion. For where in the surge of poetry, reverence, nationalism, virtue, and regionalism which now, as in the Babylonian confusion of tongues, buzz vacillating to and fro is a secure *center*, from which all of this can arrive at a clear understanding, at a *living whole*?[25]

The closure of Eichendorff's plots, however, is not strictly typical of romantic novels. For while nature is a great circle, it is only closed at an all-embracing, infinite distance. And what is true of space and of the great circle of the landscape is equally true of time and of both personal and world history. The book of nature never ends, and the path of a man's life is rounded only in death and centered only in the other world:

Many imagine the path to perfection as a straight line and undoubtedly support themselves therein with the conception of its extension *in infinitum*. But where could it lead to draw a line which arrives at no point? We should strive forward in a straight line to infinity where the actual line *in infinitum*, the line of time ends, and produces a circle.[26]

The line of life, even the line of a good life, looks straight and open to human eyes. From the divine perspective its completeness becomes visible, but to a human eye (unless supported like Eichendorff's by religious faith in incarnation and transcendence) all lives look linear and incomplete.

The conception of a life of continual striving helps to explain the fragmentary character of so many romantic novels. What is the complexity of a romantic intrigue, left in suspense at the end of a never-continued "Part One," if not the exact equivalent of the chaotic wealth of nature itself, unified only in an ideal infinite hori-

25. Page 827, my emphasis. For parallels to the world's chaotically revolving gears in this passage, see Schelling, *Werke* I, 162 (quoted above on p. 41); the wheel of time that goes nowhere in "Ein wunderbares morgenländisches Märchen" and in the poem "Die Töne" (both in Wackenroder and Tieck, *Phantasien über die Kunst*); and especially the long satire on romantic philosophy as blind circling and as self-deceiving centrality in Brentano's essay "Der Philister vor, in und nach der Geschichte," *Werke* II, 967–70.

26. Isidorus Orientalis (Heinrich Otto Graf von Loeben), *Lotosblätter* (Bamberg and Leipzig, 1817) I, 14. The finite closure of Friedrich's circle, it may be added, reflects the action of grace made flesh in Christ, leading to the possibility of fulfillment in this world.

zon beyond the limitations of any individual's experience? Tieck reports that the half-finished *Heinrich von Ofterdingen* was to be the first of a cycle of *seven* novels.[27] With the flamboyance characteristic of Novalis, this typifies the conception of the romantic novel as a fragment whose completion is relegated to a mythically distant future.[28] But the most revealing example is, I think, Tieck's novel, *Franz Sternbalds Wanderungen*.

Tieck sounds the theme of open nature very early on, in the third chapter of the first book:

"Traveling," he said to himself, "is something excellent, this freedom of nature, this liveliness of all creatures, the pure broad heaven and the spirit of man, who can sum all this up and collect it into one thought—oh, fortunate is he who early leaves his narrow homeland, to test his wings like a bird and rock himself on unknown, yet more beautiful boughs." [P. 129]

Going beyond one's limited native perspective means increasing one's powers, not dissipating them; it confers the ability to integrate ever more experience into a meaningful totality. Tieck praises active seeking, rather than retirement; his "fortunate is he" thus inverts the customary values of the Horatian "beatus ille." Yet Tieck still has one point in common with Horace: he turns the landscape into a metaphor, or better an allegory, expressing an ethic of living. Much later in the novel Sternbald goes to meet his first Italian painter—once a fellow student of the great Raphael—the hermit Anselm, who teaches him the true allegorical nature of art. And on the way to the hermit's cell he finally discovers the landscape that satisfies his desires, an infinitely vast, infinitely full, unceasingly active landscape, yet one that is unified circularly around him as a focal point:

There lay the splendor of the rivers spread out before him, he seemed to perish at the sudden sight of the broad, infinite, various nature, for it was as if it spoke up to him with heart-piercing voice, as if it looked out toward him with fiery eyes from heaven and from the shining river, pointed to him with its giant limbs. . . . The clouds moved down below on the horizon

27. See Novalis, *Schriften* I, 359.
28. It seems all the more doubtful that Novalis could ever have completed his project, since he is said to have changed his mind constantly; see Friedrich Schlegel, quoted in Novalis, *Schriften* I, 187.

through the blue heaven, the reflections and shadows stretched out on the meadows and changed their colors, strange and wonderful sounds went down the mountain, and Franz felt himself as though enchanted, like someone spellbound, whom the enchanting force causes to stop, and who cannot tear himself from the invisible circle, in spite of all his efforts.[29]

Nature is both the giant and the magician, and the invisible magic circle is not the petty machinery of a stage devil, but the great circle of nature herself. On the verge of an initiation into the mysteries of artistic and religious fulfillment, Sternbald has a preemptive revelation of natural fulfillment; in an ecstatic outburst he compares art unfavorably to the world harmony, the "full harmonic organ song" of the landscape (p. 294). He views the living totality of nature; he views a landscape that is an allegory of God—and the subjunctive and comparative forms ("like a . . .") all through the description reflect the merely allegorical character of the experience—and he acknowledges his own finitude: "The hieroglyph that designates the highest, that designates God, lies there in front of me in ceaseless activity, at work to resolve itself and express itself, I feel the motion, the riddle about to vanish—and I feel my humanity" (ibid.). The experience of natural fulfillment, the perception of the circle of nature, is also an experience of death, an experience in which Sternbald is paralyzed and spellbound and almost seems to perish. But of course the spell is only momentary and not eternal, as the revelation is only allegorical and terrestrial; Franz steps forward on his journey, which can never be completed in this life, whose end he will never see, except in his dreams.

The path of life, for Tieck, is truly an open circle, an arc that can never be closed, for fulfillment is destructive.[30] The lesson of the book, for Sternbald as well as for the often bewildered reader, is to learn to live "in uncertainties, Mysteries, doubts."[31] Once it has been conceded that Tieck, in truly romantic fashion, unites chaos

29. Pt. II, bk. i, ch. 5, p. 293.
30. That fulfillment is destructive is likewise the final lesson of the *Herzensergießungen* by Tieck's close friend Wackenroder, for Wackenroder's collection ends with the story of the musician Joseph Berglinger, whose first successful composition is also his last.
31. Here I borrow Keats's famous phrase, from the letter to his brothers dated Dec. 21, 1817.

with order and that this labyrinthine novel has a plan, it is, I think, relatively easy to show that the plan is to teach this lesson. Sternbald begins with a fixed course and what seems to be a small circle in mind: go to Italy, become a great painter, return to bring the blessings of art to Germany. "Franz now left Nürnberg, his native city, to expand his knowledge abroad in order then after a laborious journeymanship to return to Germany."[32] The cockiness of this resolution lies in its ready anticipation of the journey's conclusion. In the German the infinitive phrase could be equally well one of purpose or one of result: in grammatical terms, then, the sentence's beginning (the purpose of the journey) is also its end (the expected outcome). No greater force of will echoes here than in Eichendorff's "Taugenichts"; what Sternbald envisions is, or would be, truly a "short circuit."

Yet the difficulty is that truly educative, "laborious" experience is not so readily at hand. Sternbald begins, rather, by encountering a long series of pleasurable temptations: a rustic idyll, the offer of a well-paid job as overseer in a factory, the urging of his mother to remain with her in another idyllic situation, the flattering opinion of Lucas van Leyden that he is too talented to be helped by Italian training, and finally, as a combination of all of these temptations, the offer of marriage to the daughter of a merchant whose home is described as a place of quiet retreat in the busy city of Antwerp and whose fortune will secure for Sternbald the opportunity to paint at leisure. How is he soon to reach the stars (as his name suggests) if there are so many inducements to remain on earth? What carries Franz past these siren voices—which form the backbone of the whole first half of the novel as Tieck left it—is an irresistible forward impulse; as he explains it to his mother, "The invisible heaven draws my heart to it with magnetic force."[33] The difficulties of keeping on the path come to replace the difficulties of reaching the goal, until the path itself becomes the goal, just as we have seen "eccentric" subjectivity replace rounded objectivity as the goal for Brentano, Novalis, and the other romantics. In the epiphany on the road to Anselm's hut the dawning recognition of the reversal in

32. Pt. I, bk. i, chap. 1, p. 118.
33. Pt. I, bk. i, chap. 5, p. 142.

priorities first becomes fully conscious. There is no return home in this world, there is only moving forward. And moving forward means moving away from home and childhood, away from idyllic, self-centered ease, and out into the complexities of the world. And so in the second part of the novel Franz becomes increasingly involved in the tangled and passionate affairs of others. At the conclusion of the fragment that we possess—even including the recently published sketch of a continuation—we see him arrived in Italy to be sure, but not appreciably nearer to receiving the technical training after which he had set out.

The movement of *Franz Sternbalds Wanderungen* thus appears to be entirely centrifugal and expansive. Yet it is anchored in a central figure who remains in the foreground throughout. Further, it would be difficult to deny that this central personality gains in maturity and force. And, more important, if he does mature, the reason for it is easy to recognize. Indeed, the novel may be said to make the mechanism of development easier to recognize than the fact of development. For although Franz comes no closer to realizing his ultimate goal of returning to Germany as a master, thoughts of home and of art stay alive as a centripetal force, restraining him from overinvolvement with others. His ever broadening centrifugal experience, conversely, serves to test and correct his central purpose. And the farther he gets from home, the better his perspective on his artistic dreams. It is the interplay of these two forces, the centrifugal force of experience and the centripetal force of desire, that (if Sternbald does indeed mature) produces his growth. I will cite two examples. In chapter two of the last book, Franz receives a commission to refresh a Gothic painting for which he has no admiration. The dreariness of this realistic application of his talents leads him to revalue downward his past achievements and he recognizes, at least temporarily, the futility of his high-spirited youthful ambitions: "In a mist the figures of the great masters went past him, he cared not to stretch out his arms toward any of them; everything was soon past and ended whose beginning he was still awaiting." [34] It is true that this outburst occurs during a complicated and highly

34. Pt. II, bk. 2, chap. 2, p. 374.

melodramatic scene. It may therefore not represent any real advance in self-understanding, but *if* it does, then it does so by the action of experience on long-held but immature ideals. And similarly, to move to the other example, if the last chapter in the book is in truth the promise of more stable and mature behavior, then it is so because of the force of his ideal in pulling Franz back from increasingly giddy behavior: "Franz found the levity of his way of life until now sobering and dissatisfying, he rued many an hour, he resolved to devote himself more sincerely to art."[35] The call of his ideal does not, in the chapters we have, lead Franz back to art, but it does lead him away from his low companions and into a new, more domestic, and worthier circle of acquaintances.

I say, *if* Sternbald matures, because, of course, we as humans can never judge. Only in the highest perspective, says Moritz, can a curve be distinguished from a straight line, and only God can tell whether a course of life is leading toward integration and fulfillment or is mere dissolution. This is the lesson Sternbald learns when, after his allegorical revelation of the divinity behind nature, he finally reaches and converses with the hermit. His journey has apparently strayed from its purpose, it has become aimless, errant wandering. And so he asks Anselm to help him out of his error and back onto the right path. The hermit answers: "We all err, we must err, and beyond error there certainly lies no truth, both are also certainly not opposed, but are mere words, which man composed in his helplessness to designate something which he in no wise meant. Do you understand me?" And Sternbald answers simply, "Not so well."[36] But Anselm's words are both precise and profoundly in the spirit of his age, and they can be understood. The centrifugal movement of wandering, of error, of involvement in the labyrinth of chaotic matter, and the centripetal movement of truth, these are not true movements, but human abstractions to try to glimpse the one truth, which only God can truly mean and oversee. Kant and Hegel too said that centrifugal and centripetal forces were only abstractions to explain a single real movement. And that movement, in

35. Pt. II, bk. 2, chap. 6, p. 404.
36. Pt. II, bk. 1, chap. 5, p. 297.

Tieck's novel, is the essentially indecipherable moral pattern, the individual figure, the open circle of Franz Sternbald's life.[37]

37. In "Tieck's *Franz Sternbald*: The Loss of Thematic Control," *Studies in Romanticism* 5 (1965), 30–43, Jeffrey Sammons demonstrates that Tieck's plot raises the question whether Sternbald's "sensitivity is too great and his emotional reaction to it too powerful to permit him to be an artist" (pp. 36–37). Although he reveals the dangers that Tieck sees in overcommitment to one's own talents and desires, Sammons fails to define the dangers of overcommitment to others; the world in the novel is not "hostile, inhospitable, and philistine" (p. 35), but all too hospitable. Fulfillment, if it is to be achieved, will be found only by avoiding *any* path that is too definite and one-sided. The loss of control is not the novel's weakness, but its program.

III. The Ellipse

We have seen that the exchange of commodities comprises contradictory and mutually exclusive conditions. The development of the commodity does not resolve these contradictions, but does create the form in which they can move. This is in general the method by which real contradictions are resolved. For instance it is a contradiction that a body continually falls into another and equally continually flies away. The ellipse is one of the forms of movement in which this contradiction both manifests and resolves itself.

—Marx, *Das Kapital*

Dualism and the Doctrine of Two Centers

Jacob Böhm, a heroic poem.

—Georg Christoph Lichtenberg

> For me, too, understanding and feeling are both juxtaposed and distinct; but contact is established between them as between the poles of a galvanic pile. The most intimate life of the soul, in my view, consists precisely in that feeling which comes from the understanding, in that understanding which comes from feeling, without the two poles ever losing their identity and becoming confounded.
>
> —Friedrich Schleiermacher, letter to Friedrich Heinrich Jacobi, March 30, 1818

All aspects of romantic dialectic can be expressed in terms of an opposition between two forces, the centrifugal movement of the self and the limiting or centripetal force of the world. This metaphor has entered at some point into each preceding chapter. Thus, the culmination of what I have called the dialectic of objectivity—the recognition that true experience cannot rest on contemplative understanding but only on a constitutive act of will—was seen by Novalis as a substitution of one force for the other: "Everything seems to stream in on us because we do not stream out" (*Schriften* II, 584). The relation of poetry to philosophy can also be thought of as that of a centrifugal movement of explication to a centripetal movement of discovery. Within poetry the modes of allegory and irony constitute respectively an allusive movement toward the central truth and a chaotic centrifugal movement representing the varieties of perception. And the course of Franz Sternbald's life—like that of the hero of any romantic *Bildungsroman*—can be analyzed as the conflict between truth and error, reality and desire.

Any such analysis, however, is bound to run into difficulties; the opposing forces, as Tieck's Anselm says, are abstractions that articulate tentatively at best a more sublime meaning. As we have seen,

Herder was already turning away from explaining the world in terms of the more or less balanced interplay of contraries, and such dualistic explanations could no longer satisfy the romantics. They were engaged in a search for the "something" to which Anselm alludes, the single substratum underlying the apparent contraries, a dynamic rather than a mechanical understanding of the world.[1] Kant himself opened the way in the closing sections of the "Critique of Teleological Judgment"; there, after building his whole system on the absolute disjunction between the realms of noumena and phenomena, he began to consider the possibility of a "ground of unification," which would be "neither the one nor the other, . . . but the supersensible substratum of nature."[2] In Germany at least, the whole romantic movement can probably be seen as a common effort to overcome the dualistic presuppositions virtually uncontested since the time of Descartes.

But dualistic vocabulary and thought patterns are difficult, indeed impossible, to eliminate. For whatever the structure of the world as a whole, Kant had shown that human consciousness was inescapably dualistic and furthermore that the dualism of consciousness was not a defect to be overcome but on the contrary a great blessing. In the dualism of consciousness resides all possibility of knowledge, for knowledge, as Kant had argued in great detail, always results from the cooperation of two separate realms—a concept and a perception, a form and a content, an accident and a substance, a predicate and a subject. To renounce dualism completely would entail abandoning all of the advantages of the Kantian system, and this was unthinkable.

The romantics thus want to have their cake and eat it too. They want both the dualism of error and truth and the unity of a single principle, both the benefits of a philosophy of self-consciousness and the stability of a philosophy of the absolute. There was a traditional answer to dualistic philosophy in the assertion of a hidden parallelism between matter and spirit, of a common ground in which the opposite realms are said to be united. But although European romanticism is often credited with such a mystical belief in the

1. See for instance Franz von Baader's essay "Über den Begriff dynamischer Bewegung im Gegensatze der mechanischen," *Werke* III, 277–86.
2. *Kritik der Urteilskraft*, §78, 1790 ed., p. 362.

unity of contraries, in Germany the doctrine is actually more characteristic of the later eighteenth century, and particularly of Herder. For the German romantics no philosophy was conceivable that failed to give full weight to the dynamic conflict of opposing forces or that relegated this dynamism to the status of mere appearance. Dualism must be accepted (though perhaps only as a *necessary* illusion), and there must be an even deeper unitary reality as well. It is only with considerable qualification, then, that the doctrine of the union of opposites can be attributed to the German romantics or that "the reconciling, synthetic imagination" can be identified "as the common denominator of romanticism."[3]

The chief witness on this point is the series of lectures on the development of philosophy delivered by Friedrich Schlegel to an audience of three in Cologne in 1804–5. While they constitute perhaps the least influential major philosophical undertaking of the epoch, they do offer a revealing compendium of common aims and beliefs together with the earliest full-scale treatment of the history of philosophy by a romantic author. The critique of dualism is one of their principal aims, and a surprising collection of philosophers is accused of dualistic tendencies, including Plato and Augustine as well as Descartes.[4] But the dualistic assumption of "two worlds divided from each other, the world of ideas and the world of appearances" (*KA* XII, 216) is not the only enemy; equally at fault is a tendency to harmonize the opposing pulls of idealism and realism by seeking "a middle way that would avoid the errors of both," that often results in a mediocre compromise, in "only half" a philosophy (*KA* XII, 216). Schlegel's chief representative of this latter error is Kant himself. Whereas we might well expect a romantic to attack Kant for his failure to establish any bond between the idealistic and the empiricist sides of his philosophy, Schlegel objects even more strongly to Kant's "syncretism" and to his refusal to speculate on the implications of either philosophic system in isolation: "Kant, just as he wavers in general throughout his philosophy, chooses

3. René Wellek, referring specifically to Max Deutschbein's book, *Das Wesen des Romantischen*, in "Romanticism Re-examined," *Concepts of Criticism*, ed. Stephen G. Nichols, Jr. (New Haven, 1963), p. 203.
4. *KA* XII, 217–18, 240, and 264 respectively. See also the section on "intellectual dualism," *KA* XII, 139–44.

here the middle way between the two types of explanation, between empiricism and idealism, even though, although the saying that truth lies in the middle is not incorrect, *the truth is never found simply by avoiding the extremes.*" [5]
The romantics were looking for a philosophy that would find truth in a harmonic middle, and that would also acknowledge the dynamic interaction of irreconcilably opposing forces. What was needed then was, not a refutation, but a reformulation of dualism. Dualism, as Schlegel says, is an error, but a necessary one: "*Dualism* is error raised to the highest power, where it is about to disappear and make room for truth" (*PhL* V, 1146). The Kantian dialectic, with its apparently irrefutable proofs that experience and knowledge derive directly from the absolute separation of mind and matter, could hardly be suppressed, but it could be dethroned and subordinated to a principle of unity. In "Über das Wesen der menschlichen Freiheit" (1809), a polemic against Schlegel's recently published *Über die Sprache und Weisheit der Indier*, Schelling defines in precisely these terms the difference between romantic or "modified" dualism and the old dualism. The new dualism affects equally all branches of philosophy: thus Schelling's illustrative example is drawn from ethics, although the definition is contained in a footnote to a discussion of ontology. The discussion refers to the relationship between matter and spirit; Schelling asserts that things are "distinct from God" but not "outside God," "that things have their ground in that which is in God Himself, but is not Himself, e.g., in that which is the ground of His Existence." Schelling intended the footnote that follows to clarify the distinction between being "in God" and being God "Himself":

This is the sole true dualism, namely that which simultaneously allows a unity. Above it has been a question of the modified dualism according to which the evil principle is not correlated but subordinated to the good principle. There is hardly any need to fear that anyone would confuse the relationship here established with that dualism in which what is subordinated is always an essentially evil principle and one whose derivation from God remains for that very reason totally incomprehensible. [*Werke* VII, 359]

5. *KA* XII, 288, Schlegel's emphasis. See also the section on syncretism at the very end of the following year's lectures, *KA* XIII, 376–84.

What Schelling found startling and disturbing in the Manichean tendencies of Schlegel's new book—startling above all because Schlegel was the author—was that "there is no Jakob Böhme in it."[6] For Böhme had already become the romantics' chief ally in their advocacy of a new, organic dualism. In his works they were able to find an explanation of evil and of the dynamic opposing forces of experience as emanations of a single divinity. Böhme's doctrine of two centers, in which nature is seen as a force (or center) independent of God yet still subordinate to Him, exercised a constant fascination for the romantics, and from the moment of his rediscovery Böhme's conceptions largely dominated the romantic understanding of nature, even in the (relatively exceptional) cases where his influence was not acknowledged. There is no question that Böhme was the man of the hour; looking back in later years, Tieck speaks of his chance reading of Böhme in 1798 as a shattering revelation: "Without knowing it, I had brought into my house the firebrand which soon set aflame all these palaces of pride and profane wickedness."[7] From Tieck the enthusiasm for Böhme spread to the other romantics, and especially to Friedrich Schlegel, as has become even more evident since the recent publication of his notebooks. Novalis began almost immediately to express deep interest in Böhme, and in 1800 he borrowed a set of Böhme's complete works from the Weimar library and began to read through it.[8] He died soon after, however, and I can find no trace in his writings of the doctrine of the two centers. Independently, Franz von Baader had discovered Böhme about the same time as Tieck, and his tireless propagandizing in both essays and conversations converted Schelling to Böhme shortly after Schelling moved to Munich in 1806. From these sources Böhme's name and ideas spread throughout the romantic movement.

Böhme's commentators often compare his philosophy with that of Augustine.[9] I have already referred to Augustine's discussion of

6. Letter to A. W. Schlegel, August 26, 1808, in *Krisenjahre der Romantik*, ed. Josef Körner (Brno, 1936), I, 604.
7. "Der Aufruhr in den Cevennen," *Schriften* XXVI, 302.
8. *Schriften* III, 573, and IV, 322–23, 691.
9. One of the best commentators, in fact, compares Augustine *unfavorably* to Böhme: Horst Fuhrmanns, *Schellings Philosophie der Weltalter* (Düsseldorf, 1954), p. 120.

original sin in his commentaries on Genesis: man's fault lay in mistaking the meaning of the tree at the center of the Garden of Eden and in attempting self-mediation when he should have been submissively accepting mediocrity. For present purposes the best introduction to Böhme's doctrine therefore is the quite similar account in his commentary on Genesis, known as the *Mysterium Magnum* (1623). Böhme was fascinated above all by the mention of two trees in the center of Eden, the tree of the knowledge of good and evil and the tree of life. His solution of this ancient conundrum was that there was only one tree, seen in two different aspects: "The precious Pearle lieth in the difference of *the two trees*; and yet it is but only *one*, but manifest in two Kingdoms." [10] With regard to "the property of the Eternall *life*"—in its heavenly or inner aspect—it is the tree of life; with regard to "the wrath of the anger of God, which was manifest by the Essence of the outward world, in earthlinesse in *this Tree*," it is the tree of the knowledge of good and evil (chap. xvii, par. 13). Adam was likewise two men in one: "By the creating is understood the body, which is twofold, *viz.* a Spirituall body and a Corporeall" (xv, 10).

The twofold body is an asset rather than a liability; much to the chagrin of the Church in his own time and in the time of his romantic revival, Böhme's thought is not at all ascetic or other-worldly. He preaches full acceptance of the corporeal body and of the material world—provided only that man's corporeal side be guided by its spiritual counterpart. The material world is inherently good; it becomes evil only when it revolts against the spiritual world to which it is by nature subjugated: "The inward is holy, and the outward [life or Principle] in the Tincture were likewise *holy*, if the Curse were not come into it by reason of the awakened *vanity*." [11] The two trees in Paradise, or rather the two names of the one tree, symbolize the two realms in their proper relation to each other, in which the corporeal is wholly permeated with spirit, yet without losing its separate identity. In this connection Böhme uses the metaphor of fire (symbolizing spirit), which completely envelopes and

10. *Mysterium Magnum* xvii, 11. I quote from the English translation (London, 1654).
11. xv, 14; paragraph 13 in the English translation.

hides the material fuel on which it feeds, and yet the matter is still there, indeed must be there if the fire is not to go out. In the same way the tree of life completely absorbed the tree of the knowledge of good and evil, but not so as to destroy or nullify the working of the principles of good and evil: "For as the light swalloweth up the darknesse, so the celestiall swallowed up the Terrestriall, and changed it again into *that* whence it proceeded; or as the Eternity swalloweth up the Time, and in it, is as a nothing, so likewise were two *Centres* in Adam's mouth" (xvii, 14).

If the physical world is not inherently depraved, then the original sin did not consist of the physical act of eating from the tree. The original sin was in Adam's mind, more specifically in his attitude. Only because his mind was set on the corporeal aspect of the tree rather than on its spiritual aspect can he be said to have eaten of the tree of the knowledge of good and evil rather than from the tree of life. There is in fact no such thing as physical sin, there is only mental sin. This is Böhme's meaning when he says that "Adam also did not eat thereof in the mouth, onely with the Imagination or desire." [12]

For Böhme, then, evil is not material corruption. Both spirit and matter are central; in the *Mysterium Magnum* he speaks symbolically of the sun and earth as "the Centre of the *Astrum*" and "the Centre of the foure Elements" (xi, 31). Elsewhere he often uses the phrases "Centrum solis" and "Centrum naturae," and both are good in their place: "And even here lyeth the great Mystery of the *Creation, viz.* that the internall (*viz.* God) hath thus manifested himselfe with his Eternall Speaking Word (which he himselfe is); the externall is a Type of the internall: God is not alienate; *in him all things live and move* each in its Principle, and degree" (xi, 33). Sinfulness is not a perversion of essence; indeed, it is not a change of essence at all, only a change of attitude. It is the rejection by the material side of man of the order proper to it; that is, man's physical nature rejecting its intended submission to spiritual direction; or, the overthrow of hierarchy and the substitution of self-directing pride for humility. Or, to use Böhme's terms, evil is the "vanity" (*Eitelkeit*) or "independence" (*Eigenständigkeit*) of matter:

12. xviii, 33; paragraph 32 in the translation.

Although Adam was in Paradise, it availed him naught; for in the *imagination* or hunger for good and evil the outer man in him awoke and obtained the command; then Adam's beautiful image became powerless and neared dormancy from its effect, for the divine tincture was ensnared in earthly desire: for external desire compacted its being out of the vanity within it, from which man was darkened and lost his bright, steady eyes and sight.[13]

Virtue for Böhme, then, is nothing other than right order or consonance, and the angels are God's "strings in the All-Essentiall Speaking: and are all of them tuned for the Great *Harmony* of his Eternall Speaking Word" (viii, 31). It does not follow, however, that evil is discord; evil is simply the absence of harmony, the search of the natural center for independence from the guiding stellar or spiritual center.

This explanation immediately prompts two related questions whose answers are the heart of Böhme's originality: the question of the creation and the question of the theodicy. What led God to create an independent world? And for what purpose is the created world capable—if not of revolting against its author—then at least of abandoning him? The *Mysterium Magnum* is Böhme's most thorough and systematic attempt to raise and answer these questions, but its answers are overlaid with particularly difficult allegory and alchemical symbolism. Most often the romantics echo the more accessible versions of Böhme's theodicy found in other works.

The third of the *Quaestiones Theosophicae* (1624) deals directly with the question of creation. Not only Böhme's explanation but even his vocabulary is remarkably similar to that of the romantics. He speaks of the physical world (the "Nay") as the vessel of God's self-consciousness, as the not-self in which the divine self becomes recognizable: "If the eternal will did not flow out of itself and bring itself back in comfort, then there would be no form nor distinction, but all forces would be but One force; so too there should be no understanding: For understanding arises in the distinctions of multiplicity, where one quality sees, tests and desires the other." [14] Only in the creation does God come to see and understand his works. But this self-understanding is not a merely theoretical or disinterested

---

13. xviii, 34. My translation; the English version omits the passage.
14. *Quaestiones Theosophicae* iii, 4. The translations are my own.

action—differing thus from the *intellektuelle Anschauung* of Schelling's works before 1806—it is rather a product of God's love and desire for self-fulfillment. There is truth in pure existence, but in self-recognition there is joy, and without this joy God would be incomplete. The essential basis of creation, the motive force of the natural world, is not intellectual but emotional. Thus:

The reader should know that all things consist in Yea and Nay, be they Divine, Infernal, Earthly, or what you will. The One as the Yea is mere force and life, and is the truth of God or God Himself. He would be unrecognizable in Himself, and there would be no joy or consequence, nor sensitivity without the Nay. The Nay is an object [*Gegenwurf*] of the Yea or truth, that the truth be revealed as something, wherein eternal love may be active, perceptible, willing, that the truth be something to love.[15]

The succeeding sections analyze the mechanism of creation; they elaborate on the proposition that (in Schelling's definitive expression of it) "every being can be revealed only in its opposite, love only in hate, unity in conflict." [16] The visible world is an emanation (*Ausfluß*) of the divine will. Such an action must rest on a suspension of the primal unity; to flow out means to leave the confines of the self, to establish an existence apart from and in some way contrary to that of the divine will. The Nay of creation is not a denial of God, but it is a denial of God's unity. The natural world is a doublet of the spiritual world—and to this extent Böhme is a pantheist—but it is also distinct from God and has a life of its own. Without this independence there could be no outflow, no creation, and no satisfaction of God's benevolence. For Böhme, then, creation is an act of repetition so pronounced as to amount to an act of fission: "For One has nothing in itself that it can will, unless it du-

15. iii, 2. In other words there can be no reconciliation or *Aufhebung* in the Hegelian sense, which would lead only to torpor. Hegel's answer to this Böhmist doctrine, in the section of the *Phenomenology* on forgiveness, admits the necessity of division, but denies that conflict and negation (the Nay) are inevitable, as Böhme's dark psychology implies. See especially the very last sentence of Hegel's section VI, elaborating on the formula "Ich=Ich": "The reconciling *Yea*, in which both I's leave off from their contrary *existence*, is the *existence* of the *I* extended to duality, which therein remains equal to itself and is certain of itself in its complete alienation and opposition;— it is God appearing amongst those who know themselves as pure knowledge" (*Phänomenologie*, p. 472).
16. Schelling, "Über das Wesen der menschlichen Freiheit," *Werke* VII, 373.

plicate itself, so that it be Two; so too it can not feel itself in unity, but in duality it feels itself" (iii, 6). It would not be possible to speak of creation in Böhme's sense unless the creature had a life of its own and its own center of being—"And yet we can not say that the Yea is separate from the Nay, and that they are two things next to one another; rather they are but one thing, but divide themselves into two beginnings (*principles*) and make two *centers*, where each acts and wills for itself" (iii, 3).

Another essay, the first of the *Viertzig Fragen von der Seelen* (1620), supplements this account of the principle of division with a formidable pictorial representation of the two centers as the two eyes of God—one light, the other dark—and with a discussion of the nature of evil as represented metaphorically by fire. God in essence, says Böhme, is light. But light itself is ethereal, and it can only be produced (or revealed) by material means, through fire. Light and fire are therefore two mutually supporting aspects of God:

The Fire-life is the cause of Light-life, and the Light-life is Lord of the Fire-life and herein lyeth the Great Mysterie. For if there were no Fire, there would be no Light, and also no Spirit, and if there were no Spirit to blow up the Fire it would be smothered, and Darknesse would be, and the one would be a Nothing without the other. . . . One of them affordeth life, and the other affordeth food for that life.[17]

God, in other words, is an eternal reality, and also a reality that must be continually generated or produced. And while the subsistence of divinity poses no problems, the *production* of divinity entails division. Fire needs fuel to consume, and this fuel is a dark substance at the heart of any fire, the "ground" or "abyss" of Schelling's philosophy. While light and fire are both aspects of God, they have opposing characteristics: they are Yea and Nay, God's love and God's wrath. When the principle of life remains contained within its matter and subservient to God's love, its manifestation is organic growth: "Then the fire of Light desireth the wrathfulnesse no more, for it is dead to the wrathfulnesse, and it is a peculiar Fire in it selfe, and it sendeth forth its life out of it selfe, which is a

17. *Viertzig Fragen* i, 62, 65. In the English translation, *XL. Questions Concerning the Soule* (London, 1647), these are sections 100 and 101.

sprouting." [18] But it is also capable of breaking out as fire, of seeking to be too much like the God of light, and in so doing, consuming its own substance and ground: "Thus the Fire-will is a seeking of the high swelling Pride, and a Contempt of the darknesse: it contemneth its owne roote; it is covetous and would devoure more than it hath, or more than it should." [19] The outbreak of pride and evil, however, in no way threatens the goodness of the created world. Ultimately fire destroys only itself; it uses up the dark matter from which it lives and it burns down. Indeed, the process, even at its worst, is a dialectical one, for as the fire returns to the darkness of matter, its fuel, or "ground," is transformed into living ether: "Now you also see very well, that a fire must have fewell to burne, or else it is a Darknesse, and though it devours it selfe (by its eager attraction), yet that fire is nothing but a torment in the Darknesse, which we understand to be the Abysse of the Anger of God, which is not manifest in God, but is onely as a cause of the Life in the Kingdome of God." [20]

God, to recapitulate, exists in two forms: self-contained and emanated, cosmic and terrestrial, eternal and temporal, subsistent and productive. Both modes are good in the proper relation to each other, but the revealed material image of God—which is also God's productive, dynamic, and emotional side—must be formed out of matter that is dark and chaotic in origin. Matter is potential divinity, spirit is actual divinity. But in spirit divinity is present only inwardly, it is not revealed. Only by overcoming the inertia of matter, by forming the inchoate, is divinity revealed. The name for the inertia of matter, for its weight, its propensity to fall, is evil. Evil, in this sense, is indispensable to God's joyful purpose; it is the ground of revelation.

The popularity among the romantics, of Böhme generally, and precisely of the doctrine of the two centers, is attested by Brentano's satiric essay, "Der Philister vor, in und nach der Geschichte." This essay contains, in an imitation of Böhme's style, a condensed para-

18. Ibid., i, 97 (English, i, 149).
19. Ibid., i, 72 (English, i, 115).
20. Ibid., i, 89 (English, i, 135). I have altered "source" to "torment," since the German text reads "Qual," not "Quelle."

phrase of Böhme's essential views. Although the remainder of the essay is quite facetious, this portion is largely serious, and Brentano specifically declares his acceptance of the ideas it contains: "What I have spoken, that I believe." [21] As the essay is little read, I would like to present a substantial portion of the material received from Böhme:

God is the eternal unity outside of nature and creature, in himself, and in his outwelling is the will. The eternal unity dwelleth in the creatureless abyss of all things, in the groundless nothing, and the I of nothing [das Ichts des Nichts] is God himself, and when the unity opens itself, it is the pure will, which can will only itself. This movement, the welling of the will and the sensation of himself going out in the joy of willing, is the spirit of divine life, and so the will is the father, and love the son, but the procession of willing love is the spirit and they are the eternal unity, the light of the inward lighting with nothing appearing or having appeared, the eye of the eternal seeing, the eternal Yea, the eternal unity, which willing itself in the will withdrew to feel itself, and this is the eternal Nay or the eternal particularity. The Yea and the Nay are one, but have two centers. The Yea as the outflowing hath no ground, the Nay as the drawing in maketh the ground. The center of the Yea is love, the center of the Nay is wrath. But before all creation the eternal unity lay in these two centers, of Yea and of Nay, as the self-desiring begetting of all creatures, as the self-conception, as the idea; but when the particularity moved out of itself, the idea became an image of unity, and the visible creation stepped forth, the likeness of the idea.[22]

   The documentary value of this passage is considerable, for although the essay is largely incomprehensible to a modern reader, in its time it was highly topical.[23] It was intended for a select audience, but of this audience Brentano was evidently complete master: Varnhagen von Ense reports that when the essay was read "the company was beside itself, cheered, and shouted for joy." There is

21. Werke II, 972. The ninth of Brentano's Romanzen vom Rosenkranz is another, unquestionably serious paraphrase of Böhmist doctrine.
22. Werke II, 970. The rest of the paraphrase concerns the fall, a manifestation of the particularity of matter.
23. It was written to be read to the Christlich-Deutsche Tischgesellschaft (the nationalist association that included Arnim, Kleist, Adam Müller, and Fichte among its leading members) in March 1811, and only 200 copies were printed. The material information in this paragraph and the quotation from Varnhagen come from Brentano's Werke II, 1209.

no reason to suspect that the long paraphrase of Böhme was a blemish on the otherwise flawless calculation of the essay; and since the first part alone of the paraphrase—after which Brentano finally names Böhme as his source—would have taken almost five minutes to read, it is evident that Brentano must have counted on recognition from his audience. This passage proves (if proof were needed) that by 1811 a cultured German with romantic leanings could be expected to have a ready familiarity with Böhme's ideas and manner. But it shows more than that. For the essay was originally written in 1799 (with the title "Naturgeschichte des Philisters") and was read about 1800 to the circle around Tieck and the Schlegels. The same conclusions with regard to the preparation of the audience may be drawn about this earlier reading: almost immediately after Tieck's chance discovery in 1798 Böhme became known and accepted—not perhaps the whole of Böhme, but at least that doctrine of two centers which served the later romantics as the ground of the dialectic of objectivity. Indeed, the immediate appeal of this doctrine is confirmed by another appearance of Böhme in Brentano's early writings. In the farce *Gustav Wasa* (1800) Böhme himself walks on. He speaks one sentence from his first work, *Aurora*. In this work Böhme's theodicy is not fully developed and the accompanying metaphor of two centers does not appear. Yet Brentano selects from this work a passage suggesting the notion that opposites are made manifest in two centers: this was the characteristically romantic aspect of Böhme's writing: "When a twofold dawn breaks at midnight and two suns rise at once, then is a great splendid day at hand, and the bridegroom draws nigh" (Böhme, quoted in Brentano, *Werke* IV, 38).

Centrifugal and Centripetal Forces

> To make the application to the so-called centrifugal tendency, it is the same indwelling principle or essence of the world body as the centripetal; to wit in the former it is absolute in itself, a universe in its particularity, in the latter it is in the absolute: this is both the same, as we have seen. Both those forces, thus falsely designated, are thus in truth only the two unities of the ideas, just as rhythm and the harmony of the movements arising from them are the reflex of the absolute life of all things.
>
> —Schelling, *Ideen zu einer Philosophie der Natur*

I have already spoken of the pervasiveness of dualistic forms of explanation and of the general desire to overcome them. The passages from Schlegel and Schelling that I quoted came, for ease of presentation, from the years when Böhme's influence was at its height: only after the new ideas had been developed could the romantics themselves clearly discern the forces that had been at work. But there was no dearth of attempts throughout the 1790s to overcome the dualistic Kantian dialectic. The whole of the dialectic of objectivity tended toward substituting a dynamic philosophy for Kant's intellectual philosophy and substituting a unitary, vitalistic, and experiential criterion of *value* for the invariably binary standard of *knowledge* (which involves comparing an idea with a fact). Novalis's programmatic statement in "Die Lehrlinge zu Sais," though it speaks against truth rather than against dualism, may be taken as typical of the later 1790s: "It cannot be said that there is a nature without saying something excessive, and all effort toward truth in speeches and conversations about nature only deviates ever further from verisimilitude. A great deal is already won when the striving to understand nature completely is refined into yearning" (*Schriften* I, 85).

A process by which the philosophical imagery was consciously refined can be traced. The process operated first of all on the image of centrifugal and centripetal forces, to which I have already alluded and which, according to Schelling, were particularly associated with the dualism of the Kantian system.[1] This association has the sanction of Kant himself. The speculations of Kant's last years—almost exactly contemporaneous with Schelling's efforts in the same direction—concerned the possibility of finding a link between the philosophy of mind and the philosophy of nature. These efforts to define the substratum (whose existence was already hinted at in the closing sections of the "Critique of Teleological Judgment") never bore fruit. The late notebooks, however, contain numerous drafts of the preface to the unwritten work. In the drafts the invariable example of the dualism to be overcome is that of the opposing central forces, and the image of unity is that of the circle. The circle, according to Kant, is the only real motion; the central forces are a superimposed abstraction, "not certain forces *proper* to the nature of a material, . . . but simply motions which are subsumed in certain other motions."[2] Hegel's dissertation on planetary orbits took up the cause in 1801 (though Hegel could not have known Kant's

1. *Ideen zu einer Philosophie der Natur*, in *Werke* II, 204. Throughout the discussion it will be observed that centrifugal force was generally described as if it were directed exactly opposite to centripetal force, that is, outward from the center. Of course the image so used contradicts the scientific fact to which the phrase properly applies, namely the momentum of a rotating body tangential to its orbit. It may well be that the (unexpressed) tension between the accepted image and the acknowledged fact contributed to the instability of the image in the 1790s. It is certain in any case that the romantics, with their deep interest in science, were aware of the correct fact, for they avoid actually defining the word "centrifugal" as a movement outward from the center. I have noted exceptions only in two relatively minor medical treatises: von Eckartshausen's *Ideen über das affirmative Princip des Lebens* (Leipzig, 1798), where the *vis centrifuga* is defined as "the expansive, effective force" working "from the center to the periphery" (pp. 102 and 28, respectively), and Karl Friedrich Burdach's "De primis momentis formationis foetus" (1814), reprinted (in English translation only) in Arthur William Meyer, *Human Generation: Conclusions of Burdach, Döllinger and von Baer* (Stanford, Calif., 1956), pp. 7–18 (see especially chap. 2, sect. 4). Ulrich Gaier attributes the same error to Oetinger in *Der gesetzliche Kalkül: Hölderlins Dichtungslehre* (Tübingen, 1962), p. 38; in fact Oetinger always correctly describes eccentric (that is, centrifugal) force as perpendicular to centripetal force, or as "tangential" (*Theoriae Musicae Analysis*, Tübingen, 1753, p. 39). Using the terminology that Gaier derives from Hölderlin, one could say that the two forces are "harmonically opposed," not "directly opposed."

2. *Opus Postumum*, in *Gesammelte Schriften* XXI (Berlin, 1936), 167.

private notebooks, of course), and he restated his arguments in the *Science of Logic* (1812) and yet again in the 1831 *Encyclopedia*.[3] By 1802 Schelling was attributing planetary motion to "preestablished harmony" rather than to opposing forces.[4] Baader too tried, in more complicated fashion, to "rectify the usual distinction of a centripetal and centrifugal direction" by means of an additional distinction between gravitational attraction and falling; and in another essay he speaks of "the indivisible connection of the existence of a star in its particularity with its orbit." The orbit, he argues, is a defining characteristic of the star or planet; it is invariable and even, in a sense, personal, and to attribute it to the interaction of invisible opposing forces is at best a mechanistic form of explanation that violates the spirit, even if not the letter, of the facts.[5]

One of the earliest and most interesting exponents of these views is Novalis. He too was led to attempt a synthesis, to discover the principle containing both forces and preceding their separation from each other: "Centripetal force—is the synthetic effort—centrifugal force—the analytic effort of the spirit—effort toward unity —effort toward multiplicity—through mutual determination of both by each other—that higher synthesis of unity and multiplicity is itself produced—through which One is in All and All in One" (*Schriften* II, 589). One of the *Blütenstaub* fragments, which were written a few months before the above fragment, is a study for such a "higher synthesis." In a dense paragraph Novalis claims first that the notions of outward and inward motion are purely relative; second that (in their transcendental application) they are merely ways of naming, which depend upon the orientation of the perceiving in-

3. For a typical quotation from the dissertation see "The Circle and the Organic World-View" above. In the *Wissenschaft der Logik*, see the note "Über Zentripetal- und Zentrifugalkraft"; in the *Enzyklopädie*, §270.
4. *Ideen zu einer Philosophie der Natur*, in *Werke* II, 199. The first edition of this work (1797) hedges somewhat, denying the reality of the central forces, but at the same time admitting their didactic value and their validity in the phenomenal world (see especially II, 5, pp. 227–39).
5. The first quotation is from "Elementarbegriffe über die Zeit," *Werke* XIV, 40–41; the second from "Über den verderblichen Einfluss der herrschenden rationalistisch-materialistischen Vorstellungen auf die höhere Physik und Kunst," *Werke* III, 292–93. See also "Rüge einiger Irrthümer . . . ," *Werke* III, 316–22. Baader often refers with approbation to Hegel's views on the subject.

tellect rather than any objective judgment of the circumstances; and finally that physical life is just as centripetal—just as much a return into the self, a reflexion—as mental life is:

To return into oneself signifies for us to abstract from the outer world. For spirits earthly life means analogously an inner contemplation, an ingoing into oneself, an immanent activity. Thus earthly life arises from an original reflection, a primitive ingoing, a collecting in the self, which is as free as our reflection. Conversely, spiritual life in this world arises from a breaching of that primitive reflection. . . . Here we see how relative going out and going in is. What we call going in is actually going out, a resumption of the original form.[6]

The obscurity of expression in this fragment reflects a struggle to come to terms with the ideas of others. In particular, Novalis is attempting to respond to a challenge implicit in the fifth section of Fichte's most important treatise, the *Grundlage der gesamten Wissenschaftslehre* of 1794−95. In that section, which is in fact the apparent source of the popularity of the words centripetal and centrifugal, Fichte poses the question of the origin of an external object world, of a "not-self," as he calls it. This question is particularly acute in his philosophy, which begins not merely in Cartesian fashion with the self, but with a self necessarily thinking about itself, a self whose every thought is ultimately turned inward: "The self posits itself absolutely, and to that extent its activity is all returning into itself. The direction of it is—if it is permitted . . . to borrow from natural science a word that enters the latter precisely from the present transcendental point, as will be shown in due time—solely *centripetal*."[7] But the ability to reflect, he argues, presupposes the existence of something to think about, something that stands in the way of immediate and infinite self-knowledge. Reflection thus always brings with it the thought of its own potential limitation, of something outside the bounds of the self. And this thought that

6. *Blütenstaub* 45. Note the affinity to Heideggerian vocabulary of Novalis's "Sammeln in sich selbst."

7. *Werke* I, 273. In a note to *LN* 812 Hans Eichner derives Schlegel's use of "centripetal" and "centrifugal" from this passage. Observe that in insisting that self-consciousness must precede perception, Fichte is characteristically more rigorous than Kant, who says only that "the: *I think* must be *able* to accompany all my representations" (*Kritik der reinen Vernunft*, 2d ed., p. 131, Kant's emphasis).

moves beyond the self is the centrifugal aspect of the self. The movement toward the self, in other words, must be accompanied by a movement away from the self: "There is no one direction, without there being a second directly opposed to the first" (*Werke* I, 273). This is the movement that "posits" the not-self and establishes the real world, which, Fichte goes on to say, is in fact necessarily infinite.

This is a circular argument. Fichte recognized as much, for he supplemented it with a discussion defending its circularity. He acknowledges that both directions of thought are equally located in the self. He also acknowledges that the self is limited only because it freely recognizes a limitation, in other words only by its own act and not by any demonstrable not-self. To this extent—and here is the inspiration for Novalis's fragment attacking a dualistic ontology—both directions are really the same: "Therefore the centripetal and centrifugal direction of activity are both founded in the same way in the nature of the self; they are both *one* and the same" (*Werke* I, 274). The proof that an external world exists is therefore no proof, it has only persuasive force at best. Consequently Fichte adds "an important remark" explaining that although "the principle of life and consciousness" is "of course contained in the self," there must be a not-self because the absence of a not-self (that is, of a real world) is "totally unthinkable" (I, 278–79). The two "directions," then, will never support a true proof; for when the self goes out and returns in on itself, this constitutes both an experiential and a logical "circle," which only a "dogmatic" philosophy could ever claim to overcome:

This, that the finite spirit must necessarily posit something absolute (a thing in itself) outside of itself and nevertheless on the other hand must recognize that the thing is only there *for it* (a necessary noumenon), is the circle which it can expand to infinity [the infinite circle again!] but out of which it can never emerge. A system that takes no cognizance of this circle is a dogmatic idealism; for it is actually only the indicated circle that limits us and makes us finite beings; a system that claims to have gone outside of the circle is a transcendental realistic dogmatism. [*Werke* I, 281]

The basic fact of experience for Fichte is then a circle consisting of the outward movement of exploration (but this may be only self-projection) followed by the returning movement of recognition (which may be only self-recognition). Prior to the existence of this circle, he says, no experience was possible. The circle is what we might call a necessary illusion; it is infinite and embraces the whole world in its scope. Hence there can be no independent confirmation that either the world or the circle that produces it has substantive reality. In claiming to have reached the limit of the provable, Fichte betrays his weakness by the truculence of his tone: "Here we see clear as daylight what so many philosophers who, despite their alleged Kantianism [*Kritizismus*], have not yet freed themselves from transcendent dogmatism cannot understand, *that* and *how* the ego can develop solely in itself everything which is ever to occur in it, without ever going outside of itself and breaking through its circle" (I, 289). Significantly, the appeal here is not to reason but to intuition (what "we see clear as daylight"). For the problem (to which Novalis among others was responding) is that Fichte himself continually risks the dogmatism he rebukes in others. Much as he wished to establish the self firmly as the sole and central principle of experience, the argument must repeatedly posit what it cannot prove; and the circle remains in danger of disintegrating into the dualism of opposing forces out of which it is compounded. Indeed, the historical importance of the book arises, it seems to me, directly out of the failure of its argument, which lays bare the struggle between two conceptual systems at the moment of transition.

Two contradictory tendencies thus control the form of the book: the zeal to persuade the reader that the structure of experience is necessarily circular and the constant provocation to find a sure ground for a linear argument. The two tendencies lead to Fichte's two irreconcilable claims that the *Grundlage* is a perfect sphere presenting the totality of knowledge and that it is the "very imperfect" (linear) first step toward the elaboration of the *Wissenschaftslehre*. The very style of the book is flamboyantly circular; as hallmark it has numerous statements of mutual exclusion couched in the verbal formula, "no A, no B, no B, no A," as well as countless epicycles, such as the (undemonstrated) claim that the word "centripetal" was borrowed from philosophy by the scientists and is now being reclaimed. The overall structure is also a circle, though the appearance of a continuously unfolding argument does much to conceal this fact. The theoretical part, as Fichte comments (I, 222–23), is a continuing ascent to first principles, the practical part a redescent to reality; the theoretical part, he says at another point (I, 285), is concerned with the how of knowledge, the practical part with the what. The whole arch is neatly rounded when the final pages return to the concept of an action that establishes the not-self, harking back to the notion of a "deed-action" (*Tathandlung*) at the opening of the treatise. Yet in spite of these circularities, the progresssive tendencies remain. The theoretical portion, in particular, consists of a dazzling succession of dialectical arguments constructed on a single model, each leading to the unveiling of a circle that must be resolved in a higher dialectic. Such constant refinement of the dialectic leads to the conviction that circularity is both inescapable and dissatisfying; an unshakable first principle is continually sought and yet never found. The "Deduction of Representation," which closed the first installment of the book and which was therefore sure to make a strong impression on its early readers, is especially insistent in its search for a "firm point" to ground the dialectic. To be sure, the book continues to relapse into its dualistic governing principles (centrifugal and centripetal movements of the self) and into the circle that they imply; the principles are defined successively as the imagination's "suspension" (*Schweben*) between extremes, as "reciprocity" (*Wechselbestimmung*), and as the "drive for reciprocity." Yet the closing pages introduce a spate of new terms, each attempting once again to reduce to a single name the reciprocal relationship between self and not-self, or, as Fichte also calls them, between the "determinant" (*das Bestimmende*) and the "determinate" (*das Bestimmte*). Of these new terms, "applause" (*Beifall*), "harmony," and "satisfaction," the second is particularly telling. For Fichte had earlier labeled as "inconsistent" the similar Leibnizian notion of preestablished harmony (I, 147–48). He had also declared in the thesis of section 2 that self and not-self are not merely opposites but "absolutely opposed" (I, 104). Consequently, it cannot be said that the concept of harmony at the end of the treatise (which is supposed both to resolve the opposition of forces and to establish a linear terminus for the dialectic) issues from a consistent chain of reasoning. Rather, Fichte has abruptly emancipated a pun that was repressed during the whole of the preceding argument. "Harmony," accompanied by a "feeling of applause" and leading to "satisfaction," can become a final stage only because the key verb "bestimmen" has implicitly shifted from its technical meaning (determine) to its musical meaning (tune). Thus, the *Grundlage* neither completely closes its circle nor decisively opens it to a linear deduction from a fixed principle; instead, it concludes with the mere illusion of a resolution, arising out of a punning evasion and artfully sidestepping an ultimate decision.[8]

Novalis's struggle to resolve the Fichtean centrifugal and centripetal forces into a single principle can therefore be seen as response to an ambivalence already present in Fichte's work. Novalis died before discovering the solution to which most of his contemporaries soon adhered, but—perhaps for that very reason—his efforts constitute the most interesting evidence of the direction in which the romantics were looking. I would like to refer to three texts—Novalis's early Fichte studies (1795–96), a group of fragments from the manuscripts known as the *Allgemeines Brouillon* (late 1798), and then less briefly Novalis's unfinished story "Die Lehrlinge zu Sais" (probably 1798).

Novalis's earliest references to Fichte's two directions treat them as opposed: a typical comment is "nothing outgoing, but an ingoing" (*Schriften* II, 139, see also II, 135). He thus begins by accepting Fichte's assumption that experience can be explained only on the unprovable assumption of a real world that resists the self. Even in these first references, however, Novalis is looking for a "synthesis" (II, 139), that is, for a way to develop Fichte's hint that the two

8. Dieter Henrich, *Fichtes ursprüngliche Einsicht* (Frankfurt, 1967), p. 35, describes the mixture of certitude and indefiniteness as follows: "Fichte was very concerned to make the fundamental principle as clear as possible, . . . [to provide] an unshakable assurance of the precedence and dignity of conscious freedom. But such assurance does not bring the peace of secure knowledge. It only awakens a heightened desire to ground it in a theory that always remains capable of improvement." Of interest also are Henrich's discussions of Fichte's introduction of the phenomenologists' term "gleich ursprünglich" (p. 24), the return to a metaphorical style to express the absolute (p. 47), the doubling of consciousness (p. 49); these correspond to Novalis's conception of "suspension" (discussed below), the romantic defense of allegory, the doctrine of two centers. For a thorough conceptual analysis and defense of Fichte's circle see Giuseppe Duso, *Contraddizione e dialettica nella formazione del pensiero fichtiano* (Urbino, 1974).

directions, though apparently contraries, are really one and the same. A later entry indicates that Novalis continued to look for this synthesis and anticipates the *Blütenstaub* fragment that equates inward and outward movement: "The direction [of force] is at once centripetal and centrifugal" (II, 190). Finally another, much longer entry redefines Fichte's notion of "suspension" as something not merely free, but truly central and primary: it is the unity, prior to any opposition between self and world or subject and object, from which the apparent divisions spring. The image of a unifying central sun to which Novalis here alludes reveals the influence of Schelling's early work and marks a tentative step beyond Fichte's standpoint:

All being, being in general, is nothing but being free—*suspension* between extremes which are necessarily to be united and necessarily to be separated. All reality streams out from this light point of suspension—everything is contained in it—object and subject exist through it, not it through them. . . . It is something thoroughly real, for the suspension, its cause, is the source, the *mater* of all reality, reality itself.[9]

   This treatment of suspension is only an embryonic solution to Fichte's circle—Novalis resolved, after the fashion of these note-books, to think more "about the nature of this suspension" (II, 266). But in its attempt to relate opposition to a prior unity and to treat the dualism of the two extremes as the outward form of a single underlying principle the concept is a prophetic one. Another attempt occurs in the course of a group of fragments about music, dating from 1798. Novalis had just read a treatise on acoustics by Ernst Florens Friedrich Chladni. He was obviously attracted by the idea that vibration offers a physical analogy to the opposing directions of movement that produce Fichte's circle—one fragment actually says that "Fichte did nothing but discover the rhythm of philosophy and express it in verbal acoustics" (III, 310)—and a long series of entries speculate with characteristic whimsy on the implications of vibration (III, 283–311 passim). Toward the end the associations become increasingly fanciful as Novalis gropes for

9. *Schriften* II, 266. For philological evidence of Schelling's influence on the Fichte studies see the editors' note to II, 116. The image of the central sun re-appears later in Novalis's work as the shining carbuncle produced by the teacher in "Die Lehrlinge zu Sais" (*Schriften* I, 106).

a unifying term. For instance, the last of the whole cluster, headed "Musical Physics," contains the following sentences: "The center is a consonant like the periphery (of the universe). . . . Absolute unity of bass and descant. This is the systole and diastole of divine life." [10] In an earlier fragment we can see even more clearly that Novalis was pursuing the ideal of a single source for both inward and outward movement, for both the intellectual and physical world: "Is not reflection on oneself, or abstraction from the external world—consonant in nature. Song toward *the outside—external world—song toward the inside—internal world*" (III, 310). Novalis draws from Fichte the notion that music is to be taken as the source of experience, though he conceives of music primarily as melody rather than as Fichte's harmony. His desire to apply the conceit "categorically" to experience in general, and not just to acoustics, is evident from the rather surprising fact that the fragment is headed not "Music," but "Philosophy." [11]

These continued speculations reached partial fruition in "Die Lehrlinge zu Sais." Novalis was unable to arrive at a fully satisfactory formulation of the relationship between the world of the self and the world of nature; and he left the story unfinished while he pursued a solution in fragments such as those just quoted. Nevertheless it remains a sensitive account of the state of philosophical controversy in the late 1790s. It consists of discussions among characters representing various current viewpoints and is unified by a rather obscure allegorical plot. Its extreme condensation makes it impossible to summarize; I will simply draw attention to aspects related to the present topic.

The brief opening chapter, "The Apprentice," contains the discussion of the path of life to which I have already alluded. Novalis's opening sentences establish the correlation between a man's life and

10. III, 311. The fragment identifies the descant with the center and the bass with the periphery. Both are "infinite," and observation may start from either. This true reciprocity distinguishes the German romantics even from the myth of the divine heartbeat in Poe's *Eureka*, where only the central point is divine.
11. The Neckar bridge, "which resounds with wagons and men," in Hölderlin's "Heidelberg" is a similar example of a unitary response. The bridge is topographically in the center of the poem's landscape; it is a semidivine manifestation ("light and powerful the bridge swings across the river") and a source of ultimate, visionary experience; it is associated with pulsation and music ("schwingt" suggests *Schwingung*, the technical word for vibration).

geometrical figures to which a symbolic significance is attributed: "Many routes are traveled by men. He who pursues and compares them will see wonderful figures arise; figures that seem to belong to that great cipher which is everywhere to be glimpsed: on wings, egg shells, in clouds, in the snow, . . . in the lights of heaven, . . . in the filings around the magnet, and in strange conjunctures of fate" (I, 79). This beginning is a necessary preparation for the story, whose narrative portions consist of sketchy accounts of experiences of wandering and exploration. The reader is alerted that these accounts mean something, that they are allegorical representations (in "cipher") of universal significance; and he is encouraged to relate them to one another and to the philosophical discussions that make up the bulk of the story. Almost immediately the first of these accounts follows, the parablelike story of a clumsy apprentice who had disappeared one evening but had returned the following morning with a remarkable stone. The teacher at that time indicated the significance of the discovery by a symbolic action: "He placed the little stone in an empty spot which lay in among other stones, exactly where many rows touched one another like rays of light" (I, 81). Not knowledge or experience, but the naiveté of the untutored apprentice fills the central spot. As slender as the anecdote is, it serves to define Novalis's philosophical ambition: to replace Fichte's philosophy of reflection with a philosophy of innocence and thereby to find the middle that can link the two incommensurable extremes (thinking self and limiting world) of Fichte's universe. The ambition is by no means negligible—it amounted to a rejection of the whole Cartesian tradition of beginning with the *thinking* self—but the modesty of the parable itself, and indeed of the whole of the "Lehrlinge," attests to the sobriety and seriousness of Novalis's intentions.

The second and much longer of the story's two chapters is called "Nature." It opens with a dissertation and a philosophical conversation about reality. The dissertation expresses Novalis's dissatisfaction with Fichte's conception of nature as a resistant not-self. "Round about us," says Novalis, "lies the wonderful sensory and supersensory nature," and whenever we perceive it we feel "an attraction of nature, an expression of our sympathy with it." In order to explain this affinity between the self and nature, Novalis translates into conceptual terms the teacher's symbolic comment on the parable of the apprentice: "There is a secret pull to all sides in our inner self, spreading round about from an infinitely deep center" (I, 85). The dissertation gradually merges into the conversation —the absence of a sharp division is of course programmatic—in which various views of the relation of man to nature are presented: that nature is deadly; that nature must be conquered; that man's great asset is his independence from nature; and finally that freedom is only possible through moral action, which in turn will lead inevitably to full knowledge and utilization of nature. This conversation is brilliantly laid out; each speaker simply elaborates on the preceding one, yet the later statements are nevertheless directly opposed to the earlier ones.[12] In spite of the lyrical flow of the dialogue from one speaker to the next, the logical mode of argumentation achieves only dissent and discord. The dialectics, in other words, interrupt the very continuity ("spreading round about," in the teacher's words) that Novalis is trying to establish as the basic principle of his philosophy. In fact, the break in continuity becomes the exception that proves the rule that continuity is superior: far from being productive as the opposition between self and not-self is for Fichte, disagreement results only in the confusion of the apprentice who is listening to the "clashing voices."

After what is described as a temporary emotional storm, the apprentice becomes quiet and "sunk into himself." Intellectual activity leads to introspection cut off from the very nature toward which it is ostensibly directed. "A lively playmate" comes to restore the apprentice's spirits; the apprentice, as he says, should turn outward rather than inward. "Stop brooding; you are going the wrong way." [13] Abstract intellect must yield to emotional fullness; the dissonant voices of reason must be brought into harmony. The word *Stimmung* used by the playmate in reference equally to the

12. The second speaker—actually a group—expresses agreement with the first by beginning "Well then." Another group speaks third, beginning "You are right." Finally, an individual speaks "to these last" (with whom he agrees), beginning "The others speak wrongly."

13. "'Du Grübler', rief er, 'bist auf ganz verkehrtem Wege'" (I, 91). A *Grübler* is one who digs into his own mind.

unity of man with nature and to the emotional basis (the "mood") of this unity is perhaps the key to the whole story.[14] The playmate tries to restore the apprentice's feeling for nature and for "the spirit . . . which surrounds you like an invisible beloved." He tries to re-center the apprentice in nature, so to speak. And because the center, for all the romantics, can only be hinted at, the playmate's method is to tell an allegorical story, a fairy tale. This is the famous story of Hyacinth and Roseblossom (I, 91–95), two characters human in their actions, but fully natural in their names.

It is the story of two children who love each other and are at home in nature. But one day an alchemist comes from far away, tells Hyacinth wonderful, incomprehensible things, and takes him exploring "in deep pits." The combination of eccentricity (coming from far away) and introversion (delving) infects Hyacinth; he becomes both melancholy and restive. His happy childhood harmony thus gives way to the unhappy extremes of immersion in self and immersion in nature, and he leaves home on a vague quest. He quickly discovers, however, that his true motive force is not intellectual and reflective, but emotive; it is his "yearning" for nature and his "love" for the lost Roseblossom. His journey takes him away from the rude, violent landscape of the West and toward the orient, which lacks abrupt shifts of season and is characterized by lush, gradually maturing plant forms. And in this landscape what Novalis had described in the *Blütenstaub* fragment comes true. What on the physical level is Hyacinth's centrifugal movement is equivalent to a centripetal movement on the spiritual level: as he moves toward the realm of the flowers and of the "family of spirits" (*Geisterfamilie*) who seem to rule them, he discovers to his eternal delight that his wandering has brought him back home to Roseblossom, but to a home now transfigured by the change in setting and "surrounded" by "a distant music."

Novalis substitutes for Fichte's circle of opposing directions of movement a single emotional movement that is simultaneously cen-

14. For the background that resonates in this word, see Leo Spitzer, *Classical and Christian Ideas of World Harmony* (Baltimore, 1963). There are nuanced treatments of *Stimmung* in the romantics by Paul Böckmann, "Formen der Stimmungslyrik," *Formensprache* (Hamburg, 1966), pp. 425–52, and by Martin Wettstein in his brilliant study, *Die Prosasprache Joseph von Eichendorffs* (Zurich, 1975), pp. 61–65.

trifugal and centripetal, which leads away from home and yet—mysteriously, for the return lies under the aegis of the mystery goddess Isis—back to home. The motive force of Fichte's circle, except perhaps at the very end of the *Grundlage*, is reflection on the difference between man and nature; that of Novalis's single movement is, from its inception, harmony and the desire for harmony. The listeners—for the apprentice, emerged from his isolation, has been mysteriously joined by others—draw the musical moral of the tale: "'Oh! would that man,' they said, 'understood the inner music of nature and had a sense for external harmony. But . . . he can leave nothing be, he divides us tyrannically and flails about him in sheer dissonance'" (I, 95). The remainder of the story is taken up by another philosophical conversation in which more and more new arrivals participate. The discussion, which I will not analyze in detail, concerns the way nature can be understood by a central self whose observations emanate in all directions (I, 97). With the proper love such an observer will recognize in nature neither the Fichtean object world nor simply a narcissistic reflection of his own desires and abilities, but another subject—an *alter ego* in the truest sense—to respond to him and confirm him in his sympathies for the world around: "Does not the rock itself become an individual 'thou' in the moment when I speak to it?"[15] The lover of nature feels that it is separate from himself, but also feels their "wedded" unity. This fusion of two in one, but in which the two maintain their distinctness—two motions in one, the back-and-forth vibration of a string that produces one tone, two subjects united in one love—is one of the great discoveries (or rediscoveries) of romanticism: "I call this son, this favorite of nature fortunate whom she allows to consider her in her duality, as procreating and begetting power, and in her unity, as an infinite, eternal wedding" (I, 106).

During the conversation the teacher has quietly appeared. As at the end of the fairy tale, "a music was heard in the distance" (I, 106). The reuniting of the teacher and his pupils near the temple of Sais is a conscious parallel to the gathering of Hyacinth's family in

15. I, 100. This conception of the beloved as a separate person who is linked to the self yet recognizes its separate identity is a romantic commonplace. Thus, in Schlegel's *Lucinde*: "Only in the answer of his thou can each I fully feel his infinite unity" (*KA* V, 61).

the same temple. All of the descriptive passages in the "Lehrlinge" are in fact clearly emblematic, and the parallel to the fairy tale draws further attention to the allegorical character of the whole story. The story is abstract throughout; it contains no concrete realization of the ideal that it describes. In this sense is is true to the nature of romantic allegory: it alludes to but does not exhibit a central verity. The whole discussion following the fairy tale, including the teacher's long closing address (I, 107–109), is devoted, not to the description of a lover of nature and to the ways to educate men to love nature, but only to the conditions that a nature-lover must meet. The tone of the whole is optative. Novalis has not yet found the way to fulfill the demands that he placed on whoever was to correct Fichte's work. Indeed, one of the participants in the discussion argues that there is no concrete fulfillment, only poetic fulfillment, expressed and perceived with infinite insubstantiality: "Only poets have felt what nature can be to men, . . . and here too it can be said of them that humanity finds itself in the most complete dissolution in them and therefore every sense impression is propagated toward all sides, pure in its infinite variations, through their crystal clarity and mobility" (I, 99). The teacher is both more and less optimistic; he looks forward to a concrete and communicable (that is, teachable) experience of the affinity of man and nature, but he must project this achievement into an indefinite future. Here, in the closing lines of the story, is his description of the teacher of the future:

> With the help of these insights he will form a system for applying these means to each given individual, founded on experiments, analysis, and comparison; he will assimilate this system until it becomes second nature and then begin his rewarding business with enthusiasm. Only he will be rightly called a teacher of nature, for every other mere naturalist, like any natural phenomenon, will only awaken the sense for nature randomly and sympathetically. [I, 109]

"Die Lehrlinge zu Sais" thus takes the form of "an indispensable answer to a secret question, or the question to this infinite answer" (I, 99); it defines a set of conditions governing an as yet unsolved equation that was to produce a figure different from Fichte's circle.[16] In this sense it is more complete than many romantic "fragments." It seems indisputable that the parallel between the end of the fairy tale and the end of the whole story reveals an intention to round off the narrative. If the story seems incomplete, that is not because it lacks an ending, but because it lacks a fully realized meaning. Like all romantic allegory it points to an unrevealed truth.

Along with *Franz Sternbald* and *Hyperion* (discussed below), it belongs to the generation of romantic works that attempt to respond to the questions raised by Fichte's works but that still have an indeterminate or "eccentric" curve. It is true that in 1800 Novalis was already planning to finish the "Lehrlinge." But the context in which he speaks of doing so is highly revealing: he talks about his plans, not merely in the same famous long letter, but in the same portion of that letter to Tieck of February 23, 1800, in which he also reports on his recent study of Böhme. Here are his words: "I am reading Jakob Böhme now in context and am beginning to understand him as he must be understood. . . . So much the better that the 'Lehrlinge' is now resting—which now will have to appear in an entirely different way" (*Schriften* IV, 322–23). The solution to the problems raised by Fichte was to be found in Böhme. The solution, had Novalis lived, would perhaps have permitted him to finish the fragment and to close the circle. But the work would then have been entirely different. And its curve, we may be almost certain, would no longer have been the Fichtean circle of experience, but the Böhmist curve with two centers or foci—the ellipse.

In Goethe's works may be found an essay that illustrates how the ellipse came to replace the open circle as the "romantic" curve. Entitled "Problem und Erwiderung," the essay consists of a "Problem" formulated by Goethe and a longer "Reply" by a scientific

16. The open-ended or allegorical character of the "Lehrlinge" also has implications for hermeneutics. The figure of a man's life written in "cipher," like "the filings around the magnet," like a "constellation" (I, 79), or like the thread in a labyrinth (I, 103), is both textile and text, an open weave of significance designed to contain a loose but infinite meaning. A proper understanding of an allegorical text or figure requires a generous empathy rather than cool, precise knowledge. After the fairy tale the listeners describe this kind of understanding as "the sweet passion for the weave of nature. . . . Thought is but a dream of feeling, an extinct feeling" (I, 96).

friend of his, Ernst Meyer.[17] It proposes the ellipse in quite specific terms as the answer to the problems raised by Fichte's analysis of the opposing central forces of experience. The essay is relatively late (1823), but its even and unpolemical tenor makes it a valuable witness to the romantics' own understanding of the intellectual history of their period.

It should not be surprising to discover Goethe intimately involved in romantic speculations. Indeed, Novalis's interest in the philosophical significance of polar alternations (vibrations, systole and diastole, for example) runs closely parallel to Goethe's. The curve with which Goethe is most commonly associated, the spiral, is in fact peculiar to him. But the spiral itself is associated with a second motion, the Fichtean alternation of in and out. Here is an example of Goethe's urge to represent the rotation of the earth simultaneously as a spiral and as a pulsation, in this case the regular twice-daily rise and fall of the barometer:

We imagine there to be a rotating motion inside the earth which forces the immense ball around itself in twenty-four hours and which may be conceived as an endless living screw.

But this is not enough: this motion has a certain pulsation, an increase and decrease, without which no life would be thinkable, it is likewise a regular expansion and contraction which repeats itself [twice] in twenty-four hours.[18]

There are, as Goethe says, "two fundamental movements of every terrestrial body" (*Werke* XX, 931).

The metamorphic spiral is, as I have said, the more familiar of these two Goethean curves. In "Problem und Erwiderung," however, it is subordinated as one pole under the more general curve of expansion and contraction. The "Problem" (XIX, 347–49) is how nature can be understood, that is—since our understanding is always organized—how a system comprehending the infinite variety of nature is possible: "Nature has no system, it has, it is, life and continuity from an unknown center to an unknowable limit." The concept most nearly adequate to this infinite variety is that of meta-

---

17. Goethe, *Werke* XIX, 347–61. At the time Meyer was a Privatdozent in Göttingen; he later became professor of botany in Königsberg.
18. "Versuch einer Witterungslehre," *Werke* XX, 930–31.

morphosis; but metamorphosis has its dangers too—confusion and loss of control over the material to be studied: "The idea of metamorphosis . . . is like the *vis centrifuga* and would be lost in infinity if a counterweight were not given to it."[19] The counterbalancing "*vis centripeta*" is the "tendency to specification, the tenacious capacity to persist." The problem that Goethe raises resembles the Kantian problem of the compatibility of causal and teleological explanations of nature: Goethe says that although both forces operate at all times and it is impossible to study either in isolation without falsification, nevertheless it seems impossible to think in terms of both at once. The problem is again one of balancing between two apparently incommensurable extremes: "Our whole attention must be directed toward eavesdropping on nature's procedure, so as not to make her refractory through coercive precepts but also so as not to let her caprice separate us from the goal." While the two forces cannot logically be *conceived* together, Goethe asks for a way to *imagine* them together, for a comparison with which to represent their interaction: "A symbolism is to be erected!" It is to this demand that Meyer responds in the "Reply."

He begins by dismissing the possibility of a divine central viewpoint from which everything could be seen to be in harmony: "We shall not ask whether there must be a standpoint from which, if it were accessible to us, nature and system would appear to correspond to each other as image and reflection. . . . It has not been reached, that is certain" (XIX, 350). The absence of a central viewpoint means, for Meyer as for Novalis, that the requirement can never be literally fulfilled, and in order to explain the impossibility Meyer adopts the Kantian description of a regulative ideal: "In the demand for a natural system human reason seems to exceed its limits, yet without being able to give up the demand itself" (XIX, 352). From this proposition Meyer draws the proper Kantian consequences (and again the resemblance to Novalis, and to other ro-

19. The tendency of the metamorphic spiral toward chaos is illustrated by the sorcerer's apprentice, who loses control over the broom he has transmuted, and by Makarie in the *Wanderjahre*, a spinster whose mind is spiraling off into the solar system. On Makarie, see Jane K. Brown, *Goethe's Cyclical Narratives* (Chapel Hill, N.C., 1975), pp. 69–75, and on the contrasting forces in Goethe in general see the excellent discussion by Georges Poulet in *The Metamorphoses of the Circle*, trans. Carley Dawson and Elliott Coleman (Baltimore, 1966), pp. 111–18.

mantics, can hardly be overlooked). Kant had taught in the *Critique of Aesthetic Judgment* that the only means of representing a transcendental ideal is in poetry, and it is precisely for a poetic symbolism that Meyer calls: *"The true mediatrix is art"* (XIX, 355).

After these preliminaries he loses no time in presenting his symbolism, which is also that of nearly all the romantics. The symbolism fulfills all the conditions placed on it: it allows for equal emphasis to both poles, it does not lay claim to a single central viewpoint, and it transforms the "circle of metamorphosis" (XIX, 354) into a different and more adequate figure:

As a schema of such a symbolic natural science of the plant kingdom the ellipse offers itself. The metamorphosis of life and the persistence of species would be its foci. Thought of as at rest the radii which proceed to the circumference might indicate the system of plants which, going out from the center of the simplest infusorial plant forms, develops round about, but not equally far in all directions. Thought of as the path of an ordered movement it might signify the life of the primal plant, the circumference that encloses all real and potential radii. In the one case the latter, in the other the former center, would be the original determinant, which, however, *so that the circle might be expanded to an ellipse*, must never lack the opposite, symbolically mediating center. [XIX, 356–57, my emphasis]

What Fichte and Novalis stood to learn from Böhme could in principle have been taught them by any schoolboy: the characteristic product of centripetal and centrifugal forces in this universe is an ellipse.

The Eccentric Path

The German admirer, however, not led astray, followed
attentively so strange a life and poetry in all its eccentricity,
which indeed was all the more striking since its like was
scarcely to be discovered in past centuries and we were de-
prived of all the elements for calculating such a path.
—Goethe, "Zum Andenken Lord
Byrons"

It grieves me when my researches make the well-disposed
botanist uncomfortable. My eccentric path will some day
enter this scientific system, and I must be satisfied not to
find everything which I ask.
—Goethe, letter to Zelter, July 19,
1830

By rejecting the metaphor of the central forces the romantics expressed their dissatisfaction with Kant's dualistic, polarized dialectic. Their search for a new symbolism was rewarded with Böhme's
ellipse. But between the rejection of Kant and the rediscovery of
Böhme was a brief period of uncertainty, which corresponded
exactly, as it happens, to the philosophical ascendancy of Fichte.
We have already seen that it is impossible to determine the true
curve of Tieck's Franz Sternbald, to distinguish good and productive actions from bad or morally indifferent ones. The ambiguity in
Sternbald's case is both moral and geographical: does he return to
himself? does he return home? The image usually correlated with
such uncertainties was astronomical rather than geographical. I
have alluded to it in connection with Franz Sternbald; it is the "eccentric path," a phrase familiar from Hölderlin's *Hyperion*.

The word "eccentric" is a technical term from astronomy, referring to any noncircular orbit. It was originally applied by Ptolemy
to the apparently irregular orbit of the sun around the earth, and
after Copernicus it naturally came to be used of planetary paths.
With the growing interest in astronomy in the later eighteenth century, the concept of orbital eccentricity came to be extremely famil-

iar. Even in its everyday meaning ("peculiar") the original technical
meaning was more readily perceived than it is today. Matthias
Claudius furnishes an example of this in the introduction to his influential translation (1782) of *Des Erreurs et de la vérité* by the
French mystic Louis Claude de Saint-Martin: "His hints and utterances are indeed great and pleasing like the summits of the paternal
mountains, but at the same time so *ec-centric* and wonderful, that
our reason can nowhere plot their circle" (*Werke*, p. 212).
   Eccentricity is the measure of an orbit's approach to a perfect circle; the more nearly circular, the less eccentric. The phrase "eccentric path" therefore tended to suggest less the nearly circular planetary orbits than the wildly deviant, highly eccentric orbits of comets,
which had long been a principal subject of speculation and research.[1] Newton himself devoted the final chapter of his *Principia
Mathematica* to the study of comets and lent the weight of his authority to the special association of eccentricity with comets when
he wrote, "Planets move all one and the same way in Orbs concen-
trick, while Comets move all manner of ways in Orbs very excen-
trick."[2] Here is a typical example, taken from Kant's pioneering
Allgemeine Naturgeschichte und Theorie des Himmels, of the way
in which the idea of eccentricity leads inevitably to the thought of

1. Ulrich Gaier, *Der gesetzliche Kalkül* (Tübingen, 1962), p. 38, considers and
   then rejects the "modern" meaning of "regellos, krumm," for Hölderlin's
   "exzentrisch." But this sense is by no means exclusively modern. Cf. Milton,
   The Reason of Church Government I, 1: "Our happiness may orb itself into a
   thousand vagancies of glory and delight, and with a kind of eccentrical equation
   be, as it were, an invariable planet of joy and felicity." C. S. Lewis, who quotes
   the passage, glosses "eccentrical" as "beyond all predicting" (*A Preface to Paradise Lost*, London, 1942, pp. 79–80). Novalis himself gives a comparable gloss
   in one fragment: "Eccentric and concentric constitutions. (Very variable—
   calmer—steadier)" (*Schriften* III, 410).
2. Newton, *Opticks* (New York, 1952), p. 369 (Part III, Query 28). See also the
   Scholium generale in the *Principia*. Two other English passages that associate
   eccentricity with comets are Pope, *Dunciad*, Book IV, note to lines 76–101
   (the third or "excentrical" class of the dull have the same use "in the moral
   World, as that of *Comets* in the natural"); and the first sentence of De Quincey's
   "English Mail-Coach" ("eccentric people in comets"). Many of the examples
   under "eccentric" and related words in the OED refer to comets. Unfortunately,
   Grimm's *Deutsches Wörterbuch* does not record loan-words such as *exzentrisch*, but a passage in Gustav Freytag's *Soll und Haben* (Bk. II, chap. ii, pars.
   2–3) shows that the association of eccentricity with comets was still familiar,
   indeed clichéd, in 1855.

comets: "The eccentricity in the movements of the planets increases with their remove from the sun, and the distant planets thereby approach more nearly to the condition of comets."[3] Whereas planets have many symbolic and mythological attributes, comets have primarily their eccentricity. Eccentricity thus comes to be regarded as the "most distinctive criterion" of a cometary nature (p. 56). So Joseph Görres says in "Glauben und Wissen": "As the impress of their deep origin comets all bear in their paths the great eccentricity as an eloquent proof of the considerable difference between themselves and the sun" (*Schriften* III, 28). A curious inversion, which shows perhaps most convincingly of all how infallibly eccentricity suggested comet, occurs in a scientific theory proposed by Johann Wilhelm Ritter to his new friend, the great Danish physicist Hans Christian Ørsted. Ritter proposed a series of values relating the orbital times and the distances of planetary and cometary orbits to one another. Since his figures for orbital eccentricity could be extrapolated so as to apply to the sun as well, Ritter concluded "that the *sun* itself is a member of the series like every other, that it lies on the cometary side, itself is a former comet, that Mercury is likewise a comet, whence the great eccentricity of the orbit."[4]

The age was in agreement, not only that comets were the chief example of eccentricity, but also about the significance of cometary eccentricity: the accord reflects the fact that comets are tantalizingly ambiguous. It was, and still remains, extremely difficult to distinguish on the basis of visual observation between comets with elliptical orbits and those with parabolic orbits. The leading textbook of the time, Friedrich Theodor Schubert's *Theoretische Astronomie* (3 volumes, St. Petersburg, 1798), maintains an agnostic attitude on the subject. Schubert, whose treatise is always cited by the romantics in technical discussions of comets, supposes that the "parabolic hypothesis" is, for all practical purposes, "concordant" with the elliptical (II, 329, §307). He contends that cometary orbits are

3. 1755 ed., p. 18. See also Herder's *Ideen* I, ii (*Werke* XII, 16): "The earth has two planets, Mercury and Venus, under it, Mars (and if perhaps yet another is hidden above it), Jupiter, Saturn, Uranus above it; and whatever others there may yet be until the sun's regular circle of activity is lost, and the eccentric path of the last planet jumps over into the wild ellipse of the cometary orbits."
4. *Correspondance de H. C. Örsted avec divers savants*, ed. M. C. Harding (Copenhagen, 1920), II, 18 (letter of July 25, 1802).

actually elliptical (II, 329, §308), but he strongly recommends calculating them as though they were parabolic, since the elliptical calculation is much more difficult (II, 331, §310).[5] Similarly, Gotthilf Heinrich Schubert's greatly admired lectures, *Ansichten über die Nachtseite der Naturwissenschaft* (Dresden, 1808), devote much of the sixth lecture to "the only partially understood realm of comets" (p. 16). After quoting his namesake without acknowledgment, G. H. Schubert concludes that "the path of comets appears as something indeterminate, still formless—fluid" (p. 140). Cometary orbits are indeterminately either open (parabolic) or closed (elliptical), and there is no clear dividing line between planets, asteroids (to which G. H. Schubert devotes a great deal of attention), returning and nonreturning comets.[6]

Thus, the solar system provides the image of a spectrum of moral values in which good merges insensibly into bad. "It is certain," writes Schelling's disciple Henrich Steffens in his first major work, "that the planets themselves constitute by far the smallest, the eccentric comets the largest share of our planetary system. Thus if Mercury forms the most contracted side of the system, so do the comets show its more expanded side, just as the coherence too indeed decreases on the whole, through all the planets, down to those comets in which a firm kernel can hardly be discerned."[7] The more eccentric the path, the more unstable the object. So Novalis says that "comets are truly eccentric beings—capable of the highest illumination and the highest darkening—a true Ginnistan—inhabited by good and bad spirits" (*Schriften*, II, 619–20). Schlegel's notebooks make appropriate use of this continuum of noncircular orbits.

For Schlegel, as for Novalis, eccentric paths are associated with

5. These are also the views of d'Alembert's long article "Comète" in the *Encyclopédie*.
6. Cf. Richard Brinsley Sheridan, letter to Thomas Grenville, February 24, 1773, in *Letters*, ed. Cecil Price (Oxford, 1966), I, 77: "The Track of a Comet is as regular to the eye of God as the orbit of a Planet." This passage illustrates the waning of the ancient superstition that comets are omens of disaster, a belief attacked by Pierre Bayle in his popular compendia, *Pensées diverses sur la comète* (1681 ff.). The shift in attitudes toward comets is documented by Gibbon in chap. 43 of *The History of the Decline and Fall of the Roman Empire*, ed. J. B. Bury (New York, 1946), II, 1426–27.
7. *Beyträge zur innern Naturgeschichte der Erde* (Freiberg, 1801), p. 249.

poetry (Novalis's "Ginnistan"), but there is apparently a decrease in merit as the eccentricity increases: the inner planets are "more religious," the outer planets are "very romantic" (*PhL* III, 372), but the comets are "probably completely irreligious, merely poetic and philosophical, eccentric disharmonies" (*PhL* III, 375). In his account of the Creation in the *Ideen*, Herder gives a paradigmatic description of these related alternatives, ellipse or parabola, planet or comet, order or dissipation. He says that the universe began when ethereal matter started to organize itself under divine guidance into solid matter. Some ether fell into the sun, and other particles accreted into other bodies, planets or comets. The distinction between planets and comets is thus subordinate; primarily they are related as eccentric matter in contrast to central matter (the sun). Herder subdivides the eccentric bodies into elliptical and parabolic (or hyperbolic), but this subdivision is clearly less important, and the nature of cometary orbits is ultimately left somewhat vague:

Down to the center of the whole, the sun, flowed whatever could nowhere find its own path, or what on its powerful throne the sun drew to itself with prevailing force. What found another center of attraction clustered in a similar manner around it and either went in ellipses around its great focus or flew away in parabolas and hyperbolas and never came back. So the ether was clarified; so out of a swimming, confluent chaos arose a harmonious cosmic system in which earths and comets in regular paths throughout eons revolve around their sun. [*Ideen* XV, ii; in *Werke* XIV, 213–14]

All authorities agree, first, in using eccentricity as the symbol of life (understood as the wavering interplay of opposing forces) and, second, in using cometary eccentricity as the symbol of the moral uncertainty of human life. There may well have been a common source in the Dutch philosopher Hemsterhuis, whose *Lettre sur l'homme et ses rapports* compared the human mind to a comet: "The science of man, or the human mind, seems to move around perfection like comets around the sun, describing highly eccentric curves."[8] This comparison is known to have particularly intrigued Novalis, who excerpted the passage in 1799 (*Schriften* II, 368) and

8. *Oeuvres philosophiques* (Paris, 1792) I, 230, quoted in Novalis, *Schriften* III, 912.

referred to it again in his encyclopedia late in the following year (III, 275). In his *Lehrbuch der Naturphilosophie* Lorenz Oken duly registered the association of eccentricity with physical life, as opposed to the ideality of light: "The more lifelike a planet is, the more eccentric its path must be, because it comes into great opposition with light" (§231). And as late as 1827, in his *Philosophie des Lebens*, Schlegel continued to associate orbital eccentricity—which might follow either a dissipated parabolic path or a virtuous elliptical path—with vigorous action. He says that men are characterized by an "eccentric unfolding" of consciousness; "not as if the spirit in the sex most often called to external activity ought to leave its higher center of inner life or wander with genius and lose itself in distant irregular paths like comets, although this too is observed often enough; but the masculine spirit can and should move in broad circles" (*KA* X, 40).

When we turn to more strictly literary texts, we find precisely the same ambiguities in the conception of the eccentric path. Indeed, Schlegel's late description of masculine activity—sometimes moving off into space and sometimes remaining faithful to its original mission and closing the circle of its actions—accords perfectly with his account of Lessing's career in the essay "Über Lessing" of 1797. Schlegel was anxious to claim Lessing as a romantic *avant la lettre*, as a philosophical humorist, and therefore as a thoroughly individual, isolated, and eccentric figure. In describing the "extremely characteristic" epilogue to the *Hamburgische Dramaturgie*, Schlegel portrays it as a work with no organization and no center, but which sails off—after the manner of a comet leaving the solar system for a distant sun—toward a vague and distant goal. It is, he says,

a work which, in this respect unique in its kind, proceeds from a mercantile occasion and from the premise of a weekly conversation and, before you know it, has flown infinitely far beyond the popular horizon and, unconcerned about all relations of time, absorbed in the purest speculation, sets out full tilt for the paradoxical goal of a *poetical Euclid*, but is also executed on its eccentric path in so individual, so lifelike, so Lessingian a manner, that it could even be called a *monodrama*. [*KA* II, 113]

According to the original close of the essay, Lessing's "eccentric career" ("exzentrische Laufbahn") nevertheless did not transcend all bounds, but arrived at a "goal" that was both limited and concrete, namely, the play *Nathan der Weise*. This play, says Schlegel, corrected the false stylistic direction of Lessing's earlier plays: whereas these contained an artificial and inorganic combination of styles, *Nathan* returns to a more organic and, we must conclude, more central form. We are left with the impression that Lessing's career was not parabolic, but was rounded into a naturally closed form:

So *paradoxically* did Lessing *end* in poetry, as everywhere else! The achieved goal explains and justifies the eccentric career; *Nathan der Weise* is the best *apology* of the whole of *Lessing's poetry*, which without it must needs seem only a *false tendency* where applied poetic effects of rhetorical stage dramas are clumsily confounded with the pure poetry of dramatic works of art and thereby progress is uselessly hindered until it becomes impossible. [*KA* II, 125]

In both these quotations Schlegel associates eccentricity with paradox; Lessing's career was eccentric because it was unpredictable, incalculable. Yet another example of the prevalence of this conception of an unpredictable path in the literature of the 1790s is the old man's description of the imagination in Goethe's *Unterhaltungen deutscher Ausgewanderten*. The old man, it should be remembered, is the spokesman for Goethe, and this is his introduction to the "Märchen," the work's triumphantly allegorical conclusion: "[The imagination] makes no plans, decides on no road in advance, but is carried and led by its own wings, and in soaring back and forth describes the most wonderful paths which are always changing direction and turning" (*Werke* VI, 695).

Only in this context is it possible to understand the two controversial draft prefaces to *Hyperion* in which the phrase "eccentric path" occurs. Commentators invariably explain the phrase with reference to related ideas in Hölderlin's work; as a result their discussions are pertinent but overlook the phrase's crucial nuance of indeterminacy. Thus, Wolfgang Schadewaldt speaks of "periodicity" and of an alternation between two distinct poles; Wolfgang Binder and Lawrence Ryan claim that a dialectical movement is in antithesis to a first principle and leads to a resolution, a movement for which Binder coined the phrase "eccentric path from the center to the center"; Maria Cornelissen writes of an organic development away from childhood.[9] Because such distortions of the phrase have repeatedly led readers to overlook a crucial element in the development of romanticism and in Hölderlin's own development, I should like to comment separately on the passage in each draft.

In the introduction to the early "Fragment of Hyperion" (1794), Hölderlin writes, "The eccentric path that a man traverses, in general and in particular, from a point (of more or less pure simplicity) to another (of more or less perfect culture) seems *in its essential directions* always to be the same. Some of these, together with their rectifications, are to be represented in the letters of which the following are a fragment" (*Werke* III, 163). Ryan treats the phrase as if it said that the eccentric path (the path away from the center, the antithetical path) is essentially the same in all men. But the structure of the sentence is antithetical: culture is the reverse of simplicity, and the eccentricity of the paths is outweighed by their resemblance. Men's lives are widely variable, but nevertheless they have important resemblances and the overall course tends to fall into a recognizable type.[10] In "Über den Begriff der Wissenschaftslehre" also written in 1794, Fichte describes the mechanism of such an unpredictable yet self-correcting development:

It seems that a hairbreadth deviation from a straight line must necessarily lead to an infinitely increasing deviation: and so it would in fact be if man had to employ clear thinking to bring to pass everything which he knows; and if the basic disposition of reason did not rather rule in him without his consciousness, leading him through new aberrations from the straight path of *formaliter* and logically correct reasoning back to the *materialiter* sole true result, at which he would never have been able to arrive through correct inference from incorrect premises; and if feeling did not often correct the old aberrations through causing a new aberration from the straight path of reasoning, leading him back again whither he would never have come through correct inference. [*Werke* I, 78]

9. W. Schadewaldt, "Das Bild der exzentrischen Bahn bei Hölderlin," *Hölderlin-Jahrbuch* (1952), p. 16; W. Binder, *Hölderlin-Aufsätze* (Frankfurt, 1970), pp. 125 and 229; L. Ryan, *Hölderlins Hyperion* (Stuttgart, 1965), p. 12; M. Cornelissen, *Hölderlins Ode "Chiron"* (Tübingen, 1958), pp. 24–53.

10. Cf. Fr. Schlegel, "Über die Philosophie. An Dorothea," *KA* VIII, 50: "The true middle is only the one to which a man ever and again *returns* from the eccentric paths of enthusiasm and energy, not the one which is never left." Here, too, eccentricity is corrected by uniformity, and eccentric paths are considered to be multiple and divergent.

The second passage appears in the preface to Hölderlin's penultimate version of the novel: "This Hyperion will perhaps irritate with his contradictions, his aberrations, his strength and his weakness, his anger and his love. But offense must come — We all traverse an eccentric path, and no other way is possible from childhood to perfection" (*Werke* III, 236). Taken in its context, as I have quoted it, there can be no doubt that the eccentric path here is irritating, aberrant, unpredictable. A straight path or even a clear dialectic would be preferable if it were possible, but we are forced to make do with the confused "way," which is barely a path at all. This applies both as an ethical principle and as an aesthetic warning to the readers of the novel.

The final version of the novel refers at one point to comets (III, 42), but eliminates explicit reference to the eccentric path. Nevertheless, the conception of an unpredictable and yet directed movement persists: "Again this time, as formerly, I had had my heart's joy in watching this spirit on his bold vagation, where he pursued his way so irregularly, in such unrestrained good cheer, and yet on the whole so surely" (III, 30). So surely and yet, it must be said, so indeterminately. Contradictory utterances from the year when he was writing the novel leave the question as unclear as it was for Fichte whether Hölderlin thought of his goal as the "infinite approximation" of an "indefinite line" (III, 236) or as the "infinite approximation, like the approximation of the square to a circle" (letter to Schiller, September 4, 1795, *Werke* VI, 181). Hölderlin embodied this uncertainty in the closing words of the novel, "more later," for the reader remains unsure whether the work is finished or fragmentary, whether (because the novel is cast in a complex autobiographical form) the words point back circularly to the state of the narrator at the beginning or point ahead to the future of the mature narrator who writes them, whether the hero's life is a failure or a success.[11]

Such indeterminacy characterizes much German writing of the last five years of the century. This was the period of the great collections of fragments, of major unfinished novels by Schlegel, Novalis, Tieck, and Goethe as well as Hölderlin, of wildly eccentric literary

11. On the ending, cf. Lawrence Ryan, "Hölderlins 'Hyperion': ein 'romantischer' Roman?" in *Über Hölderlin*, ed. Jochen Schmidt (Frankfurt, 1970), p. 208.

experiments like Jean Paul's early novels and Tieck's absurdist comedies.[12] The ethics of open nature thus found its counterpart in the aesthetics of indeterminate form. The unfinished business of life becomes a never-ending novel, going nowhere or everywhere at once. Novalis wrote to Caroline Schlegel on February 27, 1799:

> For I feel like devoting my whole life to one novel—which alone should make up a whole library—perhaps contain the apprenticeship [*Lehrjahre*] of a *nation*. The word *apprenticeship* is false—it expresses a definite *orientation* [*ein bestimmtes* Wohin]. But in my case it should signify nothing but—*transitional years* from the infinite to the finite. I hope at the same time to satisfy my historical and philosophical yearning. A journey to south and north is still indispensable to me, as a preparation for this. [*Schriften*, IV, 281]

"A journey to south and north"—an indeterminate path in preparation for an interminable novel, even more drifting in its course than Wilhelm Meister's sprawling *Apprenticeship*; a summa of individual and collective experience designed to lay out the course of a nation and to give finite, poetic expression to the infinite, transcendent, central intuitions of philosophy. In this arch-romantic program a conception of literary form and a moral imperative fuse with a particular reading of the historical and political situation. These were the crucible years of romanticism, a revolutionary period in which no one was certain of its direction, but all were sure that it was a time of transition and that a great work was about to be realized. And so we can take the "eccentric path" to be not only a popular phrase *in* the period, but an appropriate description *of* the period. We can see even more clearly now what was already felt at the time—that a new movement was under way, still casting about for its direction but expecting the necessary rectifications that would establish it in its new course.

12. See Nicolai's comments to Tieck about *Die verkehrte Welt*, which harp like a leitmotiv on the play's eccentricity, quoted in *Die verkehrte Welt*, ed. Karl Pestalozzi (Berlin, 1964), pp. 133–34.

The World-Ellipse

> Anyone who had ever plumbed or even inquired into the
> depths of life knew that the business with a simple mid-
> point—he was avoiding the word center on purpose—was
> false, and that life did not move in a circle, but rather in an
> ellipse. Whence two turning points were naturally given.
>
> —Fontane, *Frau Jenny Treibel*

After 1800, the open curve characteristic of the works of the late
eighteenth century disappears. The absence of a well-defined course
is no longer regarded as characteristic of human life; no longer will
a character say, after the fashion of Tieck's Anselm, that "we all
err." On the contrary, Ottilie's confession in Goethe's *Wahlverwandtschaften*, "I have stepped out of my path" (*Werke* VI, 562
and 578), indicates an individual and tragic error, a personal deficiency in her character. For purposes of comparison it is particularly
significant that Schlegel altered his essay on Lessing according to the
changing conception when he reissued it in 1801. He suppressed the
last two paragraphs of the original version, including the description of *Nathan* as the "achieved goal" of Lessing's "eccentric career," and added a long conclusion emphasizing the fragmentary
character of Lessing's achievement. The new conclusion repeats the
identification of eccentricity with paradox, but the notion of eccentricity itself has changed. Instead of an indeterminate path, possibly
open or closed, Schlegel now sees Lessing's career as decidedly incomplete, indeed as a parabola, one of "those curved lines, which,
hurrying forward in visible steadiness and regularity, can never appear otherwise than as a fragment because one of its centers lies in
infinity."[1]

The changes in the Lessing essay are nevertheless atypical in one
respect: the curve that becomes dominant after 1800 is not the
parabola of irony, but the Böhmist ellipse. This is true even for
Schlegel himself. Thus, in one fragment {LN 2071) Schlegel de-

---

1. *KA* II, 415. In his edition of Schlegel's *Kritische Schriften*, Wolfdietrich Rasch
misleadingly prints the suppressed paragraphs along with the later conclusion.

scribes his novel *Lucinde* as a work that leads from "revolutionary poetry," which he characterizes by drawing a parabola ⊂, to romantic poetry, which will be "organized," and therefore presumably a closed curve. *Lucinde*, he says, is "only a transition," but the age of closed forms was imminent. Even the modern curve, however, would not be perfectly regular, Schlegel says: it would be also "chaotic," that is, eccentric rather than perfectly circular. The metaphor underlying this fragment is unquestionably the progression from a parabola to an ellipse.

Schlegel's rare published references to such mathematical metaphors would hardly support such a conclusion.[2] But now that copious portions of his private notebooks and of his philosophical lectures have been edited, we are in a better position to appreciate the importance and influence of such underlying ideas. In the age of Fichte and Schelling, according to one fragment, philosophy is conceived "as an ellipse with two centers, an ideal one of reason, a real one of the universe."[3] The significance of this historical development was undoubtedly to make philosophy more eccentric—as any reader familiar with romantic philosophy will surely agree— but it was also to bring the structure of philosophy closer to that of life. For life, too, "is an elliptical process" (*PhL* III, 554). The ellipse is not the only curve, but it is the fundamental curve: "The ellipse, the circle, the parabola and hyperbola are but explosions, developments of the point, which must be conceived in a highly mystical fashion. In the primitive point is duality. Ellipse the first symbol of the same; circle and parabola but deviation."[4] This meditation would doubtless have been less mystifying to Schlegel's friends than it is liable to be to a modern reader; it reflects the Böhmist conception that the energy of life results chiefly from the existence of two motive principles or centers, not inimical to each other, but sufficiently different to arouse considerable tension and

2. The principal references are the 1801 conclusion of the Lessing essay—"the presently existing philosophical forms are mathematical in nature," by which is meant circular ("kreisförmig"), triangular ("Schema der Triplizität"), elliptical ("Ellipsen"), "and much more"—and *Ideen* 117 ("philosophy is an ellipse").

3. *PhL* IV, 1322. *PhL* V, 217 contains the same idea: "Philosophy is an ellipse that has two centers."

4. *PhL* III, 398. Similarly *PhL* V, 1151: "The sphere can be explained only from the ellipse."

uncertainty. The ellipse, in other words, replaces the comet as the symbol wherever the tension between two definite forms replaces an unspecified eccentricity or subjectivity as the characteristic definition of life: "Perhaps the center in every universe is *double* in its proper sense of *heterogeneous*, One out of two, two at once from different orders, e.g., the earth does not live from the sun alone but from the sun *and* the central ether. Therefore it lives *elliptically*, as all life is *curved*."[5]

Nearly all treatises on *Naturphilosophie* begin with astronomy, the "night side of natural science" (in G. H. Schubert's catchy phrase), because the writers have in mind the idea that "ellipses are symbols of increasing life."[6] Inevitably they include an explanation of the significance of planetary orbits. The theme is always the same; God in his totality is perfect and therefore circular, but the world is only the visible portion of God, only a fragment in other words, and so deviates from pure circular perfection:

Through the elliptical paths of the planets their relative difference is indicated, so that no heavenly body by itself, but rather all together describe the complete circular path, which cannot reveal itself to the senses (with which all relative differences are necessarily posited to infinity), but which rather is absolute only for intellectual perception in the eternal essence of reason.[7]

Lorenz Oken's *Lehrbuch der Naturphilosophie* contains the key to such extravagant metaphors. His universe is aggressively circular. God is a central point, and the world is the circular expansion of the divine point; as he says, in a novel variation of the old mystical definition of God as an infinite sphere, "Mundus est Sphaera, cujus centrum ubique, circumferentia nusquam" (§131). With the consistency that is his special distinction, he remains absolutely

5. *PhL* III, 551. I have not found any text where cometary motion is explicitly rejected in favor of elliptical motion. But Schlegel's subordination of the parabola to the ellipse comes close, as does Brentano's subordination of comets to the moon in "Erklärung der Sinnbilder," *Werke* II, 1052–53.
6. Friedrich Schleiermacher, *Hermeneutik*, ed. Heinz Kimmerle (Heidelberg, 1959), p. 37. The passage concerns rhetorical, not geometrical, ellipses. I quote it to suggest how the rhetorical conception may be related to the geometrical metaphors analyzed below.
7. Henrich Steffens, *Grundzüge der philosophischen Naturwissenschaft* (Berlin, 1806), p. 33.

faithful to this initial premise: space is spherical (§112); geometry is the "doctrine of the sphere" (§137); "the world is a rotating ball of ether" (§162) and also of fire (§197); indeed, "all motion is circular" (§134).[8] Nevertheless, this homogenization does not prevent Oken from conceiving a theory of polarity to account for the dualism of spirit and matter. Every living thing participates in both realms; "all *individuals* must have a double life" (§171). In a sentence that, although meaningless, is undeniably memorable, he impresses the principle on his readers: "All real lines are polar; all are rooted with one end in God, with the other in finitude" (§120).

Although he often describes this polarity—of spiritual and natural, ideal and created—in terms of the contrast between center and periphery, the relationship is not one of mere opposition; notwithstanding their polarization the two realms are interdependent and intimately connected. Oken accounts for their relationship by a theory of creative emanation grounded in mathematics; "Theology," as he explains, "is personified arithmetic" (§98). Zero, he says, is "the fundamental principle of all mathematics" (§19), and it contains all the other numbers "in an ideal manner, not *actu*, but only *potentia*" (§25). Zero is the absolute, the "substratum of everything that follows" (§60). But since it is unlimited, it has no positive qualities. It is unreal; "the eternal is the nothing of nature" (§33). In order for it to become real it must be "posited" or "affirmed." Thus, "numbers are identical with zero; they are the extensive zero, it is intensive numbers" (§26). More precisely, "nothing posited once as nothing = 1" (§41), and the other numbers are repetitions of this first finite act (§34). The world is constructed— here the analogy to mathematics becomes determining—out of a succession of such acts; "Time is nothing other than the eternal repetition of the positing of the eternal, corresponding to the numerical sequence $+1+1+1+n$" (§61). To illustrate this conception, Oken uses a homely metaphor: time "is a repetition of one and the

8. Several of Oken's worst excesses, including this one, can be traced to Saint-Martin. The French mystic also says that "there is not a single straight line in nature" and that "all extension is circular," *Des Erreurs et de la vérité* (Edinburgh [Lyons?], 1782) II, 107 and 121; *Irrtümer und Weisheit*, trans. Matthias Claudius, II (Stuttgart, 1922), 123 and 139. Oken's *Abriss des Systems der Biologie* more sensibly limits the locale in which linear motion is impossible to the atmosphere.

same act, namely, of the primal act, like a rolling ball, which always returns into itself" (§63). Creation is thus not the opposite of a pre-existing chaos, but the unfolding of preexisting capabilities: "The eternal becomes real or appears as extension" (§33). As an affirmation of the eternal, creation is logos, "the speech of God" (§73). It would be difficult to overestimate the importance for the romantics of this notion of creation. The essential character of the finite world is that of a repetition; and its essential impulse is to return to the eternal realm, which is recognized as its model and source.[9] (Oken calls this "mutual love" and assigns the minus sign to it—§58—as opposed to the plus sign of creative affirmation.) "Real and ideal are one and the same, only in two forms" (§25), namely as essence and existence, idea and appearance, imagination and verification. Or, in a more distinctly Böhmist formulation, "the ideal becomes real through fission" (§37). Whereas the movement of nature, therefore, may seem circular to a naive observer, who is only aware of its created, visible aspect, in fact "nothing finite is absolutely spherical" (§223). The world partakes of both spheres and fluctuates between them: "The sun cannot be in the absolute center, because of the contrast with the planets, which equally desire to become the center. . . . Since the real universe can only exist bicentrally, so there is in this respect too no universal central body. . . . Only God is monocentral. The world is the bicentral God"

9. Cf. Paul de Man, "The Rhetoric of Temporality," in *Interpretation: Theory and Practice*, ed. Charles S. Singleton (Baltimore, 1969), p. 190: "The meaning constituted by the allegorical sign can then consist only in the *repetition* (in the Kierkegaardian sense of the term) of a previous sign with which it can never coincide." J. Hillis Miller's "The Still Heart: Poetic Form in Wordsworth," *New Literary History* 2 (1971), 297–310, suggestively illustrates this principle in English poetry. A highly indicative document is Baader's essay "Über den Einfluss der Zeichen der Gedanken auf deren Erzeugung und Gestaltung" (*Werke* II, 125–36), which appeared in Schlegel's periodical *Concordia*, especially p. 128: "Everything external in things can be considered a sign (announcement—praesagium—index) of their inside. . . . It can be said concerning this that in general a sign is firstly and in itself the announcement of a thing or essence that is still separate and therefore still hidden (closed off) from us." Emerson's essay "Experience" contains a rejection of the bicentral viewpoint: "Life will be imaged, but cannot be divided nor doubled. Any invasion of its unity would be chaos. The soul is not twin-born but the only begotten, and though revealing itself as child in time, child in appearance, is of a fatal and universal power, admitting no co-life. Every day, every act betrays the ill-concealed deity" (*Works* III, 79).

(§222–23). To be aware of the true bicentral nature of the universe means to know one's status as finite being and to feel the attraction of the infinite realm. And conversely to be aware of one's nature means to feel the attraction of both poles, of both centers. This reasoning, finally, leads Oken to formulate with eminent and conspicuous terseness the principle that was usually enunciated much more tentatively and laboriously: "Self-consciousness is a living ellipse" (§223).

This notion of self-consciousness was first publicly elaborated, to my knowledge, by Friedrich Schlegel in his Jena lectures of 1800–1801. Self-consciousness, in his view, is primarily consciousness of the existence of a spiritual or intellectual world. It is the consciousness that the visible world is the realization of a prior ideal, and indeed only an imperfect and fragmentary realization. Thus, one of Schlegel's principal conclusions is "that the world is as yet incomplete" (*KA* XII, 42), a statement whose novelty lies in the allegorically previsional "as yet." This in no way means that the world is a defective or disfigured copy; in fact it would be meaningless to suggest as much. For the ideal has no physical existence; we can know it only by inspecting our own experience in the light of reason. To claim that the world is a defective copy can therefore prove only that we have the wrong ideal in mind. As Baader says, if a physical phenomenon seems to conflict with a spiritual truth, the reason can only be that it has been associated with the wrong spiritual truth. Such a "mésalliance" does not mean that matter ("the flesh") is inherently weak or false; on the contrary, every phenomenon will, in time, be matched with "its ideal." [10]

Since it is senseless to speak of the world as a faulty copy, it is also impossible to regard evil in the usual way as a harmful and injurious force. Reality is always a realization, and therefore there can be no true destruction and no anarchy.[11] There can be no turning away from God, only a turning toward. Even when it is non-Christian (that is, nonsacramental), later romantic thought thus remains

10. "Über die Analogie des Erkenntniss- und des Zeugungstriebes," *Werke* I, 45–46.
11. Of course such a view could be embraced only after coming to terms with the French Revolution; indeed, for some of the romantics, such as Goethe and Eichendorff, bitter memories of revolutionary destruction tinged this optimistic belief in the unreality of evil with an element of deep-seated fear.

strictly Augustinian in its conception of time. Evil cannot refer to any defect in the fabric of the universe, only to a deficiency (this may help to account for the often noted absence of conflict in much romantic fiction). Evil is nothing more than incomplete revelation, and revelation is incomplete because, as repetition, it takes place in and through time. Or, as Schlegel said in the Jena lectures, evil *is* time; "the philosophy of religion should view time as the evil principle" (*KA* XII, 41).

Self-consciousness, then, is the awareness that man lives in two worlds and must serve two masters. The two worlds, the eternal and the temporal, are not in conflict, but they do make different demands. The eternal (man's spiritual side) seeks self-expression and demands constancy. The temporal (the physical world) seeks organic change and fulfillment. Since the ideal, however, is regarded as the source of the real world, the movement toward fulfillment is essentially negative, a movement back to the source. It is seen as the removal of imperfection, leading eventually to self-abolition; or, as Schlegel says, "the return of the definite into the indefinite" (*KA* XII, 11). Self-consciousness is, ultimately, temporal consciousness. It is awareness of the two worlds in their movement toward realization and completion; it is awareness of the asymptotic movement of the real toward the ideal, which takes place throughout time— which is, in fact, the definition of time—but which obviously can never be consummated without abolishing time itself.[12] It is in this authentically Hegelian sense that Schlegel can say—six years before the *Phenomenology*—that "consciousness is history"[13] and that "the true life is only in death" (*KA* XII, 40).

This theory of the movement of time provides the link between Oken's explanation of the ellipse and that of Görres. For the act of creation is a sudden eruption into reality, an eruption that is discontinuous just as the set of positive integers is discontinuous. It is followed by a slow, indeed an endless, ebbing back to the

12. See, as early as 1782, Herder's essay on Hemsterhuis, "Liebe und Selbstheit," *Werke* XV, 326.
13. *KA* XII, 11. Schlegel here radicalizes an idea broached with more philosophical refinement in the early works of Fichte and Schelling, for instance in Fichte's claim that "The *Wissenschaftslehre* should be a pragmatic history of the human spirit" (*Grundlage der gesamten Wissenschaftslehre*, in *Werke* I, 222); see further Ulrich Claesges, *Geschichte des Selbstbewußtseins* (The Hague, 1974).

source. Emanation and return is the structure of the world. For this Oken's notorious formula was $+-=0$.[14] Neither the centrifugal, positive reality principle nor the centripetal, negative ideal principle can exist in isolation (except, for more orthodox thinkers, in some mythical pre-Adamitic past); it is the simultaneous, though variable, action of both that constitutes the world as we know it. Figuratively speaking, the intelligible world revolves dynamically around both centers; the world is spirit *and* nature, pattern *and* product. The unfolding of spirit in nature, however, is only partial, so that the world may be more accurately described as the absolute spirit engaged in realizing itself. Or, finally, in the correspondence and reciprocal confirmation of its two aspects, the world is nothing other than the self-recognition, the self-consciousness, of God:

> The act of creation and the act of absorption are therefore both equally bound to the divine act of self-consciousness and this to the essence of divinity itself; both are not an external alteration of this essence, but only as it were an inner creative ferment, without visible change of the unvarying divine essence. Figuratively, therefore, the center of superabundance decomposes into two foci, and the infinite circle of the unnameable becomes objective to itself in the infinite ellipse, the oval of reality.[15]

Baader, too, sees in the ellipse the symbol of the natural world in so far as it is a revelation of the divine. His description of the real world, as will be seen, corresponds closely to that of the other romantics; the background explanation, however, rests on a highly individual epistemology. God, says Baader, is wisdom. Although we usually think of wisdom as timeless disinterested contemplation, it is in fact demeaning to attribute to either God or man what Baader calls the "blind and stupid gawking or gaping of mindlessness" ("jenes blinde und stupide Angaffen oder Anstaunen des Unverstandes").[16] Wisdom cannot long remain contentedly indifferent, but immediately seeks verification. Indeed, until it is verified, that is, until it has a real content, it can hardly be called wisdom at

---

14. As late as 1833 Baader could reproduce and criticize this formula without naming the author: "Über den Begriff der Zeit und die vermittelnde Function der Form oder des Maasses," *Werke* II, 520.

15. Görres, "Glauben und Wissen," *Schriften* III, 13.

16. "Über die Analogie des Erkenntniss- und des Zeugungstriebes," *Werke* I, 41. This essay was published in 1808 by Schelling, who admired it greatly.

all. By its very nature then, significant (not "stupid") contemplation must be translated, or "sublimated," into the emotional forces of the desire to produce verification and the pleasure of achieving verification. This is obviously true of human knowledge, according to Baader; science progresses only because hypotheses are uttered and pride and prestige are engaged in confirming them.[17] But it is also true of God and of the world as a total entity. The intelligible, or spiritual, world can exist only in collaboration with an "outlet" (as Böhme called it).

This would be the physical world, which is ultimately shaped into the crowning triumph and "glorification" of the ideal by dint of an output of energy, above all sexual energy. As the circle is Baader's symbol for the eternal and invariant divine repose of the intelligible world, so the less regular ellipse symbolizes divinity driving the physical world along its allotted path:

If even the self-manifestation of God (through eternal nature as light, and so on) is conceivable only as a sublimation and division of unity (out of the *circle* into the *ellipse* with two foci), so an analogous but deeper sublimation and division must found the creature, only that here it is that spoken Word (wisdom, Idea), which by dividing (into desire and pleasure as J. Böhme expresses it) sublimates itself and herein calls forth the creature to solve and complete this crisis of the creative orgasm or creative conflict and, by becoming autonomous, not only to restore but to glorify the Idea.[18]

17. See the essay just cited along with Baader's "Fragmente zu einer Theorie des Erkennens," *Werke* I, 39–48, 49–56.
18. Baader, *Fermenta Cognitionis* III, 9, in *Werke* II, 255–56. A few necessarily inadequate words should be added about Hegel's relation to these ideas. It was Hegel's greatness to have preserved the dynamism of the romantic world view without presupposing either Cartesian dualism or Böhmist bicentrality and therefore without admitting discontinuity in the form of either the Kantian antinomies or doctrines of creative emanation. For the Böhmist ellipse he substitutes the notion of the unitary concept or "inside of things" (*Phänomenologie*, p. 110; see also p. 106 and Schlegel, *LN* 691), and he avoids speaking of two centers even where, as in the discussion of celestial mechanics in the *Encyclopedia* (§262–271), it would have been obligatory for the *Naturphilosophen*. Two passages in the *Phenomenology* are particularly relevant, first the definition of consciousness not as an ellipse but as "the determinant or middle" (p. 477) and second the refutation on pp. 266–67 of the notion of centroperiphericity and of the related conception of personality as the fluctuating balance struck by each individual between spiritual and physical motivations for his actions.

IV. Romantic Temporality

Ich harre, mich umkreist die Zeit.

—Goethe, *Faust*

The Human Condition

> "But, my lady, what if precisely the new charm of this beautiful sphere produced a division within me, if the heart's inescapable inner sympathy stood in the way of the much more general interest of the spirit, if, rather than returning into myself calmed and strengthened, I felt only the passionate longing to collect all the rays of my human and artistic existence in the center of so lovely a group . . . ?" "It lies," answered the countess . . . , "in the nature of men like you to be one-sided in everything. . . ."
>
> —Mörike, *Maler Nolten*

The themes and forms of romantic poetry after 1800 developed in response to the bicentral world view. This is emphatically not a matter of influence in any conventional sense, as if the theory were simply a source from which the poetry derived or the poetry simply an offshoot of the theory. Neither common sense nor chronology will support the priority of a mostly unreadable philosophy that emerged quite suddenly in 1799–1800 over a splendid body of literature whose major form—the novel with inserted poems—can be traced back at least as far as Goethe's *Wilhelm Meister* (1795–96). Rather, poetry and philosophy mutually conditioned each other in an almost seamless continuity. If, within this symbiosis, poetry seems to function as a *response* to philosophy, it does so only in a special, quasi-medical sense. We have already seen how, according to the romantics, poetry was to give form to the intuitive energies of philosophy; later romantics, more psychological in their orientation, would say that poetry stabilizes the uncontrolled passions of the intellect. Ultimately, poetry can even be seen as a cure for the twin philosophical diseases, melancholy and insanity. Poetry thus becomes an indispensable outlet for the romantics, a "central" activity, to which even the philosophers gladly turned.[1] Yet it should not be supposed that the poetry came after the philosophy,

1. Nowhere can this better be seen than in the case of Wilhelm von Humboldt: see my essay, "Humboldt and the Mediation between Self and World," *Genre* 6 (1973), 121–41.

as response normally follows stimulus or cure follows disease. They originated in tandem, much as in science progress often consists of the simultaneous and inseparable discoveries of a new problem and a new solution.

In place of the classical and humanistic notion that poetic passion is to be tamed by philosophic calm, or poetic madness balanced by philosophic wisdom, romantic poets and philosophers alike see art as the place where the ferment of consciousness is quieted. As Schelling says in the conclusion of the *System des transzendentalen Idealismus*, art produces "the feeling of infinite contentment" (*Schriften*, III, 615). This notion, too, has its classical antecedents, of course, and both the spirit and the letter of Winckelmann live on in Schelling's claim that "the external expression of the work of art is thus the expression of calm and of quiet greatness, even where the greatest tension of pain or of joy is to be expressed" (III, 620). In furtherance of this ideal, much German romantic poetry aims at a smooth exterior, with a willed simplicity of structure, theme, and style. Tension is present, but concealed, and we must look to the theorists for help in discovering it.

Speculative writing thus plays much the same role in the period of German romanticism that poetry plays in other periods. This is the key to understanding and utilizing the effusions of the philosophers of nature. *Naturphilosophie* is metaphorical in style, arbitrary in its reasoning and its procedures for verification, and often shy of concreteness in its conclusions. Given to personifications of natural phenomena, psychological rather than logical even where the organization is at its most drily schematic, it has human nature as its foundation. And in human nature it gives as much recognition to the peripheral, irrational components, tending even to madness, as to the rational ones. Never convincingly quantitative—Oken is typical when he uses the real number system as a mere metaphor for the divine personality—even in the classical scientific disciplines it appeals to the intuitive imagery of geometry rather than to arithmetic calculation. It is a product at least as much of the emotions and the imagination as of the intellect. Indeed, Oken, Steffens, and Görres were among the most popular university lecturers of their day, and their writings are invested with an intensity of feeling to which even modern readers can occasionally respond and which stimulated their contemporary adherents to passionate enthusiasm. Writings in this vein reveal more than the poetic texts themselves about the romantic state of mind and feeling and thus about the condition in which the poetry was written.

The principal contribution of Böhme's ideas to romantic episte-mology lay in their complete rejection of the category of substance. Permanence belongs only to the ideal realm; everything real is, by definition, in a state of everlasting dynamic flux. Friedrich Schlegel's Cologne lectures on the history of philosophy (1804–5) introduce the psychological implications of the bicentral world view. His statement of the principle of flux is both categorical and typical: "There is no *being*, only *becoming*." [2] Thus are abandoned the as-sumptions that something permanent must necessarily be the cause of our perceptions and that the job of philosophy is to describe this external, separate substratum. All we can know is what we per-ceive; it makes no sense to talk about a nature totally distinct from the perceiving self, about the "not-self outside the self," which, according to Schlegel, Fichte's dualism presupposes. The outside world makes itself felt only through changes within us; it is thus none other than the principle of inner division. It appears not as a subsisting object, but as another subject, within the self and, like the self, engaged in the temporal flux. Hence nature appears to Schlegel as "*a thou*, not as something (as in life) similar to the self and yet opposed (man against man, not animal, stone against man), but rather generally as a counterself" (*KA* XII, 337). Man's essential activity is to search out the meaning of what he perceives, to find out the course of nature so that he can associate himself with it, to produce a "loving uniting of the *I* with the thou which is the coun-terpart [*Gegenstand*] of the I" (*KA* XII, 351).

What cause is there to believe that nature has a meaning and a purpose, that a movement toward unity and cooperation with na-ture is possible, or (to use the vocabulary of Schlegel's summary, *KA* XII, 383) that two infinite curves can ever coalesce into an in-finite ellipse? In an objective sense there is no such assurance; in Schlegel's view man's most characteristic actions are utopian in character, based on hope rather than on acquired knowledge: "Pure

2. *KA* XII, 331. A relevant parallel is the speech of the "Gelehrter" (representing Oken) in the fifth "Adventure" of Eichendorff's first play, *Krieg den Philistern*.

yearning is always a striving toward something known, but indefinite . . . , it is a dark anticipation of an unknown object, a striving toward an immeasurable dark distance" (*KA* XII, 219). Schlegel here uses the common romantic motif of the journey into the distance: life is a search for meaning prompted by a dissatisfaction with the fragmentary, apparently inexplicable nature of experience. It is a search that can never completely succeed. But on the other hand it is neither unjustifiable nor ungrounded. The very passage just quoted, from the historical portion of the lectures, identifies the force that originates and justifies the search for unity and the belief in ultimate meaning—it is the Platonic anamnesis: "A pure yearning, pure love can only be explained through memory; pure yearning is always a striving toward something known, but indefinite, toward something which one has previously known, a goodness, a splendor which has already been enjoyed before."

"The concept of *unity* can by no means be deduced except out of *memory*; it can no more be explained through the senses than through reason" (*KA* XII, 381). For Schlegel, present perception is always a perception of difference, a record of the traces made by nature, by the outer or counterself on the inner self. Memory is also a perception of the distance between an immediate self and another, past self. But in memory there is no discontinuity. The self that is remembered is thus intermediate in status between the perceiving self (the I) and the external world, or thou. Memory provides a model for a kind of difference that is not divisive and thus provides the hope that the division perceived between the self and nature can be overcome in the future.

The obvious implication of Schlegel's argument is that both the stirrings of hope and the consolations of memory are temporal in nature. Immediate sense perception is spatial and static; it defines self and world in terms of inside and outside. There is no way to overcome this outer, spatial distance. But if the distance between self and other can be seen as an inner, temporal distance, as a distance between present and past self, then continuity can be restored. The outer world must be seen not as a state, but as a process; mechanical, spatial concepts must give way to an organic, temporal understanding. The present is reabsorbed into the dynamic flow of life; spatial perception, the perception of solid substances, is no more than a limitation placed on true understanding: "*Being* in and of itself is nothing; it is only *appearance*; it is only the boundary of becoming, of striving. When striving arrives at its goal, this disappears and a new goal arises" (*KA* XII, 336). One of the manuscript fragments, though dating from the time of the earlier Jena lectures (1800–1801), sums up the thoroughly temporal nature of human consciousness as the Cologne lectures were to analyze it. The present, as this fragment says, is no more than the infinitely thin dividing line between what has been achieved and what is yet to come: "Consciousness, the self, knowledge itself is a fraction *whose denominator is in the past, but whose numerator lies in the future*" (*PhL* V, 1137).

The self that knows itself in its continuity, the self that is known (*cogitor ergo sum* was one of Baader's favorite maxims), the self that finds itself in what it knows—the self is everywhere but in the present instant, everywhere but in its own *Ansich*. Life is the past and the future, in memory and intimation—memory as *Er-innerung*, or the inner distance of reflection, intimation as the anticipation of meaning in experience, or the yearning love that posits a relationship between the I and nature's thou. Between these the present is only an infinitely thin surface, a point of instability, an empty or divided center.

The immediate experience of romantic consciousness is one of alienation. Keats's Adam may wake to find his dream truth, but Keats's own struggle to awaken (in the "Ode to a Nightingale") produces only disorientation, and German authors in comparable settings find the mind torn in two. For Faust to awaken is to see his dream cloud split in half (stage direction to the opening of part 2, act 4); for Kleist's Prince Friedrich it is to confront two unfamiliar objects, a laurel wreath and a single glove, and not to know to which of two ladies-in-waiting each belongs, as he twice confesses (*Prinz Friedrich von Homburg*, lines 166, 194). Neither of the Prince's conjectures is correct, of course, for truth never lies in the spontaneity of unmediated consciousness, but only in the obscurity of dream intuition or else in the fullness of temporal understanding. In darkness we may have the illusion of immediate presence; we may well say, as Hegel imagines in analyzing "sensual certainty" at the beginning of the *Phenomenology*, "The now is the night."

But the bright light of consciousness destroys any such illusion: "If we look again *now*, *this noon*, at the written truth, then we will have to say that it has become hollow." [3] To be present is to be outside oneself, to expect truth now is to find error. Human consciousness originates in aberration, eccentricity. The abnormal is the norm.

Hence the Böhmist perspective assimilates the rapidly growing interest in mental illness. Insanity becomes a paradigm of all that is immediate or primitive in human experience. Texts dealing with this topic are legion, but one, in which the dependence on the bicentral model is fully explicit, is relatively unfamiliar. It is a long passage written by Henrich Steffens, a Danish-born scientist and follower of Schelling as well as a prolific popular novelist who was ultimately best known for his ten volumes of memoirs of the romantic period; characteristically, it is at once a scientific, philosophical, and poetic text. Opening an essay that was supposed to propound a theory of mental illness, it was first published in the *Beiträge zur Beförderung einer Curmethode auf psychischem Wege*, edited by J. C. Reil, a psychologist whose writings influenced Kleist and Hoffmann. In the passage Steffens translates the bicentral model into psychological terms and thus establishes a link between the metaphysics and epistemology of the later romantic thinkers and the anthropology (or view of man) communicated by the poets:

3. Page 81. To be sure, night and day are only examples chosen by Hegel to illustrate the pitfalls inherent in the notion of sensual certainty. I might appear to have done double violence to Hegel's text, first in allegorizing the times of day as states of consciousness, and second in treating a mere example as if it determined the thematics of the text. But (1) throughout the *Phenomenology* there is a constant symbolism of day as "reality" and as the "movement [of] consciousness" and of night as the hidden immediacy of consciousness, "the creative secret of its birth" (quotations from p. 483); and (2) Hegel has just affirmed (what a modern critic in any case would hardly dare deny) that examples pertain to essence and are not random or contingent: "A true sensual certainty is not only this pure immediacy, but also an *example* thereof" (p. 80, Hegel's emphasis). Spatial immediacy is similarly exemplified from the realm of nature ("*The here* is, for instance, the *tree*," p. 82) and undermined by an example associated with the human condition ("*The here is not a tree*, but rather *a house*"). On exemplification in Hegel, see Andrzej Warminski, "Pre-positional By-play," *Glyph*, no. 3 (1978), 98–117.

So does one man appear to another, like single glances from an alien world that appear, like stars from the universe, in seemingly chaotic confusion. Only to observation do the paths of particularity fall into place, through which all life is lost in the abyss of individuality of each and everything, even each other man, enters as a stranger into the soul of each, seized by his assimilating power, gravitating toward his center, and thus finding its place in him, and in the whole.[4]

Discernible in this wash of words that open Steffens's essay are the astronomical model, hints of the Böhmist intensity of exaltation and degradation (the bright stars and the dark abyss), and above all the translation into psychological terms of Kant's transcendental unity of apperception. Whereas for Kant the mental universe spontaneously and instantaneously organizes its chaotic sense impressions, the comparable process for Steffens begins with a perception of alienation and proceeds via the effort of observation toward an assimilation that is gradual, and (as will be seen) never complete:

Each man is thus to be considered his own world, around which all relationships of life and existence circle, and out of which he can never emerge. Orderly oscillations extend his circle to an ellipse, wherein through waking and sleep now the periphery enters the illuminating center, now the latter enters alive into the former, but so that through the compass of the entire orbit their difference is suspended and the circle of self-possessed life [*des besonnenen Lebens*] is restored.

I cannot make much literal sense of the reference to sleep and waking, which seems a bow to Reil's interests and remains nearly undeveloped in the essay as it stands. Nor does Steffens ever actually elaborate on the rectification of the ellipse to a circle, that is, on the mechanism of cure for mental illness. We are left, then, with the idea that human existence is often or always elliptical. The self is not only divided externally from the surrounding world, but also divided internally, polarized between sleep and waking and between central illumination or intuition and peripheral life. As always in *Naturphilosophie* the imagery is highly abstract and in this

4. "Über die Geburt der Psyche, ihre Verfinsterung und mögliche Heilung," quoted from Steffens's *Schriften* (Breslau, 1821) II, 137. The three extracts that follow are from the same essay, pp. 138–39.

case not entirely consistent (Steffens conflates the center and periphery of a circle with the foci of an ellipse), but it generates a subtle and characteristic analysis of the human condition. There lies a gap between the form and the contents of a man's life, or between his knowledge and his actions, and this inner distance is the root both of his individuality and of a certain inescapable restlessness. Disquiet is man's lot and his driving force.[5]

In each and every moment of a man lies his whole existence—as particular nature his past, but his future as ordering fate. But the animating center has not in man, as in nature, come to rest. Although borne by ever-resting divinity, his life is his own deed. The creative moment emerges and gives birth anew in every instant, and hence the possibility of emergence of all aspects [*Momente*] of creation, from the first of chaos until the bright one of victorious organization.

At rest in the center of the universe is a divinely bright sun. Here the poles of existence coincide, thought and deed, spiritual form and material energy. Nature is at rest because it knows no gap between conception and execution or between intention and action. We see this most clearly in the instincts of animals, whose behavior spontaneously conforms to a great and universal design, free of the restless, conflicting whims of individual particularity. And at the other end of the spectrum there would be rest in complete, conscious self-possession (*Besonnenheit*, which a foreigner like Steffens might well punningly associate with the brightness of the sun). But man's situation lies between that of the animals and that of God. He thus is a creature not of rest but of activity in time, torn between the poles of primitive chaos (brute matter, undirected energy) and final organization (spirit, form). And time is to be understood in a double sense. It is external: the time-clock of the universe and of its parts (the earth, living creatures, the individual organism, for example), each of which exhibits its own movement from chaos to order, as the remainder of Steffens's essay narrates in some detail. But man's time is also internal. He carries his past and his future within him, not only in the sense that he has a biography with its developing shape, but also because at each moment the conflict breaks out

5. I borrow a key phrase from Georges Poulet, *The Interior Distance*, trans. Elliott Coleman (Baltimore, 1959).

anew between the shaping force of the ideal, which waits to be realized in the future, and the individualizing past actions, which leave their erratic traces on the present. Human temporality is not something given; it is something experienced from within. It is an emotional state, the restlessness of eternally unfinished business. Indeed, insanity itself is nothing other than an intensification of man's peculiar temporal situation. Insanity is not a reversion to the simplicity of subhuman nature, but a violent apotheosis of human nature's inner division:

But never does man, even [when bent] in the most destructive directions, leave his own world when he calls forth chaotic time; he only enters the chaotic periphery of his own nature, and even where all the forces of the center fall lame, where the madman appears without hope of cure and the violence of the nocturnal chaos of his nature is decisive, he remains himself, never steps outside himself, for instance into the rank of animals who are admitted into the repose of the natural center. Indestructible, truly immortal, he remains himself in that terrifying paralysis, undying though he seems dead. Hence the frightfulness of the appearance, the horror that seizes us, well knowing that the nocturnal principle dwells within us too, while the higher sun of divinity, maintaining its cheerful light, still leaves everything to our own action, which never resting, even amid the firmest, wavers.

Here we have reached the end of Steffens's long introductory paragraph. At this point the cadences have become positively Goethean: the final sentence is framed by adjectives that have been turned into nouns (*das Furchtbare, in dem Festesten*) in an effort to gain a firm conceptual grasp on the uncertain fluidity of man's existence. Yet the last word of all returns to the restless "wavering" of bipolar temporality. For however anguishing may be the void "where all the forces of the center fall lame," we must recognize that this dark center is the very origin of our spontaneity, freedom, and creativity. It is given to man to traverse an eccentric orbit encircling a primitive, nocturnal reserve of individuality as well as the bright sun of universal reason.

The Centrality of Poetry

> Poetry is thoroughly central in every respect.
> —Schlegel, *Literary Notebooks*

Steffens's essay ostensibly deals with a medical problem, and its title holds out the hope of a treatment. Yet the analysis is a typically romantic one, couched in abstract and metaphysical terms. Empirical science could hardly be expected to offer help for so universal a psychopathology. Indeed, if Steffens ever proposed a practical remedy, it was not found worthy of inclusion in his collected essays. In the absence of such a remedy, it may be conjectured that the "possible cure" for the condition of the human soul lies in the very myth of psychic development which Steffens tells. The poetic imagination, not medical manipulation, is the source of human salvation and the proper sphere of man's activity. Such a conclusion may at least be inferred from the rhetorical tendencies of Steffens's style and from his gravitation toward literary activity in his later years. And this tentative conclusion is borne out by the writings of both speculative thinkers and poets among the later romantics. Poetry is no longer generally seen as the divine central point from which genius can intuit the universal order of things, but it is still the stable focus toward which man's unstable course returns to find rest and stability.

We may find such views reflected, among other places, in Franz von Baader's theory of time, which is presented chiefly in the French essay "Sur la notion du temps."[1] I begin with Baader because of the close resemblance of his views to those of Steffens. I hope the consequent repetition of certain themes will be forgiven: Steffens and Baader are among the least readable authors of the period, and the juxtaposition helps to elucidate the verbal obscurities of each.

Human time, according to Baader, is not true time, which is "always resting in its movement and moving in rest, or always new and

---

1. *Werke* II, 47–68. In a letter to Carl von Meyer, November 9, 1818, Baader called this essay his finest work to date (*Werke* XV, 351).

always the same"; it is only apparent time, unquiet, unfulfilled. There is a "void of presence" (*Werke* II, 51). The center of time is open and empty. (The marble statue of the absent mother at the center of Godwi's experience in Brentano's novel is a representative emblem of this condition.) Human time is characterized by a striving out of the imperfect present toward an external, second center (*Werke* II, 53), toward an ideal of order that remains unreachable and unrealized:

> If time is conceived as the suspension of eternity, or, insofar as it is transposition [*Versetztheit*] as a suspension of the normal positioning [*Gesetztheit*], and if this transposition is conceived as composition [*Zusammengesetztheit*], and therefore as disunity, then the character of everything temporal must indeed be that of lack of wholeness or integrity, and time must contain the dialectical progress toward another world, that is toward integrity, fulfillment, or the satisfaction of being, which unrest (in the form of an imperative) can never abandon an existing thing.[2]

Existence in (apparent) time is characterized by a consciousness that unity of purpose has been lost and that man's goals have grown complex and conflicting. There is a feeling of bewilderment, of lack of support, of falling. This very feeling is perceived as an ethical imperative: what is missing must be restored. It is an imperative of love and hope, which Baader sharply distinguishes from the constricting Kantian imperative of duty and which forms the basis of his social vision. This imperative and this temporal situation, with its disjunction of perception and idea, are specifically human; Baader comments that animals do not sense time, because they lack the characteristic feeling of transposition or displacement (*Werke* II, 55).

The crux in Baader's account is the identity of unrest and never-fulfilled hope, of the psychological dis-ease and the ethical imperative. This identity is clearly expressed, and the problem of bridging the gap is laid bare in a later essay defining time as "a continual decay together with a continual fruitless incipient formation."[3] What unites these two aspects of time? For Baader (as indeed also

2. "Elementarbegriffe über die Zeit" *Werke* XIV, 34.
3. "Über den Begriff der Zeit und die vermittelnde Function der Form oder des Maasses," *Werke* II, 519.

for Schlegel) the mediating factor—which establishes time in this form—is language. Logos is logic (*Werke* II, 528); it is simultaneously the instrument of analysis into distinct parts and the vehicle of potential understanding through the reconstruction of a whole. For the analytical function of thought Baader coined the phrase, "What speaks . . . always speaks asunder"; but this action of language, as he clarifies, applies only to the essentially static, mechanical order of nature. Language speaks asunder, in order to establish a new totality "in image," or idea, a totality of relations, not among component parts, but of things to their functions and meanings. Thought raises things from the status of objects to that of products with a purpose; it shows what they lead toward, makes them "flowing." At the same time language also raises individuals out of their isolation; through discussion of ends and of the uses of things men become members of a truly human society:

Speaking (producing) is not merely a distinguishing between the speaker (the producer) and the spoken (the product), but this latter itself immediately appears as distinguished in and among itself, and if this product relates to its producer as a being to its spirit, then it follows that no being (image) as such (in the usual sense) is simple (uniform), but manifold, and that what speaks therefore always speaks asunder. Insofar as this manifold (developed being) nevertheless can and should be whole (universal, closed, finished or perfected) again, we must observe only that it can only receive and preserve this totality in and through its distinctive relationship to its producer, whence the unity of this manifold is not to be sought within this manifold itself (as though it were closed or locked off from its producer and hence peculiarly and independently determined or not flowing, say, in the relative relationship [attraction] of this manifold within itself or intramundane), but only secondarily (in image) in this manifold.[4] Only by relating ourselves to It or Him from which I and thou came and come can we be unified and in agreement among ourselves, can thy and my I make a *We*.[5]

It is in terms of this view that the essay "Sur la notion du temps" relates language to the idea of centrality: "Direct or whole action here means *central* action, which is also many times called *the word*

4. Baader distinguished "within" (a substantive component) from "in" (an accidental component).
5. *Fermenta Cognitionis* II, 2, in *Werke* II, 241–42.

because the immediate action of the Spirit is the word of command. The original temporal action of primitive man was to unite successively all the rays of this central action (of the word) in his being, *thus to humanify the word*" (*Werke* II, 64). Thought is central, an organizing action. As an organizing force it is also an imperative that establishes priorities and goals. But language is speech as well as thought; it works in time rather than in the divine simultaneity. Man's function is to realize the divine command in the *human* way, that is, successively. This at least was the function of the mythical primitive man; it does not, however, correspond to experience as we know it. The confusion of tongues and the fragmentation of society have put an end to the community of interest and activity. The center of time has opened; that is, the organization of nature is imperceptible. In language man still has a trace of the divine spirit. Logic provides the principle of organization, and speech provides the principle that human organization will be temporal and successive. In language man still has a center, but only an external one, only the principle of organization without its realization, only the form of his destiny without its content. Man's aim must be to bring meaning to nature, to naturalize, and in so doing to humanize the Word.[6]

To thus purify language is the role of poetry. It is, I believe, because poetry was to restore integrity to our experience that the romantics so often called it central. "Wouldn't it be more correct to place poetry in the center?" Schlegel asks in his notebooks, for *"poetry is more religious than religion itself."*[7] Similarly, Tieck,

6. Baader's theory of language develops along the lines suggested by Herder's "Abhandlung über den Ursprung der Sprache," but with the addition of the doctrine of the empty center and of the characteristic later romantic melancholy and urgent yearning. Thus, according to Herder, language is the faculty of making distinctions and abstractions needed by man because he lacks the instinctive capacities of animals; according to Baader, language "speaks asunder." The following passage from Herder will illustrate the relationship between the two authors: "No thought in *one* human soul was lost; but never was even *one* accomplishment of this race all there at *once*, as in animals: the soul was always in progress, in course, as a result of its whole economy: nothing invented, like the construction of a hive, but everything being invented, ever working, striving. In this perspective, how great does language become!" (*Werke* V, 136).
7. *PhL* Beilage VIII, 81. Karl Konrad Polheim, *Die Arabeske* (Munich, 1966), pp. 90–95, asserts that Schlegel gradually substituted history for poetry as the "central" science, beginning as early as 1804.

trying to complete his fragmentary Fichtean novel, *Franz Sternbald*, writes that art "is called divine because it proceeds from God and rests in Him as its center."[8] For Joseph Görres, art is the divine center itself, as it is manifest in the world, and "the poet's imagination" is "the all-warming central fire" ("Glauben und Wissen," *Schriften*, III, 64). Brentano describes art as "the single point in the middle of the world," which commands a view of the totality of experience (*Godwi, Werke* II, 131). Humboldt says the poet's mission is "to reveal a whole world of appearances from out of a *single point*."[9] But none of these texts, perhaps, is so germane to the present discussion as the beautiful passage that suggested the title of Eichendorff's first novel, *Ahnung und Gegenwart*:

On Friedrich the quiet life had the most beneficial influence. His soul was in the state of powerful repose in which alone it is capable, like the motionless mirror surface of a lake, of taking heaven into itself. The rustling of the forest, the birds' song round about him, this green solitude, unknown since his childhood, everything called forth again in his breast that eternal feeling which sinks us, as it were, into the center of all life, where all the colored rays proceed like radii and shape themselves on the changing surface into the painful-beautiful play of appearance. Everything experienced and past once again passes yet more solemnly and with greater dignity before us, a luxuriant future, blossoming like the dawn, settles on the pictures, and so out of intimation and memory arises a new world within us, and we indeed recognize all the places and faces again, but they are larger, more beautiful, and more powerful and move in another wonderful light. And so Friedrich composed countless songs and wonderful stories out of the most deep and heartfelt joy, and they were almost the happiest hours of his life. [*Werke*, p. 605]

Here we see the origin of art in the conversion of melancholy into happiness, quietude into speech, and the perilously thin surface of the present into a glittering reflection of the profundity of human experience in time.

The representative poet in this connection is the title figure of

8. Richard Alewyn, "Ein Fragment zur Fortsetzung von Tiecks 'Sternbald,'" *Jahrbuch des freien deutschen Hochstifts* (1962), p. 63.
9. *Schriften* II, 125 ("Über Goethes Hermann und Dorothea"). Cf. the letter to Schiller of September 1800, which says that the poems of the ancients and of Goethe "expand out from the center," *Der Briefwechsel zwischen Friedrich Schiller und Wilhelm von Humboldt*, ed. Siegfried Seidel (Berlin, 1962), II, 201.

E. T. A. Hoffmann's largest collection of stories, *Die Serapions-brüder*. Serapion is a German who, living as a hermit in the Bavarian woods, believes himself to be an anchorite in the Theban desert. His history is recounted in the frame of the collection and inspires the principal characters to begin telling their stories. For while Serapion was mad, as the character Lothar says, "Your hermit, my dear Cyprian, was a true poet, he really saw what he proclaimed, and therefore his speech gripped heart and mind" (p. 54). And Lothar continues by describing this poetic madness. Although he speaks of center and circle, rather than of ellipse and foci, his concerns are essentially identical with those we have just been probing and contribute to defining the role of poetry in the economy of romanticism:

Poor Serapion, wherein else consisted thy madness, than that some hostile star had robbed thee of the knowledge of the doubleness [*Duplizität*] by which and which alone our earthly being is conditioned. There is an inner world, and the spiritual force to behold it in utter clarity, in the perfected radiance of the most active life, but it is our earthly inheritance that the very outer world in which we are encapsulated functions as the lever which sets that force in motion. Inner appearances evaporate in the circle that external ones form about us and that our spirit can only overfly in dark, secret presentiments, which never shape themselves into a clear picture. But thou, o my hermit! didst decree no outer world, thou sawest not the hidden lever, the force working from without on thy inner being; and when thou didst declare with horrifying acuity that what sees, hears, feels, what grasps deed and event, is only the spirit, and that therefore also *that* truly did occur which it acknowledges as such, then didst thou forget that the outer world on its own forces the spirit, which is enchained within the body, to those functions of perception. [Pp. 54–55]

Serapion's madness is a more than human state. It is utterly unconditioned, and its true affinities lie with divine perfection. Fulfilling the Archimedean reverie, Serapion is his own sole center and fulcrum and firmly believes in the reality of his own imaginings. He is beyond all divisions: the outer world is fully absorbed into the inner self and offers no resistance to the flights of the imagination. Mind and body are no longer at odds, as in the dualistic world of ordinary earthly life, but have become one. The poles of existence are merged.

Serapion tries to experience in the flesh this complete absorption of body by spirit. We recognize the self-contradiction of both having and denying the body, and we call it by the names insanity and hallucination. But in the spirit, if not in physical reality, such absorption is possible. It can exist as an ideal, and then its name is poetry. Poetry is the unity that encompasses the dualities of existence. Its pulse flows with the double character of human temporality. For dark and light come together in poetry; the poetic center is not only ideal, but must have its irrational aspect as well. The darkness is the pathos of the ideal that can never be realized. Romantic poetry is both utopian and disillusioned, both allegorical and ironic. Its paradoxical, twinned vision makes it the proper expression of man's polarized nature.[10]

10. An example of dual temporality in a lyric poem is analyzed in my essay, "Eichendorff's Times of Day," *German Quarterly* 50 (1977), 485–503.

Chronic Dualism: The Romantic Novel

> Blessed are the times for which the starry heaven is the map
> of the passable roads and of those to be passed and whose
> roads are lit by the light of the stars. Everything is new for
> them and yet familiar, full of adventure and nevertheless a
> possession. The world is wide and yet like their own house,
> for the fire which burns in the soul is of the same essence
> as the stars; they are sharply divided, the world and the self,
> the light and the fire, and yet never become estranged for all
> time; for fire is the soul of each and every light and light is
> the clothing of every fire. So all action of the soul becomes
> meaningful and round in this duality: complete in sense and
> complete for the senses; round because the soul rests in it-
> self during action; round because its deed detaches itself
> and, now become an entity, finds its own center and draws
> a closed circle around itself.
>
> —Georg Lukács, *Die Theorie des*
> *Romans*

To say that literature wishes to succeed where life cannot is to say
that there is, in later romantic poetry, a definite will to form: an
aspiration to create a surrogate image in words for the unification
that is impossible in experience. Deemphasizing the all-inclusive
"progressive universal poetry" of the earlier Schlegel, the poets
searched for a controlled means adequate to the task of expressing
the erratic eccentricities of life. And the remarkable thing is that
such forms were found, indeed many such forms. I have analyzed
elsewhere, at greater length than I can do here, three of these solutions: the marble image and chiseled imagery of Brentano's *Godwi*,
which subsume the polarities of life into a firm ethical postulate;
Humboldt's willed ideal of classical form, in which the self can put
its own provisional status at a distance without self-betrayal;
Eichendorff's supple rhetorical mastery, which allows the constantly varying flow of time itself to be given a firm shape. These are
some of the noteworthy individual attempts to give, in art, a centered and coherent expression to man's incoherent experience. But

beyond such individual solutions a group effort was also made to arrive at a common solution available to all. A new, quintessentially romantic form evolved, bicentral in nature. By encompassing both poles within it, literature for the romantics became truly central. This new form was the generic expression of the later romantic world view.

Schlegel's notebooks contain the most helpful comments on the nature of bicentral literary form. In order to interpret these comments correctly, however, we must make a detour for a few paragraphs to see how thoroughly the notebooks are permeated with Böhmist imagery. Beginning as early as 1799 frequent references to two centers or to two poles reflect the effort to evaluate and exploit Böhme's conceptions in many different ways. Thus Schlegel says that harmony and allegory are two centers of poetry, that Locke and Descartes are two poles of philosophy, that Sophocles and Spinoza are two poles of morals, that politics and mysticism are two poles of morals, that art and nature are the centers of morality.[1] In addition, some fragments describe a particular quality as the "other center," even though they do not clearly identify a first center (*PhL* IV, 663, 725). One fragment from 1799 is particularly interesting in attempting to relate Böhmist bicentrality to the metaphor of central forces associated with Fichte (and also Schelling): "*Mysticism* and *magic* each a center of religion, centripetal and centrifugal principle" (*PhL* IV, 1409). In another fragment Schlegel experiments with a whole series of concepts, always grouping them in pairs: "*Law* and *love* probably are the poles of immortality; both united in the classical; or law and mystery, force and generality."[2]

Although many fragments speak only of a single center, which was the customary symbol of an individual organism, Schlegel seems to have fully accepted the Böhmist bicentral or elliptical explanation of the structure of the whole universe and to have tried with considerable regularity to clarify and apply it. I have already quoted some of the most distinctive examples in my discussion of

---

1. *PhL* IV, 710, 961, 1069, 1070; *LN* 2042.
2. *PhL* IV, 59. This fragment dates from the summer of 1798 and may thus precede Schlegel's study of Böhme; if so, it indicates his readiness for Böhme's ideas.

the symbolic ellipse; another fragment gives a significant programmatic indication of the philosophy of mind suggested by a dual center: "In the center no isolated reason of any sort should be portrayed, but it should be in dialogue—reason in reciprocity with itself" (*PhL* IV, 1314). But the best evidence that Schlegel considered the bicentral explanation to be the normal and most adequate one is negative; it consists of some fragments asserting that various phenomena have only one center. In the Kantian corpus only one work is central, only nature is central, there can be only one mediator at a time (*PhL* II, 448; III, 439; IV, 744). Such things would be unworthy of remark unless it were in some way limited or unusual to have only one center; the normal condition is to have a divided or double center. In this connection a somewhat later fragment (probably from 1802) is particularly revealing, a fragment whose strong tone probably reflects exasperation rather than absolute conviction: "The *center of the earth* is SINGLE, that much is clear" (*PhL* Beilage VII, 36). That much may or may not be clear. What is clear, when this fragment is taken in conjunction with the rest of what is known about Schlegel, is that the center of the *universe* was in his eyes not single but double.

A recognition of this pervasive theme in the notebooks makes possible the interpretation of another group of fragments. These are the fragments that speak of a central center. Examples of this type are "The ideal is the center of the center," and "The encyclopedia is a textbook of universality, centrum centrorum" (*PhL* IV, 125, 706). Syntactically, this is the type of expression familiar from the Bible—as in "the holy of holies"—and in Hebrew it is merely the common form of the superlative, there being no synthetic form corresponding to our "holiest." But to Schlegel these expressions certainly meant more than just "the absolute center." Schlegel's statement that "religion is the central center, that is clear" (*PhL* IV, 1435), suggests the image of a bicentral universe with some other principle such as material causality as the "terrestrial" center of attraction and religion as the second and higher center (metaphorically the sun) around which the lower center revolves. It suggests, in other words, a bipolar universe, a double center. The abbreviation actually used by Schlegel in his notebook—"Rel ist CtCt, das ist klar"—in fact gives a visual image of the Böhmist notion that the divine center divides itself, emanates an earthly center, and in this very process verifies and recognizes its superiority and spirituality. Repetition, as incipient self-consciousness, confers status.

Two are one and one is two—that is the structural principle governing Schlegel's speculations in these years: "There is no dualism without primacy—for all dualism results from the procession of the infinite out of itself and the positing of something finite" (*PhL* IV, 1285). Or, as Novalis wrote in a late fragment which already anticipates much later speculation, "The true dividual is also the true individual" (*Schriften*, III, 451). The absolute enters this world through duplication, and the double, or "CtCt," is the finite form that represents the infinite center. This self-division of the finite world (the temporal inner distance from self to self) is associated in particular with language: in the center is the "reciprocity" of "dialogue." Language, as Baader says, divides thing from image (it "speaks asunder"), and yet this very action of fission carries within it a re-collection of the higher, original, "central action" of Creation, when the Word was made flesh. Thus, the form that best manifests the ubiquitous bicentrality of the universe will be a language of repetition.

The perfected language of repetition is poetry. A number of Schlegel's fragments exalting poetry presuppose the belief that reduplication is the finite garb that makes visible the transcendent unity of the infinite. Thus, when Schlegel calls poetry "absolutely central in every respect" (*LN* 1827), he must be understood to mean that it is the highest, repeated, central center. The common formulas π^2 (Schlegel's shorthand notation) and "Poesie der Poesie" are the graphic and syntactic representations of a poetry that has reached the level of self-reflection (as are also the formulas "der romantische Roman" and "Ironie der Ironie"). The value of true poetry resides in its reflected quality, that is to say, in its eminent centrality: "The ancients can only be understood through CtCt poetry. All prose about the most high is incomprehensible" (*PhL* IV, 723).

Repetition is a principle of representation. Hence the Böhmist orientation affects the form of romantic poetry as well as its ethos. Only reduplicated forms can be truly central and can render "the most high," and only such reduplicated forms as suggest a temporal and ontological ordering of original and derived, hidden and revealed. In verse such duplications are inherent: "The caesura is a turning point in the verse, an inner dualism" (*LN* 1735). An inner dualism is, of course, not an absolute opposition; the two halves of the verse are two foci of meaning subordinate to a single primary (and presumably allegorical or structural) meaning: "The repetition of the sound in rhyme [is] only a reduction to the language of nature" (*LN* 2089). And more generally, "There lies an *infinite duality* in the sonnet—always anew. For that very reason the sonnet is appropriate for mystical thoughts, for prayer."[3]

The main divided, mystical form of romantic literature, however, is not verse, but the novel. (It should be remembered, however, that Schlegel used the word *Roman* for any work that fulfilled his postulates for romantic literature. The characteristics I am about to enumerate are not limited to the novel but are widespread in all the "epic" forms, including stories and tales, verse narratives, and pageant dramas such as *Faust*.) It is the romantic novel that provides the adequate structural correlative to the bicentral world view and its most highly developed expression. A few fragments before speaking of the caesura as the inner dualism of verse, Schlegel had already spoken of the dualism of novels: "That the *novel* desires two centers indicates that every novel wants to be an absolute book, indicates its mystical character. This gives it a mythological character, it becomes a *person*" (*LN* 1728). The fragment preceding this one names Schlegel's model, which is *Don Quixote*, rather than a novel of the romantic period, but his description of the bicentrality of *Don Quixote* could be applied without alteration to several of the most important romantic novels: "The chief character in the second part of *Don Quixote* is the first part. It is, throughout, the work's reflection on itself" (*LN* 1727). *Don Quixote* has, and any novel desires, two centers and two levels of meaning. First comes the level of action: part one of *Don Quixote* consists of the violent adventures that befall Don Quixote and, with more serious conse-

3. *LN* 1824. For the notion of a dualism with mystical significance in poetry, see also *LN* 435, which finds "something of the spirit of Hebrew parallelism" in *terza rima*.

quences, the characters associated with the inserted novellas. Then follows the level of reflection, the second part of the novel, consisting largely of prepared charades reflecting and playing on the adventures of the first part. In this second part are unfolded the significance, depth, and, as Schlegel calls it, personality of the actions. Similar relations hold between the two parts of *Godwi*, between the two *Wilhelm Meister* novels, and (I believe) between Hegel's two major treatises as well: the *Phenomenology of Mind* was Hegel's *Bildungsroman*, while the later *Science of Logic*, more deliberate in its pacing, reflects on the *Phenomenology* so as to ground its dialectic and ultimately to serve as an introduction to it. Thus, the romantic novel leads from action to significance or—as Loeben phrases it in a nearly identical formulation—to the unification of action with significance: "The coincidence of the visible and the invisible center in the novel, in one point, can be considered as its highest moment, as its solution, its close, and indeed no novel in which a man is given as the ideal center of the poetry can close with any other resolution." [4]

Duality of form, then, is characteristic of romantic literature in general and of the romantic novel in particular. An account of the formal presuppositions of German romanticism leads naturally to a study of romantic narrative. A full-scale phenomenology of the romantic novel would require another whole volume, of course, and I do not propose to attempt that here. But I would like at least to comment on some of the salient peculiarities of the romantic novel that are related to the bicentral conception of experience, for it is here that the language of time finds its fullest realization.

Chronic dualism.   My title phrase comes from E. T. A. Hoffmann's well-known "capriccio," "Prinzessin Brambilla" (*Späte Werke*, p. 311). It names the disease from which the double hero of this bizarre narrative is suffering. In a brilliant reading Jean Starobinski has presented the story as an allegory of the human psyche, whose chronic Fichtean schizophrenia is cured by the comic theater. [5] Paul de Man has responded that the story remains ironic

4. *Lotosblätter* (Bamberg and Leipzig, 1817) I, 149.
5. Jean Starobinski, "Ironie et mélancolie (II): La 'Princesse Brambilla' de E. T. A. Hoffmann," *Critique* 22 (1966), 438–57.

to the end, with no saving reconciliation of opposites.⁶ But both agree in seeing duality exclusively in negative terms. In so doing they overlook the double meaning of the crucial phrase. For in this story, as throughout later romanticism, the Cartesian division into opposing worlds of mind and matter is replaced not (as Fichte still desired) by a unitary first principle, but by temporalized bicentrality. The disease of chronic *dualism* is in fact cured, but the cure is none other than *chronic* dualism. To the end the hero leads a double life, as the actor Giulio Fava and as the mythical prince among princes, Cornelio Chiapperi (whose guiding spirit, "the old, fabulous Prince Bastianello of Pisa," is still present in the final tableau). He does not overcome his split personality, but he learns to conduct his life on two planes at once: ideal and real, in the imagination and in the senses, in allegory (utopian myth) and in ironic, demystified self-awareness. Earlier in the story Hoffmann has already described the tempered and temporal dualism that characterizes human life: "Everyone who is gifted with any imagination [*Fantasie*] suffers, as can be read in some book fraught with worldly wisdom, from an insanity which steadily rises and falls, like ebb and flow. The time of the latter, when the waves crash ever louder and stronger, is the fall of night, as the morning hours just after awakening, with a cup of coffee, count as the highest point of the ebb" (pp. 276–77). Outsiders see as the irreconcilable poles of madness and sanity what insiders recognize as the mutually supplementary times of fantasy and earnest sobriety. Hoffmann's tone here is only semiserious, but one worldly-wise book he may have had in mind is his own *Serapionsbrüder*, whose title character is a raving lunatic at night but nearly sane in the morning. Chronic dualism is thus the sign under which all of Hoffmann's fiction stands, and indeed, it seems to me, all the major fiction of the later romantics.

This is not a story. There are many different manifestations of this chronic dualism, though in all its forms it may be said that the

6. "The Rhetoric of Temporality," *Interpretation: Theory and Practice*, ed. Charles S. Singleton (Baltimore, 1969), pp. 199–200. Günter Wöllner's discussion of Hoffmann's would-be "Überwindung des Dualismus" lies along similar lines: *E. T. A. Hoffmann und Franz Kafka: Von der fortgeführten Metapher zum sinnlichen Paradox* (Berne, 1971), pp. 13–31.

narrative exists on two different temporal levels. The most flamboyant type is Hoffmann's novel *Kater Murr*, where sections of the cat's memoirs are interlarded with fragments from the apparently unrelated biography of the musician Kreisler. Much more common are framing effects: the inclusion within the narrative of a fairy tale that recapitulates and idealizes the action or (a favorite device of Brentano's) the magical translation of a human tale into the animal realm and back again. In Kleist's tales a different, but still related dualism, is to be found. With only one set of events, careful management of the diction (combined, in some cases, with a framing effect achieved by inversion of the narrative sequence) creates a dual perspective on them, as fluctuating contingency and as driving fate. In the fiction of the 1790s chronic dualism does occur, but in characteristically indeterminate, "eccentric" forms. Thus, both the completed portion of *Heinrich von Ofterdingen* and Goethe's *Unterhaltungen deutscher Ausgewanderten* conclude with fairy tales (rather than encapsulating the tales in a finished narrative) and consequently open outward. And Hölderlin's *Hyperion* superimposes a gradually developing narrator on a gradually maturing hero, but without reaching any definite conclusion. Other dualisms pervade every level of romantic fiction. Organizationally, for instance, we find the diptych structures of works like Brentano's "Kasperl und Annerl" and Eichendorff's "Eine Meerfahrt," thematically the widespread use of *Doppelgänger* figures, and stylistically the formulaic prose that makes the fiction sound like the repetition of long-familiar patterns. Yet all these various dualisms are marked as romantic and bicentral by the fact that they never involve mere repetition or mere opposition, but always indicate variation and hierarchy. Indeed, even the most mechanical and stylized dualism, Hoffmann's ubiquitous trick of repeating the initial word of a quotation before and after naming the speaker, is often used to give a witty effect of variation or even reversal of meaning: "'Doubt,' responded the charlatan with a polite, almost respectful greeting, 'doubt not . . .'" (*Späte Werke*, p. 308). In *Kater Murr* the hierarchy is guaranteed by the sequence of events, for the cat's "opinions" belong to a later period than the portion of Kreisler's biography being reported. Other works distinguish in different ways between their two components, but the result always conforms to the bicentral ideology, with a human world unfolding through time and imperfectly reflecting a timeless ideal. Classically, in the works of Cervantes and Fielding, inserted stories are related to the principal narrative by analogy or negative analogy, but in the romantic novel the relationship is more complex, as Novalis suggests: "The state of nature is a *strange image* of the eternal realm. The world of the fairy tale is the world *exactly opposite* to the world of truth (history)—and precisely for that reason so *thoroughly similar* to it—as *chaos* is to the *accomplished creation*" (*Schriften*, III, 281). The ideal and the real, fiction and truth, are different yet somehow related, for man lives in both worlds. Hence the ideal second world of romantic fictions never appears cut off from the first world, as the Man of the Hill is from Tom Jones, or the Latin tale of the nosy Slawkenbergius from Tristram Shandy's noseless environment.[7] A characteristic reflection of the relationship of real frame to ideal insertion is the topos "this is not a story," which sometimes introduces an inserted narrative. It is not a story because it is a part of life itself, seen from a higher perspective. "Do not take my story for a fairy tale," says Bertha at the beginning of Tieck's "Der blonde Eckbert," and this is a sign not only that the story is true, but also that it unlocks the mysteries of Eckbert's soul. "Do not take the affair for a poem," says St. Boniface at the beginning of the scene "Wüste" in Tieck's *Genoveva*, and yet his narrative monologue in ottava rima stands out as a particularly poetic section of the verse drama. But it is more than a mere poem, for it is the bridge passage between the two parts of the drama and completes the transition from the neo-Shakespearian history play of the opening to the Christian mystery of the conclusion. It is not a poem because it lies above, rather than outside, the prose world of everyday experience.

Poems in prose.   Like the speech of Time in *The Winter's Tale*, Boniface's monologue comes at a dead point in the play. Seven blank years pass while the action is stopped. Boniface does report a few events from the interval, but mostly of a supernatural rather

7.   "I never was the destruction of any body's nose, said *Susannah*,—which is more than you can say," book VI, chap. 3.

than a historical character, and the steady rhythm of the stanzas joins with an irregular alternation of tenses to create a general atmosphere of timelessness. Such timelessness characterizes lyric interruptions of the flow of events in general. Thus earlier in the same play, in the scene "Garten. Mondschein," Golo and Genoveva sing a beautiful lyric describing a moment of natural stasis. The song has an unearthly, seductive effect, against which Genoveva warns Golo: "Desist, Golo, from words of flattery which captivate my ear at dead of night like a fable and poem from a distant time; moonbeams invite poetry and invention, which is distant from truth as from the sober light of day." And indeed, after a second song and a sonnet the lyric interview is finally interrupted by a trumpet call announcing news from the battle front. Poetry is the night side of history, as imagination is of reason.

Of romantic bicentral forms the most widely used combines history and poetry: it is the prose narrative with inserted lyrics. The poems are of many types: folk songs evoking an ancient national culture, or songs (like Mignon's) that are the relics of an idealized lost childhood, prophecies, the effusions of madness such as Peregrina's songs in Mörike's *Maler Nolten*, magical incantation, or the dialogue of fairy tale creatures (particularly in Brentano). The poems can also be improvisations or recent compositions that express otherwise ineffable sensations; indeed, at times, as in Klingsohr's tale in *Heinrich von Ofterdingen* or as in parts of *Godwi*, the narrative or the dialogue simply breaks into verse under the pressure of heightened emotions. Whatever the format, the poems give access to a timeless world that is the ground of our mortal existence.

The interplay of the realms of prose and poetry is a special phenomenon of German romanticism.[8] Even Hoffmann, who was much less given to poetry than Tieck, Brentano, Arnim, or Eichendorff, has Murr interrupt his narrative to deliver a verdict on the subject: "Verses in a book written in prose should perform the same

8. For a thorough, although purely external, history of the *genre mêlé*, or prose narrative with inserted poems, see Paul Neuburger, *Die Verseinlage in der Prosadichtung der Romantik* (Leipzig, 1924). In addition see the contradictory unpublished fragments assembled (and not reconciled) by Karl Konrad Polheim in *Die Arabeske* (Munich, 1966), pp. 198–204 and 233.

as bacon in wurst, to wit, strewn hither and yon in little bits, they afford the whole mixture more radiance of richness, more sweet grace of taste" (p. 638). Despite the playful simile, the judgment is well considered. We know from an incident in "Nußknacker und Mäusekönig" (*Serapionsbrüder*, 220–22) that wurst without bacon is contemptible, and poems likewise provide an indispensable higher plane (a radiance and grace, in Murr's words) without which novels are mere entertainment. At the same time Murr pinpoints the weakness of some early examples of the type, such as Moritz's *Anton Reiser* and the first version of *Franz Sternbald*, when he adds that biographical novels should not be simply a framework and an excuse for publishing a mass of inferior verse. The decorum of romantic novels differs sharply in this respect from that of the fiction that precedes and follows. In the later nineteenth century even novelists who were active poets (the French "romantics," Eliot, Melville, Keller, Fontane, and so forth) seldom or never insert poems into their prose works. And both before and after the romantic period the rare inserted poems are liable to be felt as disturbing intrusions and to be associated with danger or evil; thus in chapter 4, "L'Enigme," of Voltaire's *Zadig* the hero almost loses his head for having written a poem; in Musset's "Fils du Titien" the hero turns to verse only to confess his lack of talent; in Dickens's *Our Mutual Friend* the balladeer Simon Wegg is the villain. When Hardy then revived the *genre mêlé* at the end of the century, it was already an archaic form appropriate to the primitive and repressed passions of his characters.

Pastoral and gothic. The historical distribution of the *genre mêlé* is worth pondering. Its popularity is invariably associated with romance forms, but of two widely divergent types. An outgrowth of the *razos*, or lives, of the Provençal poets, the prose narrative with inserted poems was a late medieval invention best known from Dante's *Vita Nuova*; it reached its first flowering in the line of Renaissance pastorals, which began with Boccaccio's *Ameto* and ran through Sannazaro, Montemayor, and Sidney. Pastoral society brings man into immediate contact with nature, and the profusion of verses studding the narrative bespeaks the easy intercourse of prose and poetry, low and high, natural and artificial, primitive and sophisticated. It is "the nature of this clime to stir up Poeticall fancies," as one of Sidney's characters says:

All the people of this countrie from high to lowe, is given to those sportes of the witte, so as you would wonder to heare how soone even children will beginne to versifie. Once, ordinary it is among the meanest sorte, to make Songes and Dialogues in meeter, either love whetting their braine, or long peace having begun it, example and emulation amending it. Not so much, but the clowne *Dametas* will stumble sometimes upon some Songs that might become a better brayne: but no sorte of people so excellent in that kinde as the pastors; for their living standing but upon the looking to their beastes, they have ease, the Nurse of Poetrie.[9]

The other romance tradition employing the *genre mêlé* is the English gothic. Here, in Radcliffe and Lewis, as later in some of Poe's stories, poetry is felt to be an interruption of the prose and hence a sign of mental alienation. This can take various forms: the simple foolishness of "poetical paroxysm," in chapter 5 of Lewis's *The Monk*; revelation of a hidden secret, as in Poe's "Assignation"; or, most often, as in "The Fall of the House of Usher," subjection to a ruling passion: "They must have been, and were, . . . the result of that intense mental collectedness and concentration to which I have previously alluded as observable only in particular moments of the highest artificial excitement. . . . In the under or mystic current of its meaning, I fancied that I perceived, for the first time, a full consciousness on the part of Usher of the tottering of his lofty reason upon her throne." The novels of Scott and Cooper are more complex in their inspiration, but they likewise employ poems most often to mark the distance between the supernatural and the natural realms: the "wild and irregular spirit" of Waverly (*Waverley*, chapter 5), the ravings of Madge Wildfire, the magical simple-mindedness of David Gamut.

The *genre mêlé* of German romanticism combines the two romance traditions. A fusion of the frenzied, "impetuous time" of the gothic with the static, reflective time of pastoral has long been rec-

9. *The Countess of Pembroke's Arcadia* in *Prose Works*, ed. Albert Feuillerat (Cambridge, 1962), I, 86 and 27–28.

ognized as characteristic of romanticism.[10] And the German romantic version of the *genre mêlé* formalizes this duality of mood. Although many significant variations occur in the distribution of modes, in general it may be said that gothic elements of plot, imagery, and atmosphere are assigned to the prose,[11] and the unchanging, circumscribed pastoral world of love and nature is evoked in the poems. The poems and the prose present alternative kinds of interest, whereas in both Renaissance pastoral and English gothic the poems are in harmony with the prose. (In *Don Quixote*, the other important formal model, the poems are confined to pastoral interludes, which are represented as an alternative folly to the violent, impetuous folly of chivalry.) The prose is the focus of human action, and the poetic pastoral is the ideal focus, the higher or central center of the novels: "Aesthetics has a center and it is just that of—humanity, beauty, art; golden age is the center of this center" (Schlegel, *LN* 1382). The ideal poem is a still point of reference in an unquiet world, the tonic on which the plot sings a descant, the centerpiece within the arabesque. Such a relationship Eichendorff found in two earlier German works, Grimmelshausen's *Simplicissimus* and Müller's *Genoveva*, and described in a passage that distills many essential formal elements of the romantic novel: "A deeply religious and specifically Catholic feeling threads its way through this wide world, indeed the beautiful song of the hermit, 'Komm Trost der Nacht, o Nachtigall!' just like Golo's song in Genoveva, could be regarded as the root chord [*Grundaccord*] that sounds through the whole, until finally Simplicissimus rescues himself as a hermit on a desert island out of the shipwreck of the world, as from out of a dream in which he has lost time and virtue" (*Der deutsche Roman*, HKA VIII², 62).

Discontinuity, repetition, and variation. Eichendorff's imitation of the hermit's song, "Komm Trost der Welt, du stille Nacht,"

10. See Emil Staiger, "Die reißende Zeit," in *Die Zeit als Einbildungskraft des Dichters* (Zurich, 1939), and Geoffrey Hartman, "False Themes and Gentle Minds," in *Beyond Formalism* (New Haven, 1970), pp. 283–97.
11. See Marianne Thalmann, *Der Trivialroman des 18. Jahrhunderts und der romantische Roman* (Berlin, 1923), for an inventory of Gothic elements.

resounds during a magical moonlit interlude of the story "Eine Meerfahrt," between a demonic chase and a dark, ghostly battle scene. The song reverses many of Grimmelshausen's emphases: his echoing bird songs are excluded, and silent night appears as a protective envelope rather than a threatening blankness. Outlines are blurred, figures merge, and chronologies overlap as shade comes drowsily to shade to drown the wakeful anguish of the soul. If time (as Baader said) is a suspension of eternity, then the protected world of Eichendorff's hermit is a suspension of time in a world of inspirited things rather than living beings: "'Quiet there!' he cried; 'what drives you to break the night with this coarse noise? The wild sea only mutters in the distance at the foot of the rocks, and the blind elements had all kept peace here for thirty years in a beautiful concord of nature, and the first Christians whom I see bring war, revolt, death'" (*Werke*, p. 1305).

Although the contrast between propulsive narration and lyrical pause is not often so schematic as here, it nevertheless is fundamental in German romantic fiction. The interaction of the two worlds is explored in countless modulations: the song may be a sudden revelation or a distraction, an analogue or a pointed irrelevance; the ideal it evokes may be true or fallacious, it may continue or vary motifs from the prose context or suggest an alien world. But whatever the specific circumstances, the very regularity of rhythm and rhyme constitutes an interruption (on occasions a failed interruption) of the linear impetus of time. As a temporality without forward movement, rhythm and rhyme of themselves constitute the ground or "tonic chord" of human time.

The essence of the lyric mode, of the pastoral "central center" of time, is repetition. Something happens, yet nothing changes, for the ideal is unvarying. Not all poems in German romantic fiction are equally central (nor are all plots equally propulsive), but the lyrical high points are marked by a well-developed art of repetition. Thus, the hermit's song in "Eine Meerfahrt" repeats elements both externally (from its literary model) and also internally (through its refrain as well as through thematic duplications). "Der Abend" is actually sung twice in "Aus dem Leben eines Taugenichts," and its repetition breaks through all realistic hindrances and unleashes the comic opera "emigration to Arcadia" (Eichendorff, *Werke*,

p. 1141), which concludes the story. Within this framework of repetition, variation offers the possibility for flexibility and also the threat of decomposition. Undoubtedly, the best-known instance is the thrice-varied song "Waldeinsamkeit" in Tieck's story "Der blonde Eckbert." With each version Bertha's forest solitude preempts a new aspect of time—first eternity, next mutability, and lastly repetition—until it has become an all-encompassing demonic space from which consciousness can find no escape.

The fictional space. Over an all but unbounded landscape the wandering hero of a romantic novel traces his figure. His character is his fate; nothing external seriously impedes his progress or shapes his destiny. Even the romantic madman, such as Nathanael in Hoffmann's "Sandmann," is possessed only by his own demon, "the wild beast in the breast," as Eichendorff repeatedly called it, and not by an external power. Yet within this world of unconfined subjectivity lies a fixed point of reference, a circumscribed world of timeless stability. Man lives in both worlds, and neither may safely take exclusive possession of his imagination. His accomplishment is measured, not by absolutes, but by the distance maintained between the freedom of prose and the order of verse. Two suns shine on the romantic hero and the romantic novel, a fire within and a light without, and the life of the fiction lies in the difference between these two illuminations.

Difference is the key word, and not opposition or ambivalence. It is true that Novalis, in a late fragment, speaks of the "battle of poetry and unpoetry" as one of the "unities of the novel" (*Schriften*, III, 639). But this is a battle in which there are no losers; indeed, it is rather a contest in which both sides are strengthened through competition, "an arch-poetic game": "Throughout Shakespeare's historical plays there is a battle of poetry with unpoetry. The common appears witty and relaxed—when the great appears stiff and sad, etc. Lower life is pitted throughout against higher—often tragically, often parodically, often for the sake of contrast. . . . Just the opposite of true history and yet history as it ought to be" (III, 685). Opposition is true friendship—not because opposites are united, but precisely because they are different enough to open a space for creativity: "The art of *estranging* in a *pleasing* way, of making an object strange and yet familiar and attractive, that is the romantic poetic" (ibid.).

The last prophetic word may be left to the earlier Novalis. It is not a final judgment or even a clear one, for these are not Novalis's virtues. But in its enthusiastically evocative way, it is a programme for the bicentral novel of the romantics and for that true life situated in the differential space of fiction:

It would be a fine question, whether the lyrical poem is actually a *poem*, plus-poetry, or whether prose is minus-poetry? As the novel has been taken for prose, so has the lyric poem been taken for poetry—both in error. The highest, truest prose is the lyric poem.

So-called prose arose from the limitation of absolute extremes—It is only there ad interim and plays a subaltern, temporary role. A time is coming where it will no longer be. For out of limitation has grown interpenetration. A true life has arisen, and poetry and prose are thereby most intimately united and put in alternation. [*Schriften*, II, 536]

Appendix

"Various Sentiments before a Seascape
with Capuchin, by Friedrich"
Clemens Brentano

It is splendid to gaze out under somber skies upon a boundless watery desert from the infinite solitude on the seashore, and to this belongs going thither, having to return, desiring to cross, being unable to, missing everything pertaining to life, and yet perceiving one's voice in the murmuring of the tide, in the blowing of the breeze, in the drifting of the clouds, in the lonely cry of the birds; to this belongs a claim which the heart makes and an injury [*Abbruch*] which natures does to one. But this is impossible before the picture, and what I ought to find in the picture itself I found only between me and the picture, namely a claim that the picture made on me by not fulfilling the same; and so I myself became the Capuchin, the picture became the dune, but that toward which I looked with yearning, the sea, was wholly lacking. In order to encounter this wonderful sensation I hearkened to the expressions of the variety of viewers all about me, and communicate them as belonging to the picture, which is altogether decoration, before which an action must proceed, since it affords no rest.

A lady and a gentleman, who was perhaps very ingenious, stepped forward; the lady looked in her catalogue and spoke:
"Number two: landscape in oils. How do you like it?"
GENTLEMAN: Infinitely deep and sublime.
LADY: You mean the sea, yes, that must be astonishingly deep, and the Capuchin is also very sublime.
GENTLEMAN: No, Frau Kriegsrat, I mean the sentiment of the peerless Friedrich at this painting.
LADY: Is it so old that he saw it too?
GENTLEMAN: Ah, you misunderstand me, I am speaking of the painter Friedrich; Ossian strikes his harp before this painting. (*Exeunt.*)

Two young ladies

FIRST LADY: Did you hear, Louise? that is Ossian.
SECOND LADY: Ah no, you misunderstand him, it is the ocean.
FIRST LADY: But he said he was striking his harp.
SECOND LADY: But I don't see a harp. Really it is quite gruesome to look at. (*Exeunt.*)

Two connoisseurs

FIRST: Gruesome [*graulich*] indeed, the whole thing is all gray [*grau*]; what dry things he always paints!
SECOND: You mean to say, how drily he paints such wet things.
FIRST: He surely must paint them as well as he can. (*Exeunt.*)

A governess with two demoiselles

GOVERNESS: This is the sea off Rügen.
FIRST DEMOISELLE: Where Kosegarten lives.
SECOND DEMOISELLE: Where groceries come from.
GOVERNESS: Now why does he paint such somber air? How beautiful, if he had painted a few amber fishermen in the foreground.
FIRST DEMOISELLE: Ah yes, sometime I would like to fish together a beautiful amber necklace for myself. (*Exeunt.*)

A young lady with two blond children and a pair of gentlemen

GENTLEMAN: Splendid, splendid, this man must be the only one who expresses a mood in his landscapes, there is great individuality in this picture, high truth, solitude, somber melancholy sky, he really knows what he paints.
SECOND GENTLEMAN: And also paints what he knows, and feels it, and thinks it, and paints it.
FIRST CHILD: What is that?
FIRST GENTLEMAN: That is the sea, my child, and a Capuchin who is walking along it and is sad that he doesn't have as nice a boy as you.
SECOND CHILD: Then why doesn't the Capuchin dance around

in front here, why doesn't he shake his head like when we have silhouettes? That would be prettier.

FIRST CHILD: It must be a Capuchin that tells the weather, like the one outside our window?

SECOND GENTLEMAN: Not like that, my child, but he does tell the weather, he is the unity in the totality, the lonely center in the lonely circle.

FIRST GENTLEMAN: Yes, he is the mood, the heart, the reflection of the whole picture in and about itself.

SECOND GENTLEMAN: How divinely the accessories are chosen, they are not a mere standard for the height of the objects as in ordinary painters, he is the thing itself, he is the picture, and while he seems to dream this region as if into a sad mirror of his own isolation, the enclosing sea, free of ships, which limits him like his vow, and the barren sand shore that is cheerless like his life, seems again to force him forth symbolically like a lonely plant prophesying itself.

FIRST GENTLEMAN: Splendid, surely you are right: (*to the lady*:) but, my dear, you don't say anything.

LADY: Ah, I felt at home before the picture, it truly touched me, it is really so natural, and when you spoke like that, it seemed just as obscure as when I used to go walking on the shore with our philosophical friends; I just wished that a fresh sea breeze would blow and drive up a sail and that a sunny gleam would shine down and that the water would murmur; it feels like nightmares and dream yearnings for the fatherland: come along, it makes me sad. (*Exeunt.*)

A lady and a guide

LADY (*stands for a long time in silence*): Great, inconceivably great! It is as if the sea had Young's night thoughts.

GENTLEMAN: You mean, as if they had occurred to the Capuchin?

LADY: If only you didn't always joke and spoil the feeling. Secretly you feel just the same, but you want to ridicule in others what you honor in yourself. I say, it is as if the sea had Young's night thoughts.

GENTLEMAN: And I say Yes, and to be exact, the Karlsruhe edition with Mercier's *Bonnet de Nuit*, and Schubert's view of nature from the night side to boot.

LADY: I can't answer that better than by a parallel anecdote: When the immortal Klopstock had said for the first time in his poems, "The dawn smiles," Mme Gottsched said while reading it, "What kind of face is she making?"

GENTLEMAN: Surely not so beautiful a face as yours, while you say that.

LADY: Now you are getting *ennuyeux*.

GENTLEMAN: And Gottsched made his wife a face for her *bon mot*.

LADY: I really ought to give you a nightcap for yours, but you already are one [*Nachtmütze*, a dumbbell].

GENTLEMAN: No, rather a view of your nature from the night side.

LADY: Mind your manners.

GENTLEMAN: Ah, if we stood to each other as the Capuchin stands.

LADY: I would leave you and go to the Capuchin.

GENTLEMAN: And ask him to mate with you.

LADY: No, to throw you into the water.

GENTLEMAN: And you would stay by yourself with the good father and seduce him, and spoil the whole picture and its night thoughts; see, thus is woman, in the end she destroys what she feels, from sheer lying she speaks the truth. Oh, I wish I were the Capuchin who in his eternal loneliness looks out over the dark portentous sea that lies before him like the apocalypse, so would I eternally yearn for you, dear Julie, and miss you eternally, for this yearning is in truth the sole splendid feeling in love.

LADY: No, no, my darling, in this picture too; if you speak like that, I will jump into the water after you and leave the Capuchin alone. (*Exeunt.*)

During this whole time a gentle tall man had listened with some signs of impatience; I joggled him a little and he answered me as if I had asked his opinion. "It is good that pictures can't hear, or else they would have covered themselves up long ago; people behave so indecently with them and are firmly convinced that they have been put in the pillory here for some secret crime which the spectators simply have to discover." "But what do *you* actually think of the picture?" I asked. "I am glad," he said, "that there still is a landscape painter who pays attention to the wonderful conjunctions of the year and the sky, which produce the most gripping effect even in the poorest region; though indeed I should prefer if beside feeling this artist also had the gift and the training to reproduce it accurately in the presentation, and in this respect he defers as much to certain Dutchmen who have painted similar objects as he surpasses them in the whole disposition of his conception; it would not be difficult to name a dozen pictures where sea and shore and Capuchin are better painted. The Capuchin appears at some distance like a brown spot; and if I had really wanted to paint a Capuchin, I should have preferred to stretch him out sleeping or to lay him down praying or gazing in all modesty, so as not to ruin the view for the spectators, who are obviously more impressed by the broad sea than by the little Capuchin. Whoever looked around later for coastal dwellers would then find in the Capuchin pretext enough to utter what several of the spectators have communicated aloud to all in an excess of general confidentiality."

This speech pleased me so greatly that I immediately set out for home with this gentleman, where I still remain and may be found in the future.

Biographical List

Baader, Franz Xaver von (1785–1841). Scientist, philosopher, theologian. "Über das Pythagoräische Quadrat in der Natur" (1798), *Fermenta Cognitionis* (1822–24).

Brentano, Clemens (1778–1842). *Godwi, oder das steinerne Bild der Mutter* (novel, 1800–1802), poems and fairy tales, *Des Knaben Wunderhorn* (folksong collection, with Achim von Arnim, 1806–8).

Carus, Carl Gustav (1789–1869). Painter, physiologist, psychologist. *Briefe über Landschaftsmalerei* (1831), *Psyche: Zur Entwicklungsgeschichte der Seele* (1846).

Claudius, Matthias (1740–1815). Author of short poems and moral essays; editor of the *Wandsbeker Bote* (newspaper, 1771–75).

Eichendorff, Joseph von (1788–1857). Assistant secretary for Catholic affairs, Prussian ministry of cults. Novels: *Ahnung und Gegenwart* (1815), *Dichter und ihre Gesellen* (1834); stories, including "Das Marmorbild" (1815), "Aus dem Leben eines Taugenichts" (1834), "Viel Lärmen um Nichts" (1832), "Eine Meerfahrt" (1835); poems.

Fichte, Johann Gottlieb (1762–1814). *Grundlage der gesamten Wissenschaftslehre* (1794–95), *Die Bestimmung des Menschen* (1800).

Görres, Joseph (1776–1848). Scholar and reactionary political-religious polemicist. "Glauben und Wissen" (1805).

Goethe, Johann Wolfgang (1749–1832). Novels: *Die Leiden des jungen Werther* (1774), *Wilhelm Meisters Lehrjahre* (1795–96), *Die Wahlverwandtschaften* (1809), *Wilhelm Meisters Wanderjahre* (1829); *Unterhaltungen deutscher Ausgewanderten* (cycle of stories, 1795); *Faust* (Part I, 1808; Part II, 1833); numerous other plays and poems; *Die Farbenlehre* (1810) and other scientific works.

Grillparzer, Franz (1791–1872). Playwright.

Hegel, Georg Wilhelm Friedrich (1770–1831). *Phänomenologie des Geistes* (1807), *Wissenschaft der Logik* (1812–16, revised 1831), *Enzyklopädie der philosophischen Wissenschaften im Grundrisse* (1817, revised 1827, 1830), lectures on the philosophy of right, history, fine arts, and the history of philosophy.

Herder, Johann Gottfried (1744–1803). Preacher, student and (later) adversary of Kant, friend of Goethe. Literary, critical, philosophical, historical, and religious writings, including *Journal meiner Reise im Jahre 1769, Über den Ursprung der Sprache* (1772), *Auch eine Philosophie zur Geschichte der Bildung der Menschheit* (1774), *Ideen zur Philosophie der Geschichte der Menschheit* (1784–91), *Gott* (1787), *Kalligone* (1800), *Adrastea* (1801–3).

Hölderlin, Johann Christian Friedrich (1770–1843, insane after 1806). Schoolmate of Hegel and Schelling. *Hyperion, oder der Eremit in Griechenland* (epistolary novel, 1797–99), elegies, Pindaric and Horatian odes.

Hoffmann, Ernst Theodor Amadeus (1776–1822). Musician and author of two novels, including *Lebensansichten des Katers Murr* (1820–22), and numerous stories, including *Die Serapionsbrüder* (cycle, 1819–21) and "Prinzessin Brambilla" (1821).

Humboldt, Wilhelm von (1767–1835). Brother of the scientist Alexander, friend of Goethe and Schiller. Essays on aesthetics, anthropology, politics; Prussian ambassador to Rome, minister of education; fundamental work in linguistics. "Über Goethes Hermann und Dorothea" (1800), *Über die Verschiedenheit des menschlichen Sprachbaues* (1836).

Jacobi, Friedrich Heinrich (1743–1819). Philosophy of sensibility. *Woldemar* (novel, 1779, 1794).

Kant, Immanuel (1724–1804). *Allgemeine Naturgeschichte und Theorie des Himmels* (1755), *Kritik der reinen Vernunft* (1781), *Kritik der praktischen Vernunft* (1788), *Kritik der Urteilskraft* (1790).

Kleist, Heinrich von (1777–1811). Author of plays and short stories.

Lichtenberg, Georg Christoph (1742–99). Physicist and aphorist.

Loeben, Otto Heinrich Graf von (1786–1825; pseudonym, Isidorus Orientalis). Follower of Novalis and mentor of Eichendorff.

Mörike, Eduard (1804–75). Author of poems and stories. *Maler Nolten* (novel, 1832).

Moritz, Karl Philipp (1757–93). Friend of Goethe, professor of rhetoric and classical archaeology. *Anton Reiser* (novel, 1785–90).

Novalis (pseudonym for Friedrich von Hardenberg, 1772–1801). Geologist, friend of Tieck and the Schlegels. Aphorisms: *Blütenstaub* and *Glauben und Liebe* (1798); "Die Lehrlinge zu Sais," *Heinrich von Ofterdingen* (novel), and poems, all published by Tieck (1802).

Oken, Lorenz (1779–1851). Author of specialized and general scientific works; founding editor of the journal *Isis* (1816–48). *Lehrbuch der Naturphilosophie* (1809–11).

Richter, Jean Paul Friedrich (1763–1825; pseudonym, Jean Paul). Novelist. *Siebenkäs* (1796–97).

Ritter, Johann Wilhelm (1776–1810). Physicist.

Runge, Philipp Otto (1777–1810). Painter, friend of Tieck. Author of essays on aesthetics and theory of color and of Low German fairy tales.

Schelling, Friedrich Wilhelm (1775–1854). Philosophy of nature, science, and mythology. "Vom Ich als Prinzip der Philosophie" (1795), "Von der Weltseele" (1798), *System des transzendentalen Idealismus* (1800), "Über das Wesen der menschlichen Freiheit" (1815).

Schiller, Friedrich (1759–1805). Plays, including *Wallenstein* (1800) and *Wilhelm Tell* (1804); aesthetic and historical works. Close friend of Goethe.

Schlegel, August Wilhelm (1767–1845). Brother of Friedrich. Essays and lectures on aesthetics and history of literature, translator of Shakespeare and Calderón.

Schlegel, Friedrich (1772–1829). Essays and lectures on aesthetics, philosophy, and linguistics. *Lucinde* (novel, 1799), *Gespräch über die Poesie* (1799), *Athenäums-Fragmente* (1798), *Ideen* (fragments, 1800).

Schleiermacher, Friedrich (1768–1834). Theologian and translator of Plato, friend of the Schlegels. *Reden über die Religion* (1799).

Schubert, Gotthilf Heinrich (1780–1860). *Ansichten über die Nachtseite der Naturwissenschaft* (1808) and works on dreaming.

Steffens, Henrich (1773–1845). Danish-born scientist and author of short stories.

Tieck, Ludwig (1773–1853). Numerous literary works in all forms, including *Franz Sternbalds Wanderungen* (novel, 1798), "Der blonde Eckbert" (story, 1798), *Leben und Tod der heiligen Genoveva* (drama, 1800), *Phantasus* (cycle of works in various forms, 1812–16); translator of Shakespeare, Cervantes, Spanish romances.

Wackenroder, Wilhelm Heinrich (1773–98). Author (together with Tieck) of *Herzensergießungen eines kunstliebenden Klosterbruders* (1797).

Works Cited by Short Title

Augustinus, Aurelius [Augustine]. *Confessions*, ed. Pierre de Labriolle. 2 vols. Paris, 1966.

Baader, Franz Xaver von. *Sämtliche Werke*, ed. Franz Hoffmann et al. 16 vols. Leipzig, 1851–60.

Böhme, Jakob. *Sämtliche Schriften*, ed. Will-Erich Peuckert. 11 vols. Stuttgart, 1958.

Brentano, Clemens. *Werke*, ed. Friedhelm Kemp et al. 4 vols. Munich, 1963–68.

Claudius, Matthias. *Sämtliche Werke*, ed. Jost Perfahl et al. Munich, 1968.

Coleridge, Samuel Taylor. *Works*. 7 vols. New York, 1854.

Eichendorff, Joseph Freiherr von. *Sämtliche Werke, historisch-kritische Ausgabe*, ed. Wilhelm Kosch et al. Regensburg, 1908–.

———. *Werke*, ed. Wolfdietrich Rasch. Munich, 1966.

Emerson, Ralph Waldo. *Works*. 12 vols. Boston and New York, 1883.

Fichte, Johann Gottlieb. *Sämmtliche Werke*, ed. Immanuel Hermann Fichte. 8 vols. Berlin, 1845–46.

Görres, Joseph. *Gesammelte Schriften*, ed. Wilhelm Schellberg et al. Cologne, 1926–.

Goethe, Johann Wolfgang von. *Neue Gesamtausgabe der poetischen Werke und Schriften*. 22 vols. Stuttgart, 1950–68[?].

Grillparzer, Franz. *Sämtliche Werke*, ed. Peter Frank and Klaus Pörnbacher. 4 vols. Munich, 1960–65.

Hegel, Georg Friedrich Wilhelm. *Phänomenologie des Geistes*, ed. Johannes Hoffmeister. Hamburg, 1952.

———. *Wissenschaft der Logik*, ed. Eva Moldenhauer and Karl Markus Michel. 2 vols. Frankfurt, 1969.

Herder, Johann Gottfried. *Sämmtliche Werke*, ed. Bernhard Suphan. 33 vols. Berlin, 1877–1913.

Hölderlin, Friedrich. *Sämtliche Werke: Große Stuttgarter Ausgabe*, ed. Friedrich Beißner and Adolf Beck. Stuttgart, 1943–77.

Hoffmann, E. T. A. *Die Elixiere des Teufels* [and] *Lebensansichten des*

Katers Murr, ed. Walter Müller-Seidel. Darmstadt, 1970.

———. *Die Serapionsbrüder*, ed. Walter Müller-Seidel. Darmstadt, 1970.

———. *Späte Werke*, ed. Walter Müller-Seidel. Darmstadt, 1970.

Humboldt, Wilhelm von. *Gesammelte Schriften*, ed. Albert Leitzmann. Berlin, 1903–.

Kleist, Heinrich von. *Sämtliche Werke und Briefe*, ed. Helmut Sembdner. 2 vols. Munich, 1964.

Moritz, Karl Philipp. *Schriften zur Ästhetik und Poetik*, ed. Hans-Joachim Schrimpf. Tübingen, 1962.

Novalis [Friedrich von Hardenberg]. *Schriften*, ed. Paul Kluckhohn, Richard Samuel, and Hans-Joachim Mähl. 4 vols. Stuttgart, 1960–75.

Runge, Philipp Otto. *Hinterlassene Schriften*, ed. J. D. Runge. 2 vols. Hamburg, 1840–41.

Schelling, Friedrich Wilhelm Joseph von. *Sämmtliche Werke*, ed. K. F. A. Schelling. 16 vols. Stuttgart and Augsburg, 1856–61.

Schiller, Friedrich. *Sämtliche Werke*, ed. Gerhard Fricke and Herbert G. Göpfert. 5 vols. Munich, 1960.

Schlegel, August Wilhelm. *Kritische Schriften und Briefe*, ed. Edgar Lohner. 7 vols. Stuttgart, 1962–74.

Schlegel, Friedrich. *Kritische Friedrich-Schlegel Ausgabe*, ed. Ernst Behler et al. Munich, Paderborn, and Vienna, 1958–.

———. *Literary Notebooks*, ed. Hans Eichner. London, 1957.

Tieck, Ludwig. *Franz Sternbalds Wanderungen* [and with Wilhelm Heinrich Wackenroder] *Phantasien über die Kunst*, ed. Jakob Minor. Leipzig, n.d.

———. *Schriften*. 28 vols. Berlin, 1828–54.

Wackenroder, Wilhelm Heinrich. *Herzensergießungen eines kunstliebenden Klosterbruders*, ed. Richard Benz. Stuttgart, 1961.

Suggestions for Further Reading

Apart from the works mentioned in the introduction, most discussions of geometrical imagery are either too restrictive (tending toward the falsely positivistic) or too casual and heuristic (tending toward the fanciful). The failure is perhaps most evident in writings on Schlegel. Typical of one extreme is Paul Kluckhohn's derivation of Schlegel's "Mittelpunkt" from Jacobi's *Woldemar*, despite the fact that Jacobi's novel, of which Schlegel wrote a scathing review, contains only one isolated image of centrality (Kluckhohn, *Die Auffassung der Liebe in der deutschen Romantik*, Halle, 1922, p. 383). Similarly, a factual error (the misidentification of Raphael's arabesques on p. 229) invalidates the concluding section of Marie Joachimi's *Weltanschauung der deutschen Romantik* (Jena and Leipzig, 1905). The opposite tendency is illustrated by a merely decorative use of Schlegel's comments on parabola and ellipse in Raymond Immerwahr, "Die symbolische Form des 'Briefes über den Roman,'" *Zeitschrift für deutsche Philologie* 88, Sonderheft (Jan., 1970), 41–60. No less a scholar than Oskar Walzel jettisons precision when he writes "Schlegel's actual purpose is not served when we are instructed that the word 'Zentrum' is a concept of Jakob Böhme's. . . . What he means is self-evident without this" (*Grenzen von Poesie und Unpoesie*, Frankfurt, 1937, p. 135).

Also too restrictive is the tendency to treat romantic science as a mere source for romantic literature and philosophy. Studies of this type—such as Martin Dyck, *Novalis and Mathematics* (Chapel Hill, N.C., 1960), which is not recommended; John Neubauer, *Bifocal Vision: Novalis' Philosophy of Nature and Disease* (Chapel Hill, N.C., 1971); Peter Kapitza, *Die frühromantische Theorie der Mischung* (Munich, 1968)—are informative, but isolate the relevant facts of biography, lexicography, and imagery. Romantic science needs to be seen as an imaginative totality in its own right, the more imaginative for being poor science. The best overview of the aims and problems of *Naturphilosophie*, so far as I am aware, is the sympathetic, lucid inaugural lecture (1824) by Johannes Müller, "Von dem Bedürfnis der Physiologie nach einer philosophischen Naturbetrachtung," reprinted in Adolf Meyer-Abich, *Biologie der Goethezeit* (Stuttgart, 1949), pp. 256–81. Among modern scholars the model historian of science is Georges Canguilhem, who discusses Oken's school in "La Théorie cellulaire," *La Connaissance de la vie* (Paris, 1965), pp. 43–80. For the student of literature the best general account of romantic science is still the sequence of chapters beginning with "Neue Wissenschaften" in Ricarda Huch's turn-of-the-century *Blütezeit der Romantik*. For a serviceable introduction in English to German romantic science see Barry Gower, "Speculation in Physics: The History and Practice of *Naturphilosophie*," *Studies in the History and Philosophy of Science* 3 (1972–73), 301–56. Two highly informative, if a bit overschematic, essays on the intellectual backgrounds of romantic medicine are in Owsei Temkin, *The Double Face of Janus and Other Essays in the History of Medicine* (Baltimore and London, 1977), pp. 345–89.

My only predecessor in using bicentrality as a paradigm for the form of romantic fiction seems to be Marianne Thalmann, in the brilliant closing pages of *The Literary Sign Language of German Romanticism*, trans. Harold A. Basilius (Detroit, 1972); Thalmann does not distinguish eccentric form from ellipse, however, and consequently assimilates the well-formed bicentral structures of the later romantics to the indeterminacy of the arabesque. Esther Hudgins's somewhat haphazard typology of the romantic novel is useful in connection with my topic (*Nicht-epische Strukturen des romantischen Romans*, The Hague, 1975). On inserted poems see the heated debate between Oskar Seidlin and Herman Meyer on Mignon's song, "Kennst du das Land," in *Wilhelm Meister*: Seidlin, "Zur Mignon-Ballade," *Von Goethe zu Thomas Mann* (Göttingen, 1963), pp. 23–37, reprinted from an essay of 1949, followed by an exchange in *Europhorion* 46 (1952), 149–69, and 47 (1953), 462–9, 469–77. Gerald Gillespie, "Zur Struktur von Eichendorff's 'Eine

Meerfahrt,'" *Literaturwissenschaftliches Jahrbuch*, NF 6 (1965), 193–206 is a helpful case study, though overly dualistic.
A number of specialized studies of geometrical imagery and related topics beyond those cited in footnotes are available.

Baader. Strangely, I could find no extended discussion of centrality, only a brief one in Eugène Susini's vast systematization, *Franz von Baader et le romantisme mystique* (Paris, 1942) I, 290–92. David Baumgardt, *Franz von Baader und die philosophische Romantik* (Halle, 1927), is valuable for its rich survey of mystical currents in the late eighteenth and early nineteenth centuries.

Böhme. Of the numerous full-length studies, I used the one by the great historian of science, Alexandre Koyré, *La Philosophie de Jacob Böhme* (Paris, 1929). The doctrine of two centers is expounded, pp. 364–392; the reference on p. 400 to "three *centers* or different principles" is a red herring. For a readable if overly Hegelian introduction in English, see Emile Boutroux, *Historical Studies in Philosophy*, trans. Fred Rothwell (London, 1912), pp. 169–233. Wildly Hegelian and unreliable is Ernst Bloch's account in his recently published lectures, *Zwischenwelten in der Philosophiegeschichte* (Frankfurt, 1977), pp. 227–41.

The best studies of Böhme's influence are Horst Fuhrmanns, *Schellings Philosophie der Weltalter* (Düsseldorf, 1954), pp. 114–27, and Siegfried Krebs, *Philipp Otto Runges Entwicklung unter dem Einflusse Ludwig Tiecks* (Heidelberg, 1909), pp. 105 ff., which contains more than its title promises. Edgar Ederheimer, *Jakob Boehme und die Romantiker* (Heidelberg, 1904), which contains less than its title promises, deals only with Tieck and Novalis and is given to inaccurate source-hunting and misleading generalizations. Ernst Worbs, "Johann Wilhelm Ritter, der romantische Physiker, und Jakob Böhme," *Aurora* 33 (1973), 63–76, discusses informatively the influence of Böhme the mythmaker, but not the intellectual Böhme and the geometrical imagery. *Goethe the Alchemist* (Cambridge, 1951) by Ronald Gray has an uncritically informative chapter "Centre and Circle"; Julius Richter, "Jakob Böhme und Goethe: Eine strukturpsychologische Studie," *Jahrbuch des freien deutschen Hochstifts* (1934/5), 3–55, begins with a careful account of Böhme but ends with generalizations about mysticism from the Middle Ages onward. I did not find the comparison of Böhme and Hegel useful in Peter Schäublin, *Zur Sprache Jakob Boehmes* (Winterthur, 1963).

Brentano. Little criticism of this author is immediately germane to my approach. Franz Robert Mennemeier's essay, "Rückblick auf Brentanos 'Godwi': Ein Roman 'ohne Tendenz,'" *Wirkendes Wort* 16 (1966), 24–33, is a good account emphasizing temporal modalities.

Eichendorff. Criticism of Eichendorff still suffers from old preconceptions concerning his simplicity or (in more sophisticated critics) the uniformity of his works. For a forceful statement of the view that Eichendorff is "subtly obvious" and that his invariable rhetorical mode is euphemism with a view toward annihilating time, see Ida Porena, "Il tempo, la notte, lo scongiuro: Per una lettura di Eichendorff," *Studi tedeschi* 17 (1974), 103–17. A lone voice against such homogenization has been Leo Spitzer's in "Zu einer Landschaft Eichendorffs," *Euphorion* 52 (1958), 141–52, an essay that rarely appears even in bibliographies. Eichendorff's centers are discussed in passing in Oskar Seidlin, *Versuche über Eichendorff* (Göttingen, 1965), especially pp. 224 and 230–32 in the essay "Des Lebens wahrhafte Geschichte"; and in Alexander von Bormann, *Natura loquitur: Naturpoesie und emblematische Formel bei Joseph von Eichendorff* (Tübingen, 1968), a learned but overly schematic study from a Hegelian perspective (p. 247 associates centrality with a mistaken, dualistic reading of Böhme). The only systematic treatment of centrality is an inadequate one in chap. 4 of Lawrence Radner's *Eichendorff: The Spiritual Geometer* (Lafayette, Ind., 1970).

Goethe. In an early discussion (originally published in 1943) of "Die 'Mitte' des Werkes" in *Die Symbolik von Faust II* (Frankfurt, 1964), pp. 39–55, Wilhelm Emrich considers the symbol both as origin and as intermediary, though without fully evaluating the tension between these two aspects and without examining Goethe's use of the word "Mitte." In *Goethes Kunstanschauung* (Berne, 1957), Matthijs Jolles discusses Goethe's conception of centrality in detail, with emphasis on the nature of the central truth and the

---

mode of its unfolding. Emrich is concerned primarily with the "spontaneous totality within the image" (p. 424), Jolles with the observation that "a true conversation . . . lets the middle appear" (p. 51).

Herder. Some useful essays on the coincidence of opposites have been written, although they do not do full justice to the fruitful ambiguities in Herder's position. See two essays by Wilhelm Dobbek, "Die coincidentia oppositorum als Prinzip der Weltdeutung bei J. G. Herder wie in seiner Zeit," in *Herder-Studien*, ed. Walter Wiora (Würzburg, 1960), pp. 16–47, and "Die Kategorie der Mitte in der Kunstphilosophie J. G. Herders," in *Worte und Werte: Bruno Markwardt zum 60. Geburtstag*, ed. Gustav Erdmann and Alfons Wichstaedt (Berlin, 1961), pp. 70–78; and the section on Herder (pp. 120–84) in Ewald A. Boucke, *Goethes Weltanschauung auf historischer Grundlage* (Stuttgart, 1907). The older literature on Goethe, such as Boucke's book and Franz Koch, *Goethe und Plotin* (Leipzig, 1922), pp. 170 ff., tends rather inaccurately to relate the metaphor of centrality to the doctrine of the coincidence of opposites.

Hölderlin. A bibliography of the literature on the eccentric path is in Friedbert Aspetsberger, *Welteinheit und epische Gestaltung* (Munich, 1971), pp. 33–34. Subsequently, Friedrich Strack, in *Ästhetik und Freiheit* (Tübingen, 1976), pp. 179–96, recognized the association of eccentricity with comets, though not the association of comets with uncertainty. Another recent study, Christoph Prignitz, *Friedrich Hölderlin: Die Entwicklung seines politischen Denkens unter dem Einfluß der Französischen Revolution* (Hamburg, 1976), pp. 141–51, discusses eccentricities as aberrations on man's road toward the ideal. An older study that has been generally overlooked, Sebastian Helberger-Frobenius, *Macht und Gewalt in der Philosophie Franz von Baaders* (Bonn, 1969), pp. 243–51, relates Hölderlin's eccentric path to Hemsterhuis. Deviant interpretations may be found in Pierre Bertaux, *Hölderlin und die französische Revolution* (Frankfurt, 1969), pp. 157–58, and in Franz Nauen, *Revolution, Idealism, and Human Freedom* (The Hague, 1971), p. 52.

Hoffmann. As with Brentano, little relevant criticism is available. There is a superficial chapter on "Die Wohlgerundetheit" in Ilse Winter, *Untersuchungen zum serapiontischen Prinzip E.T.A. Hoffmanns* (The Hague, 1976), pp. 19–28.

Humboldt. I have found nothing on centrality in Humboldt, although Oskar Walzel touches on the related metaphor of art as a medium of electric contact in "Wilhelm von Humboldt über Wert und Wesen der künstlerischen Form," in *Das Wortkunstwerk* (Leipzig, 1926), pp. 65–76.

Loeben. The only critical study, Stefanie Janke, "Isidorus Orientalis: Ein Beitrag zur Wesensbestimmung der deutschen Spätromantik" (dissertation, Cologne, 1962), though not very good, refers frequently to the concept of centrality.

Moritz. Tzvetan Todorov has an admirable appreciation of Moritz's historical role in *Théories du symbole* (Paris, 1977), pp. 179–97. On centrality see pp. 165–71 of Hans-Joachim Schrimpf's essay, "Die Sprache der Phantasie: Karl Philipp Moritz' Götterlehre," in *Festschrift für Richard Alewyn*, ed. Herbert Singer and Benno von Wiese (Cologne and Graz, 1967), pp. 165–92. More limited by its topic is the chapter "Der Mittelpunktsbegriff" in Eckehard Catholy, *Karl Philipp Moritz und die Ursprünge der deutschen Theaterleidenschaft* (Tübingen, 1962), pp. 102–8.

Novalis. The only sustained discussion of centrality I have found, Maurice Besset, *Novalis et la pensée mystique* (Paris, 1947), pp. 97–102, is heavily dependent upon Dietrich Mahnke's *Unendliche Sphäre und Allmittelpunkt* (Halle, 1937), and gives the misleading impression that Novalis's orientation was strongly Böhmist. On the "Lehrlinge zu Sais," see also Jurij Striedter, "Die Komposition der 'Lehrlinge zu Sais,'" *Der Deutschunterricht* 7 (1955), 5–23 (especially good on the identity of centrifugal and centripetal movement), and Ulrich Gaier's interesting though prolix analysis in *Krumme Regel* (Tübingen, 1970), pp. 7–108 (particularly good on compositional aspects of the philosophical debates).

Saint-Martin. Annie Becque and Nicole Chaquin, "Un philosophe toujours inconnu: Louis-Claude de Saint-Martin," *Dix-huitième siècle* 4 (1972), 169–90, is a clear exposé of Saint-Martin's thought, particularly his epistemology. Ernst Benz, *Les Sources mystiques de la philosophie romantique allemande* (Paris, 1968), massively documents Saint-Martin's influence in Germany.

Friedrich Schlegel. In addition to works cited elsewhere, see two studies of the concept of objectivity: Klaus Briegleb, *Ästhetische Sittlichkeit* (Tübingen, 1972), pp. 52–62, and Klaus Peter, "Objektivität und Interesse: Zu zwei Begriffen Friedrich Schlegels," in *Ideologie kritische Studien zur Literatur*, by Klaus Peter et al. (Frankfurt, 1972), pp. 9–34.

Tieck. One of the best books on German romanticism, *Das Problem 'Zeit' in der deutschen Romantik* (Munich, 1972) by Manfred Frank, analyzes the "systematic formlessness" of Tieck's works on the basis of a thorough and lucid account of early romantic poetics and can be used to supplement my account of the "open circle" on many points.

Index

The Shape of
German Romanticism

Designed by G. T. Whipple, Jr.
Composed by G&S Typesetters, Inc.,
in 10 point VIP Sabon, 2 points leaded,
with display lines in Deepdene.
Printed offset by Thomson-Shore, Inc.
on Warren's Number 66 text, 50 pound basis.
Bound by John H. Dekker & Sons, Inc.
in Holliston book cloth
and stamped in All Purpose foil.

Library of Congress Cataloging in Publication Data

BROWN, MARSHALL, 1945 –
 The shape of German romanticism.

 Bibliography: p.
 Includes index.
 1. Romanticism—Germany. I. Title.
PT361.B76   830'.9'14   79-14313
ISBN 0-8014-1228-5